Teacher's Book contents

New
First Certificate
Masterclass

Teacher's Book

Simon Haines

Barbara Stewart

OXFORD UNIVERSITY PRESS

Oxford University Press   Walton Street, Oxford OX2 6DP

Oxford   New York
Athens Auckland Bangkok Bogota Bombay
Buenos Aires Calcutta Cape Town Dar es Salaam
Delhi Florence Hong Kong Istanbul Karachi
Kuala Lumpur Madras Madrid Melbourne
Mexico City Nairobi Paris Singapore
Taipei Tokyo Toronto

and associated companies in
Berlin Ibadan

OXFORD and OXFORD ENGLISH are trade marks of Oxford
University Press

ISBN 0 19 432830 9

Typeset by Oxford University Press

Printed in Great Britain

ADE
CALM   4308

Acknowledgements

The publisher and authors would like to thank the following
for their kind permission to reproduce extracts and
adaptations of copyright material:

p. 162 extract from 'TV Heaven or Hell?', reproduced by
kind permission of Imperial Tobacco Limited, Bristol;
p. 164 adapted from 'Stranded' by Nuala Duxbury, Woman
Magazine, © Woman / Solo Syndication, by permission;
p. 165 extract from 'Airport mix-up' by Martin Wainwright,
p. 168 adapted from 'Anti-freeze diet', p. 169 extract from
'Runaway aged 12' by Sarah Bosely, all © The Guardian, by
permission; p. 166 extract from 'Zoos', © Radio Times, with
kind permission.

The authors and publishers are grateful to all the teachers
and students who contributed to the research and
development of the course.

EXAM TECHNIQUES	READING	LISTENING	WRITING	SPEAKING
Reading: Multiple choice questions Paper 1 Part 2	A hard act to swallow	Descriptions of places	Paragraphing and punctuation	Picture discussion Problem solving Opinion Description
Reading: Gapped text (missing sentences) Paper 1 Part 3 Listening: Short extracts Paper 4 Part 1	Long life	Story about British weather Extracts about the weather	Formal and informal styles Informal letter	Opinion Prediction Discussion
Use of English: Cloze Paper 3 Part 2	Talking to Elton John	Artists and opinions on art	Giving an opinion Exam training: Articles 1	Opinion Narrative Role play interview Description
Speaking: Personal information; talking about photos Paper 5 Parts 1 and 2	Whose finger is on the button in your house?	Interview about men's and women's abilities	Describing an object Exam training: Transactional letters 1	Discussion Opinion Problem solving
Reading: Matching headings Paper 1 Part 1 Use of English: Word formation Paper 3 Part 5	I flew to Brazil by accident	News report on caving	Exam training: Stories 1	Picture discussion Discussion Narrative Opinion
Listening: Note-taking and blank-filling Paper 4 Part 2 Reading: Gapped text (missing paragraphs) Paper 1 Part 3	The shape of things to come	People talking about lying	Exam training: Reports 1	Picture discussion Opinion Discussion Problem solving Narrative
Use of English: Error correction Paper 3 Part 4 Listening: Multiple matching Paper 4 Part 3	Living dangerously	Descriptions of someone in different contexts	Exam training: Applications 1 Describing people	Picture discussion Opinion Description
Reading: Multiple matching Paper 1 Part 4	The hangman's rope	Views on tobacco advertising	Presenting an argument Exam training: Compositions 1	Opinion Discussion Debate Role play
Use of English: Vocabulary cloze Paper 3 Part 1	Eurorailing	Advice phone-in	Exam training: Transactional letters 2	Discussion of texts Discussion Role play Opinion Narrative
Use of English: Key word transformations Paper 3 Part 3	What it takes to be an astronaut	Extracts about clothing and fashion	Exam training: Articles 2 Bringing descriptions to life	Picture discussion Discussion Role play Opinion
Listening: Selecting from two or three answers Paper 4 Part 4	Living on the edge	Radio game show 'Follow that'	Connecting ideas Exam training: Compositions 2	Discussion Description Picture discussion Narrative
Speaking: Shared task; topic-related discussion Paper 5 Parts 3 and 4	ZZzzz	Radio broadcast on Bonfire Night Extracts about Bonfire Night	Reporting an opinion Exam training: Reports 2	Picture discussion Narrative Description
	Memories are made of this	Extracts about the cinema	Exam training: Set book (Paper 2 Part 2 Question 5) Exam training: Applications 2	Discussion Opinion
Taking the First Certificate Exam	The stars who did their own thing	Extracts about music	Checking your work Exam training: Stories 2	Picture discussion Opinion Problem solving Discussion

Introduction

New First Certificate Masterclass is a complete First Certificate course, preparing students thoroughly for success in all parts of the revised First Certificate examination (1996 syllabus). It consists of the following components:

- Student's Book (224 pages).
- Workbook (96 pages; 104 pages with answers).
- Teacher's Book (176 pages).
- Two C90 audio cassettes.

The Student's Book

Rationale

In addition to practising the skills candidates need to perform well in the exam, *New First Certificate Masterclass* functions like a general coursebook in that it introduces, studies and practises key aspects of grammar and vocabulary. The overall purpose of the course is to consolidate and extend students' understanding and use of language within the framework of the First Certificate examination. It also provides a comprehensive guide to the format of the exam itself, and introduces effective strategies for dealing with the particular features of the five papers. The material in the course is all at the level of the exam.

Structure

Each unit contains the same sections:

    Introduction
    Reading
    Listening
    Writing (exam training and skills sections)
    Grammar and practice
    Vocabulary
    Exam techniques

Speaking activities do not form separate sections but are integrated throughout the book. Speaking is particularly important in the Introductions, in the preparation and follow-up work related to the Reading and Listening sections and in parts of the Grammar and Practice sections.

The unit sections each have a consistent internal structure, which is clearly signposted, so your class will become familiar with the way the course works. In order to avoid too much predictability, however, the sequence of sections varies from unit to unit. Further variety is provided by each unit having two topics, which are linked by a common language theme.

Note In order to be able to cover the many new exam

formats thoroughly, many units in the revised edition are now 14 pages long.

Timing

The structure of the units, with their single and double-page sections, is designed to give maximum flexibility to individual teachers, classes and courses. Units should divide naturally into lesson-length sections. A 12-page unit may be expected to take between seven and ten hours, while a 14-page unit should take between nine and twelve hours, depending on:

- how much time is spent on speaking activities in the Reading and Listening sections;
- how much of the work is given as homework or prepared in advance.

Exam training

It is all too easy for an exam course to give repetitive exam practice in the hope that performance will improve. *New First Certificate Masterclass*, however, gives explicit exam guidance and training, including detailed guidelines for the specialized skills that each exam question demands, and structured practice in all the exam question types. This is done in the Exam techniques sections in every unit. Factual information about the First Certificate exam is given in the Exam Factfile at the front of the Student's Book (pages 4–8) and general advice about preparing for the exam is given in Unit 14 (pages 195–196). Testing is an important part of an exam course, so photocopiable tests are provided at the back of the Teacher's Book.

Skills and language training

In order to succeed at First Certificate, candidates need both to improve their general language skills, and to be trained in the specific skills relevant to the examination. To achieve this dual aim, *New First Certificate Masterclass* allows students to develop their language abilities by doing exam-format tasks. All exam exercises appear regularly and each unit of the course provides practice for every paper.

Structure of the course

New First Certificate Masterclass Student's Book consists of 14 units. There is a substantial reference section at the end of the book, which comprises:

- An explanation of grammatical terminology used in the book (page 199).
- Notes on punctuation (page 199).
- Unit-by-unit Grammar reference notes (pages 200–214).
- Unit-by-unit topic Vocabulary reference (pages 215–219).
- A list of important lexical phrases which appear in the reading and listening texts or are dealt with in the book (pages 220–221).
- A list of Irregular verbs (page 221).
- A list of important phrasal verbs which appear in the

reading and listening texts or are dealt with in the book (page 222).
- A comprehensive index listing grammar points, language functions, and main vocabulary-building areas (page 223).

The 14-unit accompanying Workbook contains additional practice of the grammar and vocabulary covered in the Student's Book, together with further exam practice material for Paper 1 Reading, Paper 2 Writing and Paper 3 Use of English. Following Units 4, 8, 12 and 14 there are Revision sections which consolidate the grammar and vocabulary of the preceding group of units.

Unit structure

Each unit of *New First Certificate Masterclass* is based on an overall language theme which is sub-divided into two topics, each with its own language and grammar focus. For example, the theme of Unit 1 is **Description**, and the two topics are **Unusual activities** and **Places**; the first part of the unit presents language used to describe activities (focusing on tenses which refer to habitual actions), while the second part deals with the language used to describe places.

New topics are warmed up in the Introduction preceding each **Reading** or **Listening** section. The **Grammar and practice** and **Vocabulary** sections which follow are based on the preceding reading or listening texts, so should be dealt with after these texts. The **Exam techniques** and **Writing** sections are more independent and so may be done out of sequence without disrupting the flow of the book.

The following table summarizes the sequence of activities and the purpose of each of the sections of a sample unit (Unit 1).

Unit 1: Description

Section	Purpose
• Introduction	Introduction to the first topic of the unit (Unusual activities)
• Reading	Reading practice, with contextualization of grammar
• Grammar and practice	Inductive grammar focus (habitual actions in the past and present) followed by controlled practice exercises and fluency tasks
• Exam techniques	Analysis of FCE question types (reading comprehension), with guidelines, models and practice
• Introduction	Introduction to the second topic of the unit (Places)
• Listening	Listening practice, with integrated skills work and contextualization of grammar
• Grammar and practice	Second, shorter grammar focus incorporating practice exercises

• Vocabulary	Systematic development of topic vocabulary, word building and knowledge of phrasal verbs
• Writing	In-depth focus on general writing skills (Paragraphing and punctuation)

The sequence of sections varies from unit to unit. (A contents box at the beginning of the Teacher's notes for each unit summarizes, in sequence, the language points and skills in that unit.) The contents are arranged so that students working straight through the course are provided with a structured language programme which is both logical and varied.

The Teacher's Book

The Teacher's Book consists of notes on the units (including tapescripts and answer keys) and photocopiable tests.

Unit notes

These provide you with the following:
- A summary of the contents of each unit.
- Suggested procedures for exploiting Student's Book activities.
- Answers to exercises; possible answers are provided for open-ended questions and other exercises which rely on individual interpretation. Reasons and explanations are included wherever it is appropriate.
- Background information on unit topics and texts.
- Extra notes on the grammar of the unit, where this is considered necessary.
- Suggestions for extra activities for the classroom and for homework.
- Definitions of unusual or colloquial vocabulary used in texts and listening passages.
- Complete tapescripts.
- Model answers for most writing exercises.

Tests

All the tests, which are contained in a section at the back of the book, can be photocopied. There are fourteen Unit tests, one for each unit, and four Progress tests, which may be done after the Revision sections in the Workbook. The Unit tests test only language from the unit to which they relate, but Progress tests are cumulative. For example, Progress test 2 should be done after Unit 8 and tests language points from Units 1–8.

Tell the class, in advance, when the Unit tests and the Progress tests will take place and encourage them to revise, referring to the relevant units and Revision sections, as well as the Grammar and Vocabulary reference sections.

Unit tests

Unit tests consist of a variety of exercises which test the grammar and vocabulary from the unit. Allow 30 minutes for each Unit test.

Progress tests

Progress tests consist of exam format exercises. Allow up to two and a quarter hours for each Progress test (this includes 45 minutes for the writing task).

Using *New First Certificate Masterclass*

It is important that you read this section in conjunction with the Unit notes. It takes you through the various parts of the units, giving you guidelines for making the most of the activities, and ideas for extending the scope of the material.

Introductions

Approach

The Introduction presents the new themes of the Reading and Listening sections through a variety of activities. These are designed to engage the class's interest, and set the scene for the reading texts and recordings which follow. They activate general knowledge of the topic, introduce related vocabulary, and provide opportunities for both general fluency practice and specific exam practice for the Speaking test (Paper 5).

Procedure

A variable amount of time can be spent on the Introductions, depending on interest, the type of task, your methods of teaching and the time available. Each unit of the Teacher's Book contains more detailed suggestions for exploitation.

Extra ideas and activities

See individual units.

Reading

Approach

The development of reading skills relevant to the exam is a feature of every unit. All the reading passages are authentic texts, with only minimum modifications within the guidelines for the exam. They have been selected from a number of sources (magazines, journals, popular and serious newspapers, brochures), and reflect a variety of registers and styles, ranging from formal to informal and serious to humorous.

Reading skills are developed systematically within an exam framework. Each text is preceded by a variety of pre-reading activities (called **Think ahead)** which develop prediction skills or activate knowledge of the topic. These are followed by while-reading activities (**Reading**) which develop the skills of skimming and scanning as well as giving a reason for reading the text.

Most of the **Comprehension** exercises which follow the texts give practice in exam tasks, such as answering multiple choice questions, fitting sentences or paragraphs into gapped texts, matching information or headings to a text. Practice in inference skills is provided by the **Reading between the lines** exercises which follow some texts. Post-reading activities include **Points of view**, which gives the opportunity for an initial reaction to the text through a wide variety of short speaking activities. There is a chance for students to engage in more detailed discussion of the topic and related areas in **Over to you**. This is sometimes followed by a short **Writing** activity, where students are expected to respond personally to the topic.

Procedure

General procedures are outlined under the following headings. More specific procedures and ideas are detailed unit by unit.

Think ahead

These activities are intended to give students the opportunity to share ideas, knowledge and opinions. Pair work is useful when the activity involves giving a personal opinion; group or whole class work may be better when the task activates knowledge that not all students may have. However, you should group the class in the way that best suits your teaching situation.

Students are often asked to make a list of ideas which they then check off as they read the text. It can be useful to get feedback from the whole class before they read, but, if you do this, do not provide the correct answers until the students have looked for themselves.

Reading

Encourage students to develop an ability to read quickly for gist comprehension (skimming) and to find specific information (scanning) by setting a time limit. A suggested time is often indicated for gist reading. Scanning activities can be made into a competition to see who can find the information first.

Remind the class that they are not expected to understand every word in texts, and that they should decide whether a word is important before trying to guess the meaning from the context. Don't explain any vocabulary at this stage: many of the reading passages are followed by vocabulary exercises which give practice in deducing the meaning of unknown words. This is an important skill, and you can help your students to develop it by eliciting ideas from them rather than telling them the meanings, and by limiting the number of words you explain from each text. For further explanations of words, students should use dictionaries.

Points of view

These activities can be done in pairs or groups or with the whole class. Their purpose is to exploit the class's interest in the text. They allow students to react to it as a native speaker would, concentrating on what it says rather than how it says it. Don't spend too much time on these sections (a few minutes should be long enough in most cases) as there are further opportunities for discussion in **Over to you**.

Comprehension

Students will need to read texts again more carefully in order to do the exam tasks:
- Multiple matching: headings (Paper 1 Part 1)
- Multiple choice (Paper 1 Part 2)
- Gapped text – missing sentences or paragraphs (Paper 1 Part 3)
- Multiple matching: information (Paper 1 Part 4)

These tasks are most usefully done by students working individually and then checking their answers with a partner. Whatever the particular task type, stress the need for students to find evidence in the text to support their answers and encourage them to identify the parts of the text which helped them to decide.

Reading between the lines: These questions require students to interpret the text, and to infer answers which are not given explicitly. Explain that they must be able to back up their answers with evidence. If they can do this, then their answer is acceptable: if they can't, or if someone else can disprove their answer, then they may have misunderstood the text. Explain to your class that improving their inference skills will help to improve their general reading ability.

Over to you

These discussion activities are best done in pairs, or small groups of three or four. Discussion topics are often given a personal, sometimes contentious angle, so that it is unlikely for everyone in one group or class to have the same opinion.

Writing

These writing activities are short enough to be done in class, and give you the chance to see how your students work when they write. If you are short of time, they can be prepared in class and written up for homework. For ideas on correction techniques and how to use the model answers, see Writing below (page 14).

Extra ideas and activities

- If you prefer, the **Reading** and **Comprehension** activities could be set for homework after you have worked through the **Introduction** and **Think ahead** in class. This method allows you to spend more time on these sections and on **Over to you**.
- You can use parts of the texts for short dictations and gap fills before students have read them, or in subsequent lessons to revise grammar points and recycle vocabulary.
- Ask students to look up any word they want to know and write a sentence of their own showing its meaning.

- Specific ideas for extension activities are given in the individual unit notes.

Grammar and practice

Approach

It is vital for anyone taking First Certificate to have a thorough grasp of basic English grammar, and to be able to use it accurately. Students will have covered this basic grammar in their previous general English classes, and for this reason the grammar syllabus of *New First Certificate Masterclass* should be seen mainly as revision and consolidation.

In order to exploit what students already know, an inductive approach to grammar has been adopted. This means that the formal rules of grammar are not presented in the first instance, but examples of target language points are given in context. Students then answer questions or do tasks designed to show what they know, or what they can work out for themselves. This approach to grammar has several benefits at this level:
- It helps you to find out what students already know and what they need to spend more time on.
- It ensures that students don't spend unnecessary time on language points they already understand.
- It allows students to use their mental abilities to formulate grammar rules. Students who have had to work out rules of form and use for themselves are more likely to understand and remember language than those who simply learn and apply ready-formulated rules.

Here are examples of typical inductive grammar tasks used in *New First Certificate Masterclass*.

- **Answering concept questions**

Concept questions can be used to check understanding of grammatical form and meaning. They help students think about how language works and about their own understanding of this process, e.g. Student's Book Unit 1, page 12:

Do these sentences from the text refer to Stevie's life now or in the past?
1 I tend to start by swallowing a light bulb.
2 I often go into a pub, order a couple of drinks . . .
3 They'd put me on my own in a room as a punishment.

- **Matching structures with meanings**

Matching tasks are useful for helping to differentiate between structures which are similar and easy to confuse, such as ways of referring to the future, e.g. Student's Book Unit 2, page 23:

Match these sentences with the kind of future they refer to.
5 That's the phone. I'll get it.
  a an action or event that has been arranged
  b a prediction or expectation
  c an instant decision about the immediate future, frequently an offer of help

- **Identifying structures in context**

These are useful for identifying and analysing sets of structures which have the same function, e.g. Student's Book Unit 14, page 186:

Underline the purpose words or phrases in these sentences.
1 People do exercise to keep themselves fit.
2 I'm going to study really hard this week so I can have Friday off.
etc.

- **Comparing pairs or sets of sentences**

Where similar structures have different meanings, an effective way to highlight the differences is to compare examples of the structures in context, e.g. Student's Book Unit 10, page 134:

What is the difference in meaning between these sentences?
1 I didn't need to hurry. There was plenty of time.
2 I needn't have hurried. There was plenty of time.
In which sentence did the speaker hurry?

Learners need a reliable means of checking their knowledge of grammar, and, for this reason, they are instructed to turn to the **Grammar reference** (on pages 200–214 at the back of the Student's Book) once they have completed the inductive parts of the **Grammar and practice** section.

Note

In some units the language highlighted in the second **Grammar and practice** section is dealt with deductively, that is, the rules of form and use are given. (Example: Unit 2, Grammar and practice, page 30.) This method is used where inductive work would be inappropriate or too time-consuming.

Following the inductive grammar questions and other tasks, there is a series of oral and written practice exercises. Usually the first few exercises in each section are intended to improve the accuracy of students' language; in other words they encourage students to use the target structures in a controlled way. Examples of controlled practice exercises include the following:

- transformations.
- supplying correct verb forms.
- gap-filling.
- making up sentences based on a model.
- using structures in a personalized context.
- completing sentences in different ways.
- making up sentences based on an illustration.

Accuracy exercises are normally followed by oral or written 'transfer' or 'production' activities. Examples of transfer exercises include the following:

- Speaking: coming to an agreement, role play, discussion, listening and predicting.
- Writing: compositions, paragraphs, letters, public notices.

Procedure

Inductive grammar tasks

There are two alternative procedures for dealing with these tasks.

- Students work through the concept questions or other tasks individually, noting down answers and ideas. They then compare ideas or answers with one or more

partners. (This discussion will help students to clarify language points.) Finally, students check their answers with you or by looking in the **Grammar reference** at the back of their books.

- You lead students through the concept questions and tasks, eliciting ideas from individuals and providing correction and clarification when necessary.

You may wish to get students to study the target language points in the **Grammar reference** before coming across them in context or doing inductive work. This is a matter of individual preference, and in this case the inductive grammar tasks will act as a check on understanding.

Grammar reference

The comprehensive **Grammar reference** section at the back of the Student's Book (pages 200–214) is organized on a unit-by-unit basis. It contains concise explanations and further examples of the main grammar points covered in each unit. This section is intended as a first source of reference when checking answers to the inductive grammar tasks, or when working through the controlled practice exercises. It can also be used as a source of grammatical information when revising for Unit or Progress tests.

Students could be asked to work through the grammar notes on their own or in pairs, or you may wish to go through them with the whole class, providing further explanations and examples.

Practice

The main aim of the controlled exercises is grammatical accuracy, so you should correct students' language wherever necessary.

Oral transfer activities are usually called **Fluency**. Although the exercises have been designed so that the recently-practised target language will come up naturally, it should be stressed that their main aim is fluency: it is more important that students tackle the task successfully than that they restrict themselves to the target language. Don't interrupt to correct students' language – make a note of errors, and deal with them after the activity is completed.

If your class finds it difficult to understand why you correct them carefully on some occasions, but not on others, point out that this is a deliberate policy and that your attitude is dependent on the purpose of each exercise. A brief explanation will help avoid the impression that your approach is inconsistent or careless.

Extra ideas and activities

See individual units.

Listening

Approach

The recordings, which cover a wide variety of topics, reflect the range of speech situations (monologue, interview, debate, conversation) and registers which can occur in the First Certificate exam. Regional accents and background noise are used to make these recordings as close as possible to those which students will hear in the exam. The material, which is scripted or semi-scripted as in the exam, is largely adapted from authentic interviews. The tapescripts are reproduced in each unit of the Teacher's Book, but do not appear in the Student's Book.

The skills of prediction, listening for gist and specific information, and inferring meaning are all practised through a variety of activities in a framework similar to that of the Reading section. Listenings are preceded by pre-listening tasks in **Think ahead** and followed by **Comprehension** questions and tasks. These reflect the full range used in the First Certificate exam and include:
- Multiple choice questions (Paper 4 Part 1)
- Note-taking or blank-filling (Paper 4 Part 2)
- Multiple matching (Paper 4 Part 3)
- Selecting from two or three answers (Paper 4 Part 4).

The comprehension section may also include an exercise on guessing the meaning of unknown vocabulary and **Listening between the lines**, which gives inference practice and is similar to **Reading between the lines**. In most units there is an opportunity for further discussion of the topic in **Over to you** and often a short follow-up **Writing** activity.

Procedure

For **Think ahead**, **Points of view**, **Listening between the lines**, **Over to you** and **Writing**, follow the same procedure as outlined in **Reading**.

Listening

This section practises the skills of listening for gist and specific information. Exercises are intended to discourage students from expecting to understand everything they hear, so it is important that you play the cassette through once only and without stopping. Elicit and check answers unless otherwise directed.

Comprehension

Before playing the recording again, it is important to give time for reading through the instructions and questions, and to check that they have been understood. Play the recording for a second time, again without pausing. Students can often usefully compare answers in pairs or small groups, but should be asked to justify their choice of answers. If they find the recording or the tasks difficult, you may want to play the cassette for a third time, pausing the cassette soon after the answers to the questions and trying to elicit them. However, make it clear that in the exam each recording will be played only twice.

Extra ideas and activities

- Students make a short summary (spoken or written) of the main points of recordings.

- Use the tapescripts for short gap-fill dictations.
- There are further ideas in the notes to individual units.

Vocabulary

Approach

Students preparing for First Certificate need to acquire an extensive vocabulary, both active and passive. The exam specifically tests students' knowledge of the following major areas: semantic fields and word families; collocations; phrasal verbs, and transformations (e.g. adjectives to nouns). It is vital for students at this level to extend their vocabulary systematically, and this is the reason that vocabulary has been given such prominent attention in this book.

As well as contextualized vocabulary work in the **Reading** and **Listening** sections, each unit contains one two-page or two one-page **Vocabulary** sections, which have sub-sections on **Topic vocabulary**, **Word building**, and **Phrasal verbs**.

Activities in Topic vocabulary, which range from multiple-choice vocabulary exercises to puzzles, quizzes and short speaking or writing tasks, are designed to facilitate the active use of the vocabulary contained in the **Vocabulary reference** at the back of the book. In **Word-building**, students explore the grammar of vocabulary and practise word formation (e.g. compound nouns, negative prefixes). Particular emphasis is placed on getting a feel for the language.

The Phrasal verbs section has a different focus in each unit. These include: different meanings of one particular phrasal verb (e.g. *put on*); verbs with different particles (e.g. *bring in / round / on*); verbs which occur in a particular context (e.g. in a relationship). A variety of exercises help students to familiarize themselves with about 100 important phrasal verbs.

The **Phrasal verbs** reference section, at the back of the Student's Book (page 222), lists all the phrasal verbs specifically practised in the unit vocabulary exercises, as well as the important phrasal verbs which occur in the reading texts and recordings. There is also a photocopiable page in the Teacher's Book (page 175) dealing with the grammar of phrasal verbs, which some teachers may wish to go through with their students.

The **Vocabulary reference**, also at the back of the Student's Book (pages 215–219), groups vocabulary under the major topic areas in the book (e.g. sport, education, health), and also gives some useful collocations. The primary condition for the inclusion of words in this list was usefulness to the First Certificate candidate. Low-level words which students should already know have not been included.

Vocabulary is recycled and tested at various stages throughout the course: in the **Unit tests, Revision** and

Progress tests, as well as in exercises which focus on other language points. You can support and encourage this process by regular use of the **Extra ideas and activities** suggested below.

Procedure

Although the vocabulary sub-sections **Topic vocabulary**, **Word building**, **Use of English** and **Phrasal verbs** stand on their own and can be done in any order, the Vocabulary sections are intended to be studied no earlier than where they appear in a unit. This is because **Phrasal verbs** and **Word building** focus on words from the reading or listening texts.

Vocabulary reference
A good way to exploit this is for students to make their own lists and groupings in a separate notebook or file along with an L1 definition, an example in context, a note of the part of speech (noun, verb, etc.), and the correct pronunciation.

In addition, the class could build up a vocabulary box. Any unfamiliar words can be written on index cards, with the information suggested above on the other side (as in the illustration below). The task of preparing the cards can be set as homework. Vocabulary cards can be used by individuals who finish tasks ahead of time, or as short warmers or fillers.

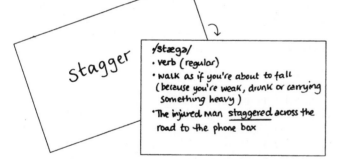

Encourage your students to consult the Vocabulary reference whenever they do a topic-based speaking or writing activity, or any of the exercises in the Vocabulary sections. Exercises in these sections are not tests; they are to help students learn. Dictionaries should be used to check meanings and pronunciation whenever necessary.

Topic vocabulary
These exercises are most usefully done in pairs, or groups of three or four students. Before doing the exercises, you could brainstorm the topic, e.g. *How many words for jobs do you know?* Set a time limit of a few minutes. Brainstorming can be teacher-directed or done as a competition between groups, and is a useful, enjoyable way of reactivating vocabulary students already know. You could sometimes ask the class to look at the topic lists the night before for homework, and then brainstorm a particular sub-section of the list in class the next day.

Word building
It is useful if students transfer their answers to this section to

their vocabulary notebooks. They can then add to it and have an easily accessible record which will be useful for exam revision.

Use of English
This heading indicates exam format exercises which appear in Paper 3, specifically Vocabulary multiple choice cloze and Word formation exercises. These are best done by students working individually.

Phrasal verbs
As well as introducing new phrasal verbs and recycling ones already learnt, many of these exercises give additional practice in choosing the correct verb form. Students can best work on their own then compare answers with a partner. Those who finish first can check their verbs in a dictionary before you give the answers.

Extra ideas and activities

- Give regular vocabulary tests. These can be formal tests, or short, informal activities at the beginning or end of the class. Some suitable activities are: Hangman; Quizzes – *What job begins with 'A' and ends in 'T' and has ten letters? (accountant).*
- Check students' vocabulary notebooks from time to time. They are more likely to stick to a system if they know you are going to look at what they have done.
- For further ideas and activities, see individual units.

Exam techniques

Approach

It is important for students to become familiar, from the beginning of their course, with the format of the exam they will be taking. For this reason, the units of *New First Certificate Masterclass* include Exam techniques sections which focus on all the First Certificate question types. This thorough, gradual training will raise students' confidence about the exam. Unit 14 has a special Exam techniques section which gives students general advice about exam preparation and suggests how to make best use of their time during the exam itself.

Exam skills are practised throughout the course and also have one Exam techniques section devoted to each of them. All the task types for Papers 1 (Reading), 3 (Use of English), 4 (Listening) and 5 (Speaking) are covered in this way.

Each Exam techniques section starts with a set of **Guidelines** which provide clear advice relevant to the particular question type. This is followed by opportunities for students to put into practice the advice they have been given. It is important that the exercises are not conducted as tests but as 'training sessions'.

The Exam techniques sections should be used in conjunction with the **Exam Factfile** at the beginning of the Student's Book. The Exam Factfile gives factual information about each paper, while the Exam techniques sections give advice and practical suggestions.

Procedure

Optional first step
Begin by getting students to read the appropriate parts of the **Exam factfile** at the front of their books. This preparatory work could be done in class or at home.

Guidelines
In the blue boxes, an arrow ◖ shows that a *don't* follows directly from a *do*. Those with a dot • stand alone.

Work through the guidelines. It is important that students fully understand these, as they will need to refer back to them regularly and use them for exam revision.
Here are some alternative ways of exploiting the guidelines:
- Once students have read the guidelines, elicit reasons for the advice given. Ask them also to think about what would happen if they didn't follow the advice. A general class discussion of these points may follow. This approach, though time-consuming, should help students to understand the language learning and exam training ideas behind the guidelines.
- Students read the guidelines and then ask you about any points they don't understand.
- Students read the guidelines to themselves, then close their books. Ask them questions to find out how much they remember. Alternatively, they could test each other.

Practice exercises
The practice exercises which follow the Guidelines should be treated as training tasks and not as tests. It is important to encourage the development of ways of approaching different exam questions, without the pressure of exam or test conditions. Plenty of opportunities for testing are provided elsewhere in the course.

As a standard procedure, students should do the tasks individually and then compare and discuss their answers in pairs. An alternative procedure is for them to work through exercises in pairs or small groups, discussing answers as they go along, or for the teacher to conduct them as whole class activities. Elicit answers to questions, allowing discussions and disagreements to develop.

Whichever way you choose to do these exercises, stress the importance of the reasoning behind the answers, rather than just their correctness.

Extra ideas and activities

1 As part of pre-exam revision, some of the Guidelines could be read out as gap-fill exercises, for example Unit 9 Use of English: Vocabulary cloze guidelines:
If you are not sure of the _____, read the sentence to yourself, filling the _____ with each of the _____ words in turn. One may seem more _____ than the others.
2 Suggest that students compile their own sets of guidelines for different parts of the exam. They could memorize the

advice given in their books or use their own wording. Encourage them to make up extra guidelines of their own. These could be listed on the classroom wall for the benefit of the whole class.

Writing

Approach

There are two kinds of Writing section: Exam training and general writing skills.

The Exam training sections focus specifically on the task types which students will meet in Paper 2. Each of the six main task types has two sections devoted to it. For example, **Articles** are covered in the Exam training sections of Unit 3 and Unit 10. In the earlier unit, the main features of the particular kind of writing are introduced. These ideas are then revised and developed in the corresponding later unit. Boxes at the end of the Exam training sections summarize the main points and will be useful to students when they revise what they have covered in the course and prepare for the exam.

The Exam training section in Unit 13 focuses on Question 5 of Paper 2, the background reading texts question.

The general writing skills sections deal with features of writing which are not specific to particular exam tasks but which are especially useful to students at this level. For example, **Formal and informal styles** (Unit 2); **Presenting an argument** (Unit 8).

The activities combine the product and process approaches to writing. The product approach is reflected in the analysis of model compositions according to their particular features (e.g. the layout and register of formal and informal writing). The process approach is reflected in the **Think, plan, write** sections, which prepare for students for their own writing – brainstorming for ideas, planning, revising and editing. Because there is also a need for regular writing practice which is not exam orientated, short writing activities have been included at the end of many reading and listening sections.

Procedure

General procedures are outlined below. More specific suggestions appear in each unit.

Models
The analysis of models is the first stage in preparing to write. The model answers which appear in the Student's Book have been written within the exam limit of 120–180 words and provide an example on which students can base their own writing. They can most usefully do the analysis exercises in pairs, or on their own before comparing ideas with a partner. Elicit ideas at the end of each stage.

Preparing students for writing
The **Think, plan, write** sections usually follow a four-step procedure:
- 1 Thinking of ideas or a personal angle on the subject or content of the task.
- 2 Planning the paragraph structure and layout.
- 3 Writing a first draft.
- 4 Editing, checking and correcting before writing a final version.

One of the biggest difficulties students have when writing their answers is a shortage of ideas. If your students have particular problems with this, it is better to start off by brainstorming with the whole class and writing up ideas on the board. This also provides an ideal opportunity for pre-teaching any vocabulary they may need. When students have gained in confidence, you can ask them to brainstorm in groups and follow this up with feedback to the rest of the class.

Though you will probably want to ask students to write their first and final drafts for homework, it is important that preparation is done in class, where you will be able to monitor and give ideas or advice.

Marking
It is particularly important that students learn to edit their own written work. You can encourage them to do this by correcting their work diagnostically, indicating with symbols the type of errors they have made, for example:
>   G = grammar.
>   S = spelling.
>   P = punctuation.
>   T = tense.
>   R = register.
>   L = layout.
>   V = vocabulary.
>   D = discourse markers.
>   WO = word order.
>   ^ = word missing.

Ask students to correct as many as possible for themselves, then correct their edited composition. An alternative idea is to get students to exchange pieces of writing and edit each other's work. The Writing skills section in Unit 14 (pages 188–189) focuses on Checking. You may wish to work through this with your class at an earlier stage.

It is also worth focusing on excerpts from students' compositions from time to time. These can be written onto overhead transparencies, or photocopied and handed out, and corrected in groups following a similar procedure.

Paper 2 scripts are marked by trained examiners. The answer to each Part is assessed according to a number of criteria, including:
- the content of the piece of writing
- the accuracy of grammar, vocabulary, spelling and punctuation
- the range of vocabulary and structure
- the organization and cohesion of the piece of writing
- the appropriacy of the format and register used
- the effect on the target reader

Students are assessed on their language abilities, not on their opinions.

Draw the class's attention to the above criteria and use them for marking those pieces of writing which are done as part of a test or mock exam.

Shorter writing activities
A length of about 80 words is suggested for most of these writing activities. You may like to treat them as fluency activities and mark them according to communicative criteria, i.e. how well they convey the students' intended message. See also ideas under **Reading** on page 10.

Extra ideas and activities

The **model answers** to the writing tasks, which are included in this Teacher's Book, could be used in the following ways:
- As dictations.
- As gapped dictations or dictated gap-fills.
- As strip stories: the text is written out in whole sentences or clauses on strips of paper, which have to be reassembled into the original form by pairs or groups.

Speaking

Approach

Each unit contains several structured speaking activities which provide opportunities for the general development of speaking skills. These can be found in the **Introduction**, **Points of view**, and **Over to you** on both topics of the unit. **Exam techniques** sections in Units 4 and 12 focus on the particular skills needed for the Speaking test in the exam (Paper 5), and extra exam speaking practice is given throughout the book: for example, there are role plays, simulations and fluency activities in **Grammar and practice**, and photo discussions in the **Introduction**. There are also many other opportunities for fluency practice. Pair and group work is suggested as the medium for many activities in this book, and students can get valuable extra speaking practice when discussing points of grammar, or simply comparing answers to exercises.

Procedure

Information gap activities, simulations and role plays
Several activities in the book are based on an information gap where Student A and Student B read different information. Notes for one of the pair are at the back of the book, and it is important to stress that they should not read each others' information.

Some activities, for example Fluency in Unit 3 (page 39), can usefully be prepared in groups before students do the roleplay. Student As exchange ideas and prepare their roles; Student Bs do the same, before splitting up to work with their original partners. Always make sure that students have understood the instructions before they start an activity.

Where the fluency activity comes at the end of the Grammar and practice section, don't worry if students don't use the particular structure they have been studying. They will probably do so, as the activities are structured to encourage this, but it is unnaturally restrictive to insist. (See also **Practice** in **Grammar and practice.**)

It is a good idea for pairs to report back at the end of the activity. This may lead on to a brief general discussion.

Photo discussion

The pictures in the Introductions can be used to give students extra fluency practice for Paper 5. Monitor discreetly while students do these activities in pairs or threes, interrupting only to suggest extra questions or discussion points when students run out of ideas. In a final feedback session, you can supply students with any vocabulary they would have found useful.

Note There are instructions in each unit for using the Introductions.

Discussions and debates

These usually work best in groups of three or four. Allow a few minutes' thinking time before starting the discussion and set a time limit. It is useful to have a 'secretary' in each group, to note down the ideas of the group and be responsible for giving feedback to the class at the end of the activity, and a 'chairperson' to ensure that everyone says something.

Monitoring

Monitor conversations discreetly and only interrupt if you are asked for help. On-the-spot correction is not advisable as it disrupts the activity and may halt it altogether. Note any major errors and deal with them at the end of the activity, or at a later stage.

Assessment

The standard format of the Speaking test (Paper 5) is two candidates and two examiners – an interlocutor and an assessor. During the test, each candidate is assessed according to the following criteria:
- use of grammar and vocabulary
- pronunciation
- ability to communicate effectively
- fluency

Keep these criteria in mind when assessing your students' oral skills, especially in tests or mock exam situations.

Extra ideas and activities

For further ideas and notes on procedure, see the notes in each unit.

1 Description

Old habits die hard

Unit focus Describing activities and places

Topic 1   Unusual activities
Reading
Grammar and practice   Present simple, present
continuous with *always*, past
simple, *would* and *used to* for
describing habitual actions
Exam techniques
    Reading: Multiple-choice questions

Topic 2   Places
Listening
Grammar and practice   *Be used to* and *get used to*
Vocabulary   Places, phrasal verbs
Writing   Describing places – paragraphs, punctuation

Introduction   Student's Book p 9

Aim: To introduce the first topic of the unit – unusual
activities.
The photographs are:
left – Stevie Starr, a professional regurgitator (a person who
swallows things and then brings them back up again);
right – a group of water diviners or dowsers (people who
search for underground water using a divining rod – a kind
of forked twig).

Start by asking the whole class to think about question A.
Elicit answers, but do not confirm or deny these; students
will find out whether they are right when they read the
text. Students then work through questions B–E in pairs or
small groups. Allow a maximum of ten minutes for this, and
then round off the activity with five to ten minutes of
feedback.

ANSWERS

A Professional regurgitator
B Objects in the photo: snooker or pool balls, coins,
   washing-up liquid, light bulb, something in a glass,
   cigarettes, Rubik Cube, padlock, balloon, mug of
   something.
C Water divining. The modern ways of detecting water
   involve electromagnetic instruments and geological
   maps.
D Suggestions:
• forecasting weather from natural signs
• navigating a ship by the stars
• alternative medicines (e.g. acupuncture, herbalism)
• making fire

Reading   Student's Book pp 10–11

1 Think ahead

The word *swallow* may help students to guess the answer,
but do not check their guesses yet – let them find out from
the article whether or not they were correct.

2 Reading

Students read the text, check their guesses and make a note
of the objects mentioned in the text which are also shown in
the photo. Set a time limit of two to three minutes if you
wish.

ANSWERS

snooker balls, washing-up liquid, light bulb, glass of
water, cigarette, padlock and key, coins, Rubik cube,
balloon

Finally, elicit ideas about the title of the article. It is a play on
words, which is a combination of two idioms: *a hard act to
follow* is a performance which the next person finds difficult
to equal; and if something is *hard to swallow*, it means that it
is difficult to accept.

3 Points of view

Students discuss the questions in pairs, groups or as a whole
class.
Question 1 requires a personal answer.
Question 2: it has been suggested that Stevie has a cleft
palate (a hole in the roof of his mouth) which he uses to
store the objects he 'swallows'.

4 Comprehension

A In Paper 1, Part 2 of the First Certificate exam, students
will have to answer multiple choice questions about specific
information in a text, as well as one or two 'general'
questions, which test their understanding of the text as a
whole. These are two examples of general questions.

ANSWERS

1 D He started life in a children's home where money
    was short and he is now financially very successful.
2 B He may do as many as four shows a day.

B ANSWERS _____

1 He would not let staff take away his pocket money for holidays – he swallowed it instead.
2 While he was in the home he learnt how to swallow and regurgitate.
3 It quietens them and makes them attentive for the rest of the show.
4 He needs people to see that he isn't cheating.

C Vocabulary

ANSWERS _____

1 staff	5 fee(s)
2 daring strategy	6 resume
3 hang on to	7 panic
4 furious	8 extract

D Reading between the lines
There are no precise answers. Students must interpret the text.

Ideas
1 Stevie was possibly an orphan, or his parents could not look after him. His childhood was probably not very happy.
2 It was probably run on strict, disciplinarian lines.
3 Because his act is very unusual, and people are prepared to pay to see the 'impossible'.
4 He might start by getting people to swallow something small, edible and not dangerous, then describe how he controls his muscles, then move on to bigger objects.

5 The show's over

Aim: Written consolidation of vocabulary.

Prepare students briefly for the task. They should write two paragraphs, using past-tense verbs, in informal letter style:
1 Brief description of Stevie's act
2 Personal reactions to the show
The final writing-up may be done for homework.

MODEL
I've just seen an incredible performance by a professional regurgitator called Stevie Starr. He swallowed everything from light bulbs to goldfish. After a few minutes he brought them up again.
   I can't say I actually enjoyed the show – it made me feel uncomfortable, but it was absolutely fascinating. You should go and see it.

Grammar and practice   Student's Book pp 12–13

1 Habitual actions and events

Aim: To revise the language of present and past routines.

A Allow students to work through the sentences.

ANSWERS _____
Stevie's life now: 1, 2, 4, 6
Relating to Stevie's past life: 3, 5, 7, 8

B Now or past?

1 **ANSWERS** _____

1 *tend to* (present simple)
2 *go, order, cough* (present simple)
3 *would* + infinitive (past routine)
4 *are accusing* (present continuous)
5 *would* + infinitive (past routine)
6 *die* (present simple)
7 *took* (past simple)
8 *used to* + infinitive

2 Explain that the repeated nature of the actions can be conveyed by the verb or by the use of time expressions.

ANSWERS _____

1 meaning of *tend to*
2 *often* + present simple
3 meaning of *would*
4 *always* + present continuous
5 meaning of *would*
6 *never* + present simple
7 *Every week*
8 meaning of *used to*

C Refer students to the Grammar reference on page 200 of their books.

2 Practice

A This is a First Certificate key word transformation exercise, but it is restricted to the grammar focused on in the previous section: the language of habitual actions. Point out to students that they must not change the word they are given and that they can use a minimum of two and a maximum of five words, including the one given, to complete the gap in the second sentence. Students can work alone or in pairs.

ANSWERS _____

1 We **used to play football** in the winter.
2 These days **I don't often play** football.
3 My father and I **always went to** a football match on Saturday afternoon.
4 When I was eight **I used to sit next** to my best friend at school.
5 My brother and I **would catch** the bus opposite the library.
6 The bus **used to be late** whenever the weather was bad.
7 My brother and I **would go into town** on Saturday mornings to spend our pocket money.
8 These days **I tend to travel** everywhere by car.

B Now and then

Elicit one or two ideas about each of the subjects. Examples:

		Then	Now
2	money	didn't have much spent without thinking	still not enough save
3	food/drinks	didn't eat fruit hated tea and coffee	eat fruit every day drink coffee
4	music/fashion	didn't think much about clothes	spend a lot of money on clothes

Students should make brief notes on the four topics, then compare their ideas in pairs or small groups. Don't force them to use specific verb forms (*used to/would*), but monitor their conversations, listening for correct and appropriate language.

Extra activity

Extra ideas for *Now and then* discussions:
1 What was life like when your parents were young?
2 How did people use to live 100 years ago?

C Elicit students' ideas for each idea listed.

Ideas

2 rush about/speak too quickly/lose their temper/panic/ forget things/make mistakes
3 shake/sweat/shiver/turn pale/go red (blush)/laugh/ speak quickly/make nervous movements/smoke/drink/ overeat
4 speak politely/look serious/dress in a suitable manner/ talk about their achievements/name-drop (casually mention important people they know)

D Repeated actions

Elicit one or two more example sentences from the class before getting them to work in pairs. Suggestions:
1 My sister's always brushing her hair.
2 I'm always forgetting to turn off lights.

3 Fluency

Aim: This fluency practice, based on an information gap, provides further incidental practice of the language of routines and habits.

Students A and B have different information. They should read the introductory notes and make sure they understand the task. Referring to the photograph, elicit ideas about the kind of people who enjoy trekking.

A Pairs of A and B students decide the kind of person they are looking for. They should try and agree. They can also decide whether they want the new member to be male or female (the three applicants can be either men or women).

B Student B now reads the information on page 13, while Student A turns to page 198. They find out different good and bad points of the three applicants and make an independent choice of team member, based on what they have read.

C Students discuss their choices in pairs and try to agree.

D Finally, pairs find out which applicant other pairs have chosen. Monitor, but do not interrupt the discussions.

Workbook: Grammar 1, 2 p 6

Exam techniques Student's Book pp 14–15

This is a regular feature of *First Certificate Masterclass* units in which students are given advice and practice related to a particular part of the FCE exam.

Reading: Multiple choice questions

Before working through the Guidelines, students could be asked to turn to the Exam Factfile on page 4 and read through the brief description of Paper 1 of the exam.

1 Guidelines

Work through the guidelines, following the ideas given in the Introduction on pages 13–14 of this book. Do not rush this process, as students may need to refer to these guidelines when doing other multiple-choice reading exercises later in the book.

Stress that students should read the text quickly before looking at the questions, and that they should find logical reasons to eliminate three of the answers. Depending on how much time you have available, you could try to elicit from students reasons for the advice given in the guidelines. Example: why is it important to skim read the passages from beginning to end?

2 Practice

Aim: To provide students with a reliable method of working through similar exercises in the future.

A Students read the text quickly, deciding where it might be from (a magazine).

B Students read the questions again and decide whether they are asking for specific or general information.

ANSWERS

Specific: 1,2,3,4,5
General: 6,7

Note: In the new First Certificate exam, general (or gist) questions relating to the whole text will usually follow specific questions. Point out to students that they may need to piece together information from different parts of the text to work out the answers to these general questions.

Students now read again, answer the questions and note their reasons for eliminating the three alternatives in each case.

3 Checking

Students compare their answers and reasons in pairs.

ANSWERS

1 C *She had long brown hair and a slim figure that I was madly jealous of.*

2 B *She'd put on her make-up in under a minute, throw on whatever clothes happened to be lying around the room, and rush off to work.*

3 A The writer says she *needed a few extra comforting dreams* and went back to sleep *to shut everything out*, and says her bed was a *favourite means of retreat.*

4 D *I overslept and was late for work every single day.* (*oversleep* = sleep later than you should)

5 D *I gave up my job.* It was the writer's decision to do this – probably because she realized that, in view of her inability to get up in the morning, it would be impossible for her to get to work any earlier.

6 B The writer is jealous of Sam's appearance, her relaxed attitude to life and the carefree ease with which she faces each day.

7 B She clearly dislikes or is ashamed of her own appearance. She seems to prefer to block out the world than to improve herself.

4 Key words

Students compare their choice of key words with a partner.

SUGGESTED ANSWERS

Paragraph 1: flat, beautiful, jealous
Paragraph 2: bed, model, teacher
Paragraph 3: weight, teeth, spotty
Paragraph 4: morning, blankets, sleep
Paragraph 5: shock, sleep, addiction
Paragraph 6: overslept, marriage, beauty

Workbook: Reading pp 4–5

Where on earth?

Introduction   Student's Book p 16

Aim: To introduce the second topic of the unit – descriptions of places.

A Get students to think about the places in the photos and guess where they are or what kind of country they are in. Elicit oral descriptions or get students to write a few sentences about each picture, following the example.

Background information
Left: the centre of Madrid (described in the example).
Top left: a village in East Africa.
Top right: a busy city scene in the Far East, showing a bicycle rickshaw and more modern vehicles.
Right: the purpose-built business district of an American city, with ultra-modern skyscrapers.

B and **C** can be done as a whole class discussion activity, or by students working in pairs.

Extra activity
Students write 100 words either:
• comparing the place they live now to one of the places in the photos
• describing which of the five places they would least like to live in.

Listening   Student's Book pp 16–17

In this first main listening section of the book students are introduced to three First Certificate listening task types: multiple-choice questions, true–false statements and the completion of unfinished sentences or notes.

1 Think ahead

Brainstorm ideas on why people move to new places.

Ideas
People move to new places:
• when they change jobs.
• when they get married or divorced.
• when they leave their parents' home.
• when they go on holiday.
• for study purposes, e.g. to learn a language.
• when they are refugees/to escape from wars or famine.
• for medical treatment.
• just for a change.

Point out that moves can be temporary or permanent.

2 Listening

Aim: Gist listening; listening for specific information.

During the first listening, students listen for the reasons why speakers 1 and 2 went to the places they talk about, and where speakers 3 and 4 are.

ANSWERS

1 She's visiting her sister.
2 He's on a business trip.
3 She's in Spain.
4 She's in Norway.

Tapescript

Extract 1

I just can't imagine what it would be like to actually live here. I mean it's a pretty interesting place, and of course, I've really enjoyed seeing my sister after so long, but I wouldn't want to settle down here unless I had enough money to live in one of the more attractive parts. I mean most of the residential areas, the suburbs, are pretty shabby, and there's terrible traffic at rush hours, so either I'd live right in the centre or I'd find somewhere further out – perhaps towards the mountains – that's a really lovely area.

Extract 2

Hi, it's me.
...
A bit tired, but apart from that I'm fine.
...
About 10 minutes ago.
...
It was okay – we landed a couple of minutes early, John met me and took me to the office. We had a very short meeting, then I got a taxi straight here.
...
Well, it could be anywhere, but it's okay. I'm on the twelfth floor, so I've got a pretty good view of the city centre.
...
Oh, you know – a small bathroom with a shower and a bath, built-in wardrobe, twin beds, air-conditioning, TV – all the usual stuff.

Extract 3

I'm just 18 and I'm from Birmingham. I came here for several reasons, I suppose. As far as my parents are concerned, I'm here to learn Spanish. Personally, I fancied something a bit different, you know, life was all a bit samey at home. I can't say I know much about Spain or the people yet, though – I mean, what with looking after the children, there are three of them under 6, and doing all the housework, I haven't had much opportunity to meet anyone my own age. Of course I do get time off – but I'm more or less broke, so I haven't been anywhere very interesting yet.

Extract 4
I = Interviewer; W = Woman

I How long have you been here now?
W Nearly five years – it's absolutely flown by.
I And what do you most like about the people?
W They're gentle, they're kind. And everyone's so hard-working. Oh and of course the Norwegian kids are amazing – I don't think I've never seen so many happy, confident children.
I How would you say it's better than your country?
W The whole lifestyle is better – for a start there's a feeling of peace. It's difficult to put my finger on it, but I feel sort of safe and secure here somehow.
I Are there any ways in which your country is better?
W Well, relationships can be a little cold here. At home personal relations are more emotional.

3 Comprehension

This is a multiple-choice listening exercise in which students have a choice of three (not four) answers for each question. Students should be given a chance to read through the questions and alternative answers carefully before listening to the recording for a second time. Play the extracts one by one with additional pauses if necessary.

ANSWERS

1 B city (residential areas, suburbs, the centre)
2 C hotel room (bathroom, wardrobe, twin beds, TV)
3 C a change (*I fancied something a bit different*)
4 B the country the woman is living in (she's been in the country for two years – longer than any normal holiday)

Extra activity

Students could be asked to work out what the other speaker says in the one-sided telephone conversation (Extract 2).

4 Listening

A Students read the eight sentences before listening to the first speaker.

ANSWERS

1 T *I went there in 1969*
2 F *everyone went there – particularly the government officials*
3 F *It was really quite inappropriate to call it Number One because . . . the first impression you got was of a place that was absolutely noisy and incredibly filthy*
4 F *The cooking corner – it wasn't really a kitchen – was actually a part of the restaurant*
5 T *just dressed in shorts and T-shirts*
6 T *they were all men, the cooks*
7 F *everything was freshly cooked*
8 F *the owner's family lived, really, at the back of the restaurant – their house . . . was just a couple of tables at the back*

Tapescript

Well, this is really about a restaurant which I used to go to when I was working in north-east Thailand, and it's back in the late '60s I went there – in 1969, and I was there for about six years – a small town in the north-east of Thailand – and it was perhaps the best restaurant in town. It was called Number One for that reason. Number One because everyone went there – particularly the government officials – but it was really *the* restaurant in town.

It was really quite inappropriate to call it Number One because, when you went into the restaurant, the first impression you got was of a place that was absolutely noisy and incredibly filthy. The building itself was pretty ramshackle – the roof was just corrugated iron, rusty and very dirty, and the floor, although it was concrete – I mean, just bare concrete – I don't think it had really been given a good clean for years and years. And with all the fat and the cooking over the years, I mean, the place had never been cleaned, so that all the – there were festoons of fat and grease and dust and cobwebs and heaven knows what hanging down from the ceiling. It was an incredibly dirty place.

The chairs and tables were just, well, basic wood, and in the case of the tables, there was a plastic top so they could be wiped clean – but hygienically, well, nothing very wonderful. And all the cooking was, was done in one corner – and the kitchen wasn't at all separate. The cooking corner it, it, wasn't really, really a kitchen, was actually a part of the restaurant – and so you had all the, the cooks there, about three or four of them, crowded into this one area with the stoves and the fires burning up so high that the area was incredibly hot.

And the cooks were all, because it was so hot, just dressed in shorts and T-shirts. They were all men, the cooks, and again the T-shirts weren't particularly clean, either. And the whole atmosphere was just one of chaos and noise – you had the cooks in the corner chopping away and clanging away with pots and pans, and the flames roaring up. The waiters would be shouting at the cooks – shouting orders to the cooks – and the cooks would be shouting back at the waiters to hurry up or get this done, or the food was ready for Number 1 or Number 2 table. There would be the sound of chopping – it was a Chinese restaurant so everything was freshly cooked, all the vegetables cooked – and the meat was chopped and peeled and cooked right there on the sides – the sizzling of the food in the pans, the roar of the flames – it was absolute chaos. And occasionally you'd get a yelp from one of the dogs that was sniffing around picking bits off the floor, and occasionally one of the diners would kick the dog to chase it away from the tables – so in the middle of all this you had this incredible noise. And the owner's family lived, really, at the back of the restaurant – their house,

such as it was, was just a couple of tables at the back. And so occasionally there would be the voice of the wife shouting down the restaurant to her husband, and the baby was crying, and so there were occasionally little bits of domestic pandemonium going on at the back.

I mean, in some ways, looking back, it seems like a scene out of hell – the flames and the noise and the dirt and the general sort of chaos – it was just like a scene out of hell. And yet, ironically, that in itself is a sort of appropriate description, because the food, when you did get it, the food, it was absolutely out of this world – it was wonderful.

B Students read the incomplete sentences before listening to the second speaker. They then complete the sentences in their own words.

ANSWERS

1 . . . the/a university.
2 . . . where he works/his work.
3 . . . a dark flat/a block of flats that was rather dark and crowded with kids.
4 . . . the temperature at night and the temperature during the day.
5 . . . the climate of/that of Southern California.
6 . . . people/you to sleep really well.

Tapescript

We've got a new chalet – it's actually on the university campus, so it only takes me about a minute to walk to work in the morning. It's really nice – it's got three bedrooms, well, two bedrooms and a study, actually, lounge-diner, nice modern kitchen. It's a very pleasant location – there's a little estate of 12 chalets at one end of the campus on a really nice piece of ground, so we're really pleased to get away from the flats, which were a bit dark at times and a bit crowded with kids. In fact, we're probably going to move again in about three weeks' time – I asked if they could give us another one 'cause it was under a large tree, which made it much more shady and they agreed.

We've just had the warmest winter of our lives – just amazing. In the deepest winter here it can probably go down to zero degrees – you can just get frost here occasionally. There was one morning when we went and there was frost on the back of the car – but of course it goes to 70 degrees Fahrenheit in the day, every day. And the trouble is, there's such a vast temperature difference that you pick up quite a lot of coughs and colds, but that's not really too high a price to pay for having such a nice winter.

People say its probably best climate in the world here in Zimbabwe – they say it's like Southern California. You just get so used to seeing the sun every day, which is really great, and of course the altitude reduces the heat, as well, and makes things fresh. And it always goes cool at night – you never have really hot sticky nights here and you can always sleep really well.

(6) When you go out into the bush you have to be careful because you can make quite nice snacks for animals, so when you go to game parks and everything, you just have to be careful. As long as you play by the rules, you're OK, and other than that, it's a really pleasant place to live. In fact, we're already used to living here. I don't think we'll ever regret leaving England.

5 Over to you

These questions should be discussed in pairs or groups.

Extra activity
Following the discussion, students could be asked to conduct a class survey to find out how much general agreement there was within the class about what people would and would not miss about their country.

Grammar and practice   Student's Book p 17

Used to

A ANSWERS
1 get used to = get accustomed to
2 we're used to = are accustomed to
3 used to go = often went

B ANSWERS
a 3rd sentence   b 2nd sentence   c 1st sentence

C Refer students to the Grammar reference on page 200 of their books.

D Verbs followed by *to* + *-ing* listed in the Grammar reference: *look forward to, object to*.
Others: *face up to, resort to*

E Practice
This should be done initially in writing. Students can then compare ideas.

Ideas
1   . . . to driving on the left in England.
     . . . to shaving in the mornings.
2   . . . to walk to school.
     . . . to go swimming every day.
3   . . . to having so much free time.
     . . . to being able to do what they want, when they want.
4   . . . to go abroad for their holidays.
     . . . to eat in restaurants.
5   . . . to standing in queues.
     . . . to talking about the weather.
6   . . . to sharing things.
     . . . to making joint decisions.

Extra activity
Get students to think of four or five questions following this pattern:
When you were a child _____ did you use to _____?
Examples:
When you were a child where did you use to live?
When you were a child what did you use to wear for school?
They could then ask each other their questions.

F Fluency
This is an activity intended to develop fluency, rather than to practise the accurate use of these verbs. If students use *get used to* and *be used to*, so much the better, but there is no need to insist on their use.

Workbook: Grammar 3, 4 p 7

Vocabulary   Student's Book pp 18–19

1 Describing places

A The place of my dreams
Students read the three descriptions and fill the gaps with appropriate prepositions.

ANSWERS

Description 1	1 on 2 in 3 close to 4 from	
Description 2	1 in 2 close to (*on* is also possible. Towns are often said to be on a river or a lake, e.g. *London is **on** the Thames*.)	
Description 3	1 in 2 in 3 on 4 from 5 in 6 close to	

B Students describe the illustration in as much detail as they can and then match it to one of the written descriptions in A.

ANSWER
The second description matches the illustration.

Extra activity
In pairs students compare where they live with the illustration.

C ANSWERS
housing: home, flat, apartment block, house, cottage
facilities: shop, pub, bank, cinema, supermarket, church, park, (open spaces)
communities: city, seaside resort, town, village
parts of a community: residential area, centre, outskirts, suburbs
natural features: mountain, coast, river, lake, countryside, hilly area, forest

Students add their own words then compare their lists with those on page 215.

D Students work in pairs.

E Aim: Written consolidation of vocabulary used to

describe places. The three descriptions in **A** should be used as models.

Extra activities

Suggestions for using the topic vocabulary lists on page 215:
1. Students draw a sketch map of their town or village and label it using as many of the words in the lists as possible.
2. Students draw a sketch map of their region and label it using words from the *Natural features* list.
3. Students write sentences about what happens at ten of the places listed under the *Other buildings* heading.
   Examples:
   At a **chemist's** you can buy all kinds of medicine.
   People go to the **theatre** to watch plays and musicals.

F Use of English

This is a multiple-choice vocabulary exercise focusing mainly on words related in some way to the sea.

ANSWERS _____

1 B resorts	4 B on	7 B blocks
2 D coast	5 A into	8 D along
3 C seaside	6 C beaches	

Note: a *pier* is a large structure built from the land out above the sea. Piers are common at traditional British seaside towns.

2 Phrasal verbs

A ANSWERS _____

1. got through (= consumed: ate or drank)
2. going on (= happening)
3. settle down (= stop moving around and live a more regular life in one place)
4. picked it up (= caught)
5. grew up / had grown up (= spent my childhood)
6. turned into (= became)

B Point out this useful reference list of phrasal verbs to students.

> Workbook: Vocabulary 1, 2, 3, 4 p 8

Writing Student's Book p 20

Describing places

Aim: To introduce paragraph writing and basic punctuation.

1 Writing in paragraphs

A Students read the description of Croydon. Do they know places like this?

B Make sure students clearly understand the importance of writing in paragraphs. Paragraph writing is a basic feature of most of the writing tasks they are required to do.

Suitable titles for three paragraphs of *My least favourite place*:
Paragraph 1: A description of Croydon (Introduction)
Paragraph 2: The reason I don't like Croydon (Main points)
Paragraph 3: Final thoughts (Conclusion)

Point out the use of *In the first place/Secondly/Lastly*.

2 Punctuation

A As students read *My favourite place* for the first time, they should divide it into three paragraphs.

ANSWERS _____

Paragraph 1 ends . . . *with whitewashed walls.*
Paragraph 2 ends . . . *traditional Breton music.*

B Before students read the text again and add necessary punctuation, check that they understand when to use capital letters, full stops, commas and apostrophes. Remind students that, in English, nationality adjectives (e.g. *French*) have capital letters.

ANSWER _____

Chateauneuf is in the centre of Brittany in north-west France and is on a hill overlooking a river. Most of the inhabitants are farmers or shopkeepers but there are a few businessmen who work in Quimper, which is 22 kilometres away. Everybody lives in stone houses or cottages with whitewashed walls.
I've visited Chateauneuf every Easter for six years now(,) because I love the atmosphere and the friendly people. Chateauneuf is not on the coast(,) so it hasn't been spoilt by tourists. There are two small hotels(,) where you can eat traditional French food quite cheaply. At Easter Chateauneuf has a festival of traditional Breton music.
If you're in Brittany, book into the Gai Logis Hotel, try the local food and then go for a walk along the river bank. You won't regret it.

Note: Commas in brackets are acceptable, but not essential.

3 Think, plan, write

Work through the suggested plan with the class and then set the writing for homework. Remind students to use the descriptions of Croydon and Chateauneuf as models.

Extra activity

When students have had their written homework corrected, they could write out unpunctuated versions. These could be exchanged by students for extra punctuation practice.

> Workbook: Writing p 9

Your students are now ready to take Unit test 1, which is on page 148 of this book. The key is on page 170.

2 Future

The outlook for tomorrow

Introduction   Student's Book p 21

Aim: To introduce the first topic of the unit – climate and weather.

A Students describe the places they see in the photographs. They then describe the weather conditions shown and discuss the probable climate of each place. They could guess where the places are. (Top: Lapland; middle left: China; middle right: North Africa; bottom left: Brazilian jungle; bottom right: Greek island of Mykonos.)

B Students discuss this second question in pairs or small groups.

C This could form the basis of a whole class discussion or be a continuation of the pair or group work started in B. Get students to think about the pattern of seasons rather than just how people behave when it is hot or when it rains. They might start by thinking about their own climate and country before moving on to one or two contrasting situations.

Some ideas
- *daily routines* – sleeping habits; work patterns; leisure activities (e.g. sports)
- *eating and drinking habits* – How climate affects what is grown or produced in various countries, as well as people's daily meals.
- *clothes* – clothes worn in different seasons; available materials for clothing; the need for protection from extremes of temperature, both hot and cold
- *homes and buildings* – available building materials; people's specific needs
- *character and attitude to life* – Does climate affect character? For example, are people who live in cold climates are less sociable than those who live in warm countries?

Listening   Student's Book p 22

1 Think ahead

Aim: To get students to make predictions about what they are going to hear.

Students should make notes individually and then compare ideas with other students. If they find it difficult to think of any ideas, ask them what they know about British weather and how they think it compares with American weather.

Note: There is a widespread perception that it is always dull and rainy in Britain, although in fact summers are often surprisingly hot and dry. The British also have a reputation for always talking about the weather – this is probably because weather conditions can vary dramatically within a short period of time.

2 Comprehension

A Before students listen to the recording for the first time, they should read through the seven statements. Play the recording twice and then check answers. (The recording is repeated on the tape, with a tone to indicate this.)

ANSWERS
1 F He says *until I'd been living here for a couple of months.* The implication is that he continued living in Britain after this two-month period.
2 T He took a pullover *in case it turned chilly in the evening.*
3 F He says *the wind got up half way through the morning.*
4 F He says *in the morning about 11 o'clock.*
5 F They left their cars to avoid accidents or getting stuck in the snow.
6 T He says *by 4 o'clock it was really warm.*
7 F Even though people listen to the weather forecasts, they know they are unreliable.

Tapescript

Everyone knows that when two British people meet in the street or on a train, the first thing they talk about is the weather. They say things like 'It's turned out nice again, hasn't it?' or 'Not too bad for the time of year, is it?'

I never used to understand why they were so interested in such a boring subject until I'd been living here for a couple of months. It was a day in July last year – July's supposed to be the height of the British summer – I remember the day really well. I got up at the usual time to go to the university – it was a bright, sunny morning, actually quite warm for Britain – so I wore my T-shirt, my oldest jeans and a pair of open sandals. To be on the safe side, I also took a thin pullover just in case it turned chilly in the evening.

On the way to the university the wind got up, then half way through the morning – about 11 o'clock – it suddenly clouded over, went really dark and began to rain. It wasn't just a gentle shower – it was a real downpour. Okay, so everyone knows it rains a lot in Britain, but that's not the end of the story. Ten minutes later, I looked out of the window again and I couldn't believe it – the rain had turned to snow. By two o'clock in the afternoon it felt like mid-December. People decided to leave their cars at work and walked home instead because they didn't want to have an accident or get stuck in the snow. I wondered how on earth I was going to manage in just my T-shirt and pullover. As it turned out, I needn't have worried – almost as quickly the weather changed again. By 4 o'clock it was really warm and I had to take my pullover off.

So that's the answer – everyone talks about British weather because it's so unpredictable. The funny thing is that even though it is completely unpredictable, most British people make sure they listen religiously to the weather forecast at least twice a day. Then, if it's wrong, which it almost always is, they complain about how unreliable the weathermen are and then go on to discuss the current state of the weather.

B This second listening activity is a matching exercise of the kind students will have to do in the First Certificate exam (Paper 4 Part 3). Make sure they know what they have to do. Get them to read the six sentences A–F and check their understanding before you play the five extracts for the first time. Students match the extracts with the sentences.

ANSWERS _____

Extract 1	D	advice about the dangers of sunbathing
Extract 2	F	country people's superstitions about the weather
Extract 3	B	a radio or TV weather forecast
Extract 4	A	a phone conversation in which someone asks to be *picked up* in a car because it's raining

Extract 5	E	a conversation about someone's holiday arrangements

Sentence C is not needed.

Tapescript

1 If you're spending your summer in a hot climate, there are a number of factors to remember. First, the heat of the sun is the greatest in the middle of the day. Second, the effect of sunburn is increased by the wind or by reflection from sand or water. Third, fair or red-haired people burn more easily; and finally, any burning is not felt at the time, but several hours later.

You don't need me to tell you to take great care. Follow your own common sense and don't stay out in the hot sun for too long at first. Over-exposure will result in painful sunburn and no tan in the end. Begin with half an hour on day one, and after that, all being well, you can double the time of the previous day.

And don't forget: there are some good creams and lotions on the market these days which will protect you from the most harmful effects of the sun.

2 **M = Man; W = Woman**
M It's been a lovely day, hasn't it?
W Mmm. And it looks like tomorrow's going to be fine too.
M How do you know that?
W Well, you know what they say: 'Red sky at night, shepherd's delight.'
M I've heard that before, but I've never been quite sure what it means exactly.
W It means a red sky in the evening shows that the next day's going to be fine – in other words, a good day for anybody working outside, like a shepherd.
M Are there any other sayings like that?
W Well, apparently cows lying down in the fields means there's going to be a thunderstorm.
M Really? I didn't know that.

3 Much of the south-east of the country will remain generally dry and cold, with any overnight freezing fog lifting slowly during the course of the day. Many western and northern parts will be cloudier with some rain at times.

Scotland and Northern Ireland will have a much milder day with some rain or patches of drizzle at times, but there will also be brighter spells.

The outlook for Thursday and Friday: it will be generally more settled with some rain or showers in most parts of Britain. Temperatures will be around normal for the time of the year, but there will still be some overnight frost, especially inland in eastern regions.

4 **T = Teenage girl; M = Mum**
T That's the phone, I'll get it.
Hello. (*Pause*) Oh hi. (*Pause*)

I don't know. Hang on. I'll ask Mum.
(*Pause*)
Mum, it's Mark on the phone. He wants to know if you can pick him up at the station. Apparently the next bus doesn't leave until 8 o'clock and it's just started to rain. Shall I tell him you'll go?

M Yes, of course. Say I'll be there in ten minutes.

5 W1 = Woman 1; W2 = Woman 2

W1 It's this Saturday you're going away, isn't it?

W2 Yeah, I can't wait. We're setting off really early and driving down to Southampton. The ferry leaves at noon and we get to France at about five in the afternoon.

W1 Whereabouts are you going?

W2 The Ardeche – same as last year and the year before. We really like that part of France. It's lovely and warm, but it never gets too hot – that's because the whole area is a plateau.

W1 What do you do there?

W2 Oh there's loads to do if you're the outdoor type. We do a lot of walking – nothing too strenuous, you know, just walking from village to village. We're going to try canoeing this year – in fact, this time next week we'll probably be having our first lesson.

C Students should read through the questions before listening to the extracts for the second time.

ANSWERS

1 **red**
   Extract 1 *red-haired people* should be especially careful of the sun (*red* here is another word for ginger or orange)
   Extract 2 *red sky at night*
2 **regions**
   Extract 3 *south-east / western and northern parts / Northern Ireland*
   Extract 5 *the Ardeche* (France)
3 **methods of transport**
   Extract 4 *bus*
   Extract 5 *ferry*

D Vocabulary

ANSWERS

1 d   2 a   3 e   4 b

3 Over to you

Students discuss these questions in pairs or small groups.
1 Elicit a few of the best stories that emerge from this question.
2 Make a list on the board of traditional sayings about the weather that anyone knows. If there is time, discuss the truthfulness of these sayings.

Grammar and practice   Student's Book p 23

1 The future

Aim: To revise the different ways of referring to the future in English.

A Students read the six examples from the recordings and match them with descriptions a–f.

ANSWERS

1 f   2 d   3 b   4 a   5 c   6 e

B Refer students to the Grammar reference on pages 200–201 of their books and, if necessary, work through the notes with them.

2 Practice

A Make sure students realize they have to fill the gaps in this letter with two different kinds of words: future verbs (1–15) and prepositions (a–j). It might be easier if they worked through all the verbs first before filling in the prepositions.

ANSWERS

1 break up (present simple – timetabled event)
2 we're having (present continuous – an arrangement)
3 we're going to start (intention)
4 going to get up (intention)
5 leaves (present simple – timetabled event)
6 gets (present simple – timetabled event)
7 we'll stop (prediction)
8 we'll drive (prediction)
9 it will take (expectation / prediction)
10 we're going (arrangement)
11 begins (timetabled event)
12 we'll get (expectation / prediction)
13 we'll probably spend (expectation / prediction)
14 I'll send (instant decision / offer)
15 Are you doing. . .? (arrangement)

a in	d in	g on	i before
b in	e for	h at	j in
c On	f On		

B SUGGESTED ANSWERS

1 I'll explain it to you. (I'll help you with it.)
2 I'm going to go to bed earlier. / I'm going to see my doctor.
3 I'll be 18.
4 I'm sorry, but I'm visiting my relatives at that time.
5 The train leaves at 8 o'clock and arrives in London at 10 o'clock.
6 It's going to snow.

C Arrangements

This is a simple role play in which two students try to arrange a meeting time one evening next week.
Explain how the exercise works. Student A information is at

the back of the book on page 198. Point out the two parts of the conversation (the holiday and next week's meeting) and check that students understand that they will need to use future verbs when they are arranging the meeting. Monitor the conversations, making a note of any serious errors, but without interrupting students.

D Predictions

This can be done as a whole class exercise or as pair or group work. Check that students understand when to use *will* and when *going to* for predictions.

Suggested predictions

Someone's going to play / put on a new CD.
The other CDs are going to fall on the floor.
Someone's going to turn the lights off.
   There will be chaos: people will fall over and spill their drinks.
   There'll be arguments and maybe even fights.
The girl's dress is going to get wet.
The cakes are going to fall on the floor.
   They'll get trodden on. The floor will be filthy.
The man who spills his wine will get himself another glass.
The man with the red tie will find himself someone else to talk to.
The woman in the purple earrings will fall asleep.

Students could also predict what the room will be like the morning after this party. Examples:
The wallpaper will be torn.
The CD player will be broken.

E Fluency

Try to involve students in this imaginary situation, in which their town is going to be hit by bad weather. Elicit a few predictions. Before getting students to work in pairs or groups, go through the list of expressions given, checking understanding and drawing attention to the word order, especially *It will **probably**. . .*, but *It **probably** won't. . . .*

Some ideas

- The river will probably overflow its banks.
- The city centre probably won't be flooded.
- Some people will almost certainly have to leave their homes.
- It's quite likely that the telephones will be out of action.
- I should think it will take weeks to repair all the damage.

F What'll happen to me

This is a writing exercise to consolidate the use of the various future forms. Check that students understand which verb forms to use for each of the three options.

- things arranged – present continuous
- intentions and predictions – *going to* and *will*
- personal and career ambitions – *going to* (*will* is less common)

Note: This is intended as a short class exercise, but could be extended. Students could be asked to write a full-length composition about their own future in 120–180 words, including all three options.

3 Articles

A This first exercise gets students to distinguish between the definite and the indefinite article. Do not try to elicit rules at this stage – these are dealt with in **B**.

ANSWERS

1 a	4 a	7 the; the
2 the	5 the	8 the
3 a	6 the	9 the

B Reasons for use of *the*

ANSWERS

2 Reason 1 (the day in July was mentioned before)
5 Reason 3 (there was only one afternoon on the day in question)
6 Reason 3 (there is only one *sun*)
7 Reason 1 (the time has already been mentioned)
   Reason 3 (there was only one *previous day*)
8 Reason 2 (the speaker and listener know which *phone* is being referred to)
9 Reason 2 (the speaker and listener know which *station* is being referred to) or
   Reason 3 (there is only one *station* that the speaker could be referring to)

C This exercise gets students to distinguish between when the definite article is used and when no article is necessary. Again do not discuss rules until students have tried the exercise.

ANSWERS

1 Ø / the	3 Ø / Ø	5 the / the / the / Ø
2 Ø / the	4 the / the / Ø	

D Having checked answers, elicit students' ideas for when no article is used. They can be given time in pairs to work out their ideas first if you wish. These are the reasons for no article being used in sentences 1–5.
1 Ireland – the name of a country
2 film reviewers – plural countable noun
3 babies – plural countable noun
   milk – uncountable noun
4 love – uncountable noun
5 on fire – an expression

E Refer students to the Grammar reference notes on page 201.

Workbook: Grammar 2, 3 pp 12–13

Vocabulary   Student's Book p 25

Weather

A Students put temperature adjectives in order.

ANSWERS

freezing – cold – cool – mild – warm – hot – scorching

Note: *to scorch* normally means to burn the surface of something by making it too hot, e.g. *An iron which is too hot may scorch clothes.*

B Gap-filling

ANSWERS

1 was falling	3 blowing	5 shine
2 poured	4 hit	

C This exercise focuses on pairs of opposite adjectives used to describe the weather.

ANSWERS

1 wet
2 dull (*dark* is possible)
3 clear (not cloudy)
4 dry

D Collocations

These are the most common combinations of the adjectives and nouns listed.

1 a light wind / a strong wind / a high wind
2 heavy / light rain
3 thick fog
4 heavy / light snow
5 light drizzle (also thin drizzle)
6 heavy / light shower
7 loud thunder
8 high / thick clouds
9 heavy downpour
10 a gentle / light breeze

E Weather adjectives ending in -y

Point out the doubling of consonants in *foggy* and *sunny*.

Adjectives

breezy	misty	stormy
cloudy	rainy	sunny
drizzly	showery	thundery
foggy	snowy	windy

F Idioms

1 *under the weather* = slightly ill or depressed
2 *go like the wind* = move / travel very fast
3 *come rain or shine* = whatever the weather is like / whatever happens
4 *to save for a rainy day* = to save money in case it is needed in the future
5 *a storm in a teacup* = a lot of excitement or discussion about something unimportant
6 *to be in a (complete) fog* = to be completely confused
7 *there's a cloud on the horizon* = something unpleasant or threatening in the future

Workbook: Vocabulary 1, 2 pp 13–14

Exam techniques Student's Book pages 26–27

Reading: Gapped text (missing sentences)

This is the first gapped text exercise students have come across in this book. Note that in the First Certificate exam, there are two types of gapped text task: missing sentences and missing paragraphs. (Missing paragraphs are introduced in the Exam techniques section of Unit 6 on pages 88–89.) Explain the general idea of a gapped text to students and then move on to the guidelines.

1 Guidelines

Work through the guidelines, following the ideas given in the Introduction on pages 13–14 of this book.
When discussing the idea of language connections between the main text and the missing sentences (fourth 'Do' point), try to elicit examples of these connections from students. Examples:
1 matching verb tenses
2 collocations, e.g. nouns and verbs which commonly go together
3 reference words, e.g. pronouns which refer back to nouns
4 sequence words, e.g. time or result words like *Finally* or *Therefore*.

2 Practice

A Students read the article quickly, thinking about the main dangers and difficulties facing explorers. They should not try to fit in the missing sentences at this stage. Students write their own lists and then compare with a partner.

Possible ideas

- very severe weather conditions, e.g. cold and very strong wind
- travel almost impossible
- open water
- cracks in the ice; splitting ice floes; risk of getting cut off
- loss of body heat; frostbite
- uncomfortable sleeping

B Gap-filling

1 In this practice exercise students are given content and language clues to help them fit the missing sentences into the text. They should first read through all the missing sentences, remembering that there is one more sentence than they need. (Missing sentence H has already been put into gap 0 as an example.) Work through the Content clues with the whole class, eliciting the answers to each clue. Then let students attempt to fit the missing sentences into the gaps.

SUGGESTED ANSWERS

Clue A   You would lose a lot of heat and become very cold.

Clue B   They were very careful and well prepared.

Clue C   In case of sudden danger.
Nervous / unrelaxed / constantly on the watch

Clue D   What happens because the ice has nowhere to go

Clue E   People would get frostbite

Clue F   When they are trying to get warm. / When they are going to sleep.
Unlikely to be available.

Clue G   Water which for some reason was suddenly exposed. / Water exposed by the cracked ice.

Clue H   Polar bears, birds and whales.

2   They should now check their answers by working through the Language clues. Elicit answers to the clues from the class. After this, students can make their final decisions about which sentences fit which gaps.

SUGGESTED ANSWERS

Clue A   This *water* must have been mentioned before.

Clue B   The explorers.

Clue C   One side or the other of the camp? or the tent?

Clue D   Another *problem is . . . / A second problem is . . .*

Clue E   A reason for this statement or an explanation of why the statement is obvious.

Clue F   Probably the *human body* / anyone's body.

Clue G   General truth / scientific fact.

Clue H   The Arctic.

C Checking

In pairs students compare answers. Finally, give correct answers.

ANSWERS

1 G 2 A 3 C 4 F 5 B 6 E
Sentence D is extra and does not fit into any of the gaps.

Note: Students will have the chance to practise this new technique again with the next reading text they do ('Long Life' on page 28).

Workbook: Reading pp 10–11

Congratulations! You're 130 today

Introduction   Student's Book p 28

Aim: To introduce the second topic of the unit – old age.

Start by discussing the photographs. How do students react to these images of old age? Students then work through the questions in pairs or groups, comparing ideas. Finish off with a brief class discussion.

A Is there a consensus in the class about when these ages start and finish?

B If students are from the same country, ask if they know how old people are regarded and treated in other countries. In Britain, for example, old people are sometimes seen as a nuisance and are put into old people's homes by their families.

C Allow **st**udents about five minutes in pairs to describe old people they know. Ask one or two students to give their descriptions to the whole class.

Extra activity

Get the class to describe old people who are famous in their country.

Reading

1 Think ahead

Brainstorm the best and worst aspects of living to be very old.

Ideas

Advantages: See future generations of your family (great-great-great grandchildren) / share your experience with younger generations / have more experiences (see more of the world)

Disadvantages: illnesses / friends die / difficult to keep up with changes in the world / nothing to do (get bored) / may be unable to move around easily / money runs out / become a burden on your family

2 Reading

This gives students a second opportunity to practise fitting missing sentences into a gapped text.

A Remind students about the Guidelines from the Exam techniques section on page 26. Allow students to read through them again or elicit as many as you can.

B Students read the article quickly, thinking about what information may be missing.

3 Comprehension

Before students start to fit sentences into gaps, remind them

---

of the need to look for content and language connections between the main text and the missing sentences.

ANSWERS _____

1 D *This belief* in D follows on from the sentence in the article *Experts. . . believe it is possible. . .*
2 G *He and his team* in G refers to *Dr Vijg* in the article.
3 A *. . . a couple more years on top of that* in A means in addition to the *30 years* mentioned in the article.
4 B *Some of the problem genes . . . already been tracked down* in B means that the process of *discovering our genetic secrets*, referred to in the article, has started.
5 E *Those given less food* in E refers back to the *animals in laboratories* mentioned in the article.
6 F *More and more are having their first child . . .* in F refers to the sentence Women *will be having babies at an older age.*
Sentence C is extra and does not fit into any of the gaps.

4 Vocabulary

The fact that some of the spaces in the table have an X in them means either that no word exists or that it is not considered important for students to learn this word. In the latter case the words are given in square brackets in the table below.

ANSWERS _____

1 confidence	[confide]	confident	confidently
2 prediction	predict	predictable	predictably
3 health	[heal]	(un)healthy	(un)healthily
4 improvement	improve	[improvable]	X
5 cure	cure	(in)curable	[incurably]
6 caution	[caution]	cautious	cautiously
7 expectation	expect	(un)expected	[unexpectedly]
8 reality	[realize*]	(un)real	really
		(un)realistic	(un)realistically

* to make real

5 Over to you

This provides the opportunity for the class to have a final brief discussion about their personal responses to the idea of living to be 130, having thought about the advantages and disadvantages in Think ahead and having read the article 'Long Life'. Leave this out if you feel that the subject has been discussed enough.

Grammar and practice   Student's Book p 30

This section continues the revision of future tenses. The paragraphs on the future continuous and the future perfect remind students of the meanings of the tenses, but do not involve any inductive work.

1 The future continuous

Clarify the two slightly different ways of using this tense:
- to describe an action that will be in progress at a specific time in the future

NOW	FUTURE
7 p.m.	9 p.m.
We're going into the cinema.	*In two hours' time we'll be coming out again.*

- to predict future trends

NOW	FUTURE
The 1990s	2020 onwards
A few people live to be 100.	*Most people will be living to the age of 100.*

2 The future perfect

Remind students that the future perfect describes an action that will already be completed at a particular time in the future. It is often used with expressions with *By . . .*, which means 'at or before':

NOW	FUTURE
1998	1999
I work in London.	*In 1998 I'm retiring.*
	By 1999 I'll have retired.

3 Practice

A Students work in pairs or groups to predict 21st-century trends. Remind students that their sentences can be negative.

POSSIBLE ANSWERS _____

- Education
  Students won't be leaving school until they are 20.
- Employment
  People will be working fewer hours.
  They'll be having longer holidays.
  They'll be retiring earlier.
- Leisure
  People will be making more use of leisure facilities.
  They'll be spending more time on their hobbies than on their work.
  They'll be making their own TV programmes.
  They'll be doing more sport.
- Diet
  People won't be eating so much meat.
  They'll be spending a larger proportion of their income on food.
  They'll be eating healthier food.
  They'll be eating more convenience foods.

B Students work individually and then in pairs. Elicit one or two more examples of future perfect sentences from the whole class before getting students to work on their own. If necessary, suggest topics for students to think about:
- friends / family • home • home town / village
- education / work

4 Fluency

Although this exercise is a chance for students to revise ways of talking about the future, do not turn it into accuracy practice by interrupting discussions to correct mistakes. Discuss the illustration. Are students looking forward to the year 2000? Do they think it is a significant date? Why? Why not?

A Students discuss their own lives in the year 2000.

B Students discuss possible and appropriate ways of celebrating the year 2000.

Monitor the discussions, making a mental note of any common mistakes. Round off the exercises with a class discussion, or by asking individual students how they intend to celebrate the occasion.

Extra activity
If students find the discussion about the year 2000 interesting, suggest that they discuss and then write about appropriate celebrations for the year 3000.

Workbook: Grammar 1 p 12

Vocabulary   Student's Book p 31

1 Age

A Prepositions
Students should try to do this exercise themselves before looking for similar expressions in the 'Long Life' article.

ANSWERS _____
  1 of 2 at 3 to 4 of 5 over

B Expressions
Brainstorm the meanings of these expressions.

ANSWERS _____
  1 It is a person's mental state or attitude to life that is important, not their age in years.
  2 Very, very old / unoriginal.
  3 Although she is young, she is as sensible or intelligent as a much older person.
  4 You can't change how a person behaves once they have certain habits and ways of doing things.
  5 A person who is like their mother or father in behaviour.
  6 She behaves and / or looks and / or seems younger than she really is.

2 Phrasal verbs

One of the definitions of a phrasal verb is 'a verb whose meaning cannot be guessed from the meaning of the verb and its particles'. This is one of the reasons why phrasal verbs are so tricky for students. Introduce the idea of literal and idiomatic meanings to students, using the examples given for *break up* and *put up*.

ANSWERS _____
  1 have put up the price of petrol / have put the price of petrol up
  2 to put three of them up / to put up three of them
  3 broke up
  4 put up your hand / put your hand up
  5 put up with the noise
  6 break up
  7 broke up
  8 broke up
_____

Workbook: Vocabulary 3 p 14

Writing

Formal and informal styles

Aim: In Paper 2 Writing of the First Certificate exam, candidates have to be able to write in a variety of styles, depending on what they are writing and who they are writing for. This section gives students the opportunity to recognize some of the differences between formal and informal language.

1 Formal or informal

Start by brainstorming ideas for common everyday situations in which people write formally and informally. Build up two lists on the board.

Ideas
Formal writing:
Letters (e.g. complaint / application / apology / requesting information / resignation / business letters, etc)
Reports (e.g. business, etc)
Compositions
Minutes of meetings
Textbooks

Informal writing:
Notes (e.g. telephone messages)
Postcards
Personal letters (general / pen friend / thank-you / invitations, etc)

2 Models

A Point out to students that the eight texts they are going to read are from a range of different sources and were written for various types of reader.

They should read the texts and then discuss them in pairs.

SUGGESTED ANSWERS

Where from?	Who for?
1 Postcard (or letter) from someone on holiday	for the writer's friend or someone in his or her family
2 Vegetarian cookery book	for people who want to learn how to cook vegetarian meals
3 Informal thank-you letter, from a brother or sister	to a brother or sister (or possibly another family member)
4 A dictionary or an encyclopaedia (possibly with a technical emphasis)	general readers – anyone interested in facts about videos
5 A fairly informal letter acknowledging a reply to an invitation	a friend who has been invited to a party
6 Part of a letter of application in which the writer is describing his or her past experience	personnel manager of a company
7 A review of a new CD or record	general readers interested in music
8 A letter, probably from a young person, thanking someone for having him or her to stay in their house	person who had the writer to stay in their house

B Elicit students' ideas about the relative formality of the eight texts. Build up an order of formality on the board. We have used the word 'neutral' below to mean neither formal nor informal.

SUGGESTED ANSWERS

1 informal   **most informal**
2 semi-formal
3 very informal
4 semi-formal / neutral
5 fairly informal / semi-formal
6 formal   **most formal**
7 semi-formal / neutral
8 informal

3 Analysis

These questions are intended to draw students' attention to a few basic differences between formal and informal writing. You could try to elicit students' own ideas without reference to the questions if you wish.

ANSWERS

1 Text 1 is more informal than Text 6; informal writing usually has shorter sentences.
2 Text 4 is more formal than Text 3; formal writing tends to have a more impersonal style.
3 Text 7 uses fewer shortened verb forms than Text 8; formal writing tends not to use shortened forms.
4 Text 5 uses more polite phrases than Text 3; writing that is less informal often includes polite phrases. Polite phrases in 5 include: *We were delighted to hear. . . / If you feel like leaving early, that's quite alright. . .*
5 Text 4 uses more passive verbs than Text 8 (*is used / are known*); formal writing tends to use more passive verbs.
   Note: Using passive verbs is often a device to convey a more impersonal style.
6 Text 3 uses more phrasal verbs than Text 6; informal writing tends to use phrasal verbs
7 Text 1 leaves out some pronouns whereas Text 2 does not; very informal writing often leaves out pronouns. This is especially true for hurried notes, postcards, letters and messages.
8 Text 3 uses some slang and colloquial expressions (*pics / brilliant / blown up*); very informal writing tends to use more of this kind of language.

Extra activity
Students write brief but clear lists of the features of formal and informal writing. They might produce lists like these:

Formal	Informal
• longer sentences	• shorter sentences
• impersonal tone	• personal tone
• full verb forms	• shortened verb forms
• polite phrases	• no especially polite phrases
• passive verbs	• active verbs
• single-word verbs	• phrasal verbs
• include pronouns	• sometimes leave out pronouns
• avoidance of slang	• some slang included

Note: The above points are generalizations which should be taken as a useful guide to students at this stage, rather than hard and fast rules to be observed at all times.

4 Practice

This exercise gives students a chance to choose appropriate formal and informal language. Students should work through each gapped text alone before comparing ideas with their partners.

A An informal reply to a party invitation

ANSWERS

1	Thanks	6	I'm really fed up
2	Sorry	7	old mates
3	I can't make it	8	ring
4	let me know	9	a chat
5	go on	10	Say 'Hi'

B A formal letter cancelling an arrangement

ANSWERS

1 I am sorry to inform you that
2 attend
3 that was arranged
4 This is due to

5 requested
6 I should make it clear
7 very interested in
8 in your company
9 a new interview date could be arranged
10 I apologize for any inconvenience

5 Think, plan, write

Read through the situation, checking that students understand what they have to do.

A Students should write notes about real or imaginary summer holiday plans. Brainstorm suitable informal expressions for thanking and apologizing.

Suggestions
- Thanking
  Thanks for the invitation. . .
  Thanks a lot for inviting me. . .
  Thank you (ever) so much for. . .
- Apologizing
  (I'm) sorry (but) I can't come. . .
  Sorry I can't make it. . .
  I'm sorry to say I can't. . .

B Work through the suggested paragraph plan which students use, together with their notes and expressions from **A**, to write their letter. (This can, as usual, be set as a homework exercise if class time is precious.)

Remind students, as usual, to check their grammar, spelling and punctuation.

MODEL
Dear Friend,

How are you? It was really great to get your letter last week and to hear all your news. And thanks a lot for the invitation to come and stay with you and your family in England next summer.

I'd really like to come, but I'm sorry to say I can't make it on the dates you suggest in your letter. I'm going on holiday with my parents then. We'll be away for the whole of July and the first two weeks of August. We're spending a couple of weeks on the coast and then four weeks staying at my grandparents' farm in the hills.

Sorry to have to turn down your invitation, but I hope we'll be able to get together again before too long. It seems such a long time since you were over here, doesn't it? What about the first week in September? Perhaps you could come here then? Let me know as soon as you can. Looking forward to hearing from you.

Love,

Workbook: Writing p 15

Exam techniques

Listening: Short extracts Student's Book p 34

This section introduces students to the kind of multiple choice listening exercise they will have to do in Part 1 of Paper 4.

Points to note
1 In the exam, there are eight short extracts. (There are only six in the practice which follows.)
2 The extracts are unconnected to each other.
3 Each extract lasts a maximum of 30 seconds.
4 There are always three answers to choose from.
5 The question and three possible answers are also recorded.

1 Guidelines

Work through the Guidelines, following the ideas given in the Introduction on pages 13–14 of this book. When you have done this, get students to read through the six questions and predict as much as they can about the subject matter of each extract.

2 Practice

Before playing the recording, draw students' attention to the clues in italics. Students will hear the questions and the three choices (A, B, C) on the tape, as in the exam, and each extract is repeated after a tone.

SUGGESTED ANSWERS TO CLUE QUESTIONS
1 A postman delivers letters to people's houses.
  A dustman collects rubbish from people's houses.
  A delivery driver delivers various things to houses or shops.
2 Schools, colleges and universities have *terms*. There are three terms in an educational year.
3 A *vet* treats animals, while a *doctor* treats humans.
4 There are *theatres* where actors perform plays and *theatres* where surgeons perform operations on patients.
5 *Coal dust* is the fine black dust that comes from coal. You might find it in and around a coal mine.
6 *Highlights* and *natural waves* refer to hair.

ANSWERS
1 B *truck / rubbish bags / go to the tip* – (a place where rubbish is taken by dustmen)
2 C *handed in / this term*
3 A *Hold Henry still / fed him / his fur*
4 C *germs or infections / theatre / cover our nose and mouth with special masks / operation / patient has recovered*
5 C *went down / morning shift / roof came crashing down / coal dust in the air / cutting equipment*
6 A *a bit off the back / natural wave / fringe / highlights*

Tapescript

1	A man is talking about a work routine. What is his job?
	A postman B dustman C delivery driver

M = Man

M We've developed a new way of working over the last few years. It's speeded things up a lot – made everything a lot more efficient. One of us, usually me, walks about half an hour ahead of the truck – collects all the rubbish bags and piles them up at regular intervals along the road. When the truck comes along, it's dead easy for another bloke to pick them up and chuck them into the back for crushing. When the truck's full we go to the tip, empty our load, and we're ready to start again.

2 What is the relationship between the speakers in this conversation?
A mother and son   B employer and employee
C teacher and student

W = Woman; I = Ian

W I'm sorry Ian, but that just isn't good enough. I clearly remember saying to you last week, that I expected everyone's work to be handed in by today.

I Sorry.

W The others have all managed to get it done – so I don't see why you should be any different. In fact, if I remember rightly, that's the second time this term that something has prevented you from doing work on time.

I It's not my fault. . .

W If you ask me, it's a simple case of you not being able to organize your time properly.

3 If you overheard this conversation, where would you be?
A in a vet's surgery   B in a doctor's surgery
C at a hospital

W = Woman; M = Man

W Now, I'd like you to hold Henry still while I examine him. (*Pause*) Fine. (*Pause*) That's lovely. (*Pause*) Good.
Now you say he's been missing for over a week?

M That's right.

W And as far as you know he hasn't eaten anything during that time?

M Well 'e probably has, but I haven't actually fed 'im.

W Hmm. I see.

M Do you know what's wrong with 'im then?

W Well, he's not starving – that's for sure. It's a guess at this stage, but by looking at his fur I'd say he was suffering some kind of virus.

4 A man is talking about aspects of his work. What is his occupation?
A actor   B dentist   C surgeon

M = Man

M It's extremely important for everyone involved to keep themselves scrupulously clean at all times. Under no circumstances can we run the risk of bringing germs or infections into the theatre. That's the reason we cover our nose and mouth with special masks. Once an operation is under way,

we've just got to keep going. Yes, it does get stressful, of course, but when it's all over and the patient has recovered, you realize what a worthwhile job it is.

5 A man is talking about a frightening experience he once had. What was the situation?
A a bomb scare   B a driving accident
C a mining accident

M = Man

M I've never been so frightened in my whole life. I went down with the morning shift as usual. It was nearly lunch time, when there was a terrible creaking noise almost directly above me – I knew what was happening. Everything went quiet for a few seconds, then the lights went out. A few of us shouted out in the darkness, then there was another rumble and the roof came crashing down. I wasn't hurt, but it was difficult to breathe – there was so much coal dust in the air. One of my mates had his legs trapped under a piece of cutting equipment.

6 Where might you overhear a conversation like this?
A at a hairdresser's   B in a clothes shop
C in a school

M = Man; G = Girl

M So, how do you want it?

G Well, I've got an interview for university tomorrow – so I need to look smart. I suppose I'd better have a bit off the back.

M Hmm – it is getting a bit long isn't it – in fact it's even lost some of its natural wave. And the front?

G Something that's easy to keep tidy.

M A fringe would be the simplest.

G Mmm – I've never been very keen on fringes – but it's not a bad idea on this occasion.

M Okay – and d'you want the highlights redone? I think it'd be worth it. It does give you a sort of sophisticated look.

Extra activity

Tell students that in this part of the exam they may be asked about any of these aspects of the recordings they hear.

1 The attitude, feeling, mood, or opinion of the speaker(s).
2 The connection between the speakers.
3 The purpose of what the speaker(s) say(s).
4 The situation or place the speaker(s) is / are in.
5 The occupation of the speaker(s).

Play the extracts again and ask them which aspect applies to each one.

ANSWERS

Extract 1 5	Extract 3 4	Extract 5 4
Extract 2 2	Extract 4 5	Extract 6 4

Your students are now ready to take Unit test 2, which is on page 149 of this book. The key is on page 170.

3 Opinion

The rich and famous

Unit focus   Expressing opinions

Topic 1   Famous people
Reading
Grammar and practice   Gerunds
Exam techniques   Use of English: Cloze

Topic 2   Arts and Crafts
Listening
Grammar and practice   Gerunds and infinitives
Vocabulary   The arts, crafts, *see* and *watch*, noun
                    suffixes, phrasal verbs
Writing   Giving an opinion
                Exam training: Articles 1

Introduction   Student's Book p 35

Aim: The discussion introduces the reading text on the pop star Elton John.

Students may discuss in small groups followed by class discussion.

A Ideas
Advantages:
You are remembered for something, adored by fans and admirers, have a lot of influence and power, VIP treatment wherever you go, make a lot of money, are able to choose the lifestyle you want and people look up to you.

Disadvantages:
You can't lead a normal life and are recognized and possibly followed by photographers and reporters wherever you go. You are expected to behave in a particular way and might be exploited. It is difficult to know who your real friends are. The pressure and demands might be too great; you might become an alcoholic, drug addict or recluse. Your personality might change; you might become spoilt or egocentric. You might even be in danger from psychopaths.

B There are many possible answers, e.g. not all famous people are rich, for example hostages, amateur sportsmen and women, explorers, scientists, politicians, religious leaders.

People who have been most affected could include Elvis Presley, who became a recluse and died of a drug overdose. Several film and pop stars like River Phoenix, Marilyn Monroe and Jimi Hendrix are thought to have died from drug abuse. Elizabeth Taylor and Richard Burton were both affected by alcoholism. Monica Seles was stabbed during a tennis match. Princess Diana had to drop out of public life because of the pressure. Many political figures, e.g. John F. Kennedy and Martin Luther King, have been assassinated. Many film stars, pop stars, and members of European royal families are constantly hounded by journalists and photographers.

Reading   Student's Book pp 36–37

1 Think ahead

Aim: To activate students' knowledge and give them a reason for reading the text (to check their predictions). It is not important how much students know about Elton John beyond the fact that he is a rich and famous pop star.

Conduct a brief class discussion, followed by personal predictions. You can use the following information to check students' ideas.
His real name is Reginald Kenneth Dwight, born 25th March 1947 at Pinner in Middlesex, England. His most famous songs include *Rocket Man*, *Goodbye Yellow Brick Road*, *Candle in the Wind*, *Nikita* and *Sacrifice*. He plays the piano, and is well-known for his elaborate costumes and glasses.

2 Reading

Students read the text quickly for gist comprehension and to check their predictions.
The text, which is from a popular women's magazine, contextualizes the grammar focus of the unit – gerunds. Interviews with well-known people are common in British magazines and are frequently written in a question-and-answer format like this one. Basically speech written down, they provide a useful example of current informal language and style. Some examples are:
plodding (line 2) – doing something slowly
stuff (line 6) – things
snacker (line 72) – someone who eats between meals
I'm a big bread fan (line 72) – I like bread a lot.

ANSWER _____

He is happy with his life. Question 4 in Reading between the lines asks for evidence of this, so don't ask students for it now.

_____

3 Comprehension

Students work on their own then discuss answers in pairs or groups, justifying their choices. Remind them to look for content clues and to check that the extra heading doesn't fit anywhere.

A ANSWERS

1 C *I like plodding . . . I love going to the supermarket*
2 D *disguise; dark glasses; hat*
3 A *I've always been a bit of a loner; I'm terribly set in my ways; Being successful . . . confidence to do things.*
4 F *look at a doughnut . . . put on a kilo; I've always had a problem with my weight.*
5 E *go on this exercise machine and walk; That burns off calories; don't snack.*
6 B *I can't keep touring and making records for the rest of my life.*
7 H *One thing I am interested in doing is writing a musical.* (from previous paragraph); *I'm not interested in going into a theatre and performing every night.*

B Vocabulary

ANSWERS

1 C 2 A 3 C 4 A

C Reading between the lines

POSSIBLE ANSWERS

1 Do you have a weight problem?
2 He may have pre-concert nerves / excitement and post-concert exhaustion / excitement, all of which take away the appetite.
3 He hates any sort of job which means following a routine and doing the same thing day after day.
4 *But I enjoy my popularity;* (line 24)
   I've lots of great friends around me. (line 33)
   I don't particularly want to (change) either. (line 37)
   Being successful has given me the confidence to do things . . . (line 38)
   (My weight) doesn't bother me too much. (line 50)
   But I'm happy with the way I am at the moment. (line 55)
   I never consider what I do as work. (line 94)

4 Over to you

Question 1 is for class discussion. Questions 2 and 3 are for pair work followed by class discussion.
If students haven't met or received a letter from a famous person, they may have seen (e.g. at a concert) or written to someone famous.
To help start the discussion for question 2, you could use the following prompts.
Would you leave them alone?
Would you write a note and ask the waiter to pass it to them?
Would you go up to them and say something?
Would you ask them for their autograph?
Ask students to say why they would choose a particular course of action.

5 A night out

This is a short follow-up writing activity, which can be set for homework.

MODEL

I have decided to go out with the American basketball player Michael Jordan because I am a keen basketball player and, in my opinion, he was the best player ever. We're going to watch a match together, somewhere in the States, possibly his old team the Chicago Bulls. After the match, he has promised to give me some tips on how to improve my game. Then we're going to have a hamburger and French fries in a typical American diner before I fly home.

Workbook: Reading pp 16–17

Grammar and practice   Student's Book pp 38–9

Aim: To revise the form and uses of the gerund: as the subject, object or complement of a clause; after most prepositions; after certain verbs.
This Grammar and practice section does three things: it sensitizes students to the different grammatical uses of the gerund, gives useful rules on when to use gerunds, and helps students to distinguish gerunds from other *-ing* forms. Students work throughout on their own, in pairs or small groups with a teacher check at the end of each stage.
The Grammar reference contains a list of common verbs which are followed by the infinitive or gerund, but asking students to memorize lists does not normally prove useful. They are more likely to learn by continuous exposure through reading.

1 Gerunds

A Form and use

ANSWERS

1 snacking b	3 being d
2 touring, making c	4 doing a; writing b

B ANSWERS

After prepositions: *being* (line 25), *eating* (line 48), *going* (line 81), *performing* (line 82), *going* (line 89).

As object or complement: *working* (line 1), *plodding* (line 2), *doing* (line 3), *going* (line 4), *going out* (line 14), *being* (heading D).

After certain verbs: after *avoid* (heading D) – also noted under object / complement.

As subject: in the title, *talking*.

-ing words which are not gerunds:

wheeling (line 11), participle (see C 2 verbs of perception in the Grammar reference on page 202); *frustrating* (line 19), adjective; *going* (line 43), participle – part of 'going to' future form; *changing* (line 85), participle – part of present continuous form; *going* (line 88), participle – part of past continuous form.

C Subject and object

Ideas

2 Wearing a disguise / Changing the way they look
3 drinking champagne / eating in expensive restaurants
4 signing autographs / being photographed
5 Being followed wherever you go / Not knowing who your real friends are
6 earning a lot of money / having no money worries

2 Gerunds after prepositions

POSSIBLE ANSWERS

2 at running
3 of winning the gold medal
4 about taking banned substances
5 of being disqualified
6 at / about competing against the best
7 with training every day
8 in winning

3 Verbs followed by gerunds

A ANSWERS

1 give up	5 mind
2 keep (on)	6 put off
3 admitted	7 risk
4 considering	8 finished

B Students should read section 1 in the Grammar reference on page 202 of their books before continuing.

4 Gerunds after verbs of liking and disliking

A The class brainstorms verbs and expressions of liking and disliking. Students, in pairs or small groups, rank these in order from extreme liking to extreme disliking.

ANSWERS

The verbs are ranked in the order given below. Where answers occur on the same line, they are of more or less equal strength.

adore, be crazy / mad about
love
like, enjoy, be into, be keen on
don't mind
don't like, dislike
hate, can't stand, can't bear
loathe, detest

All of these verbs and expressions can be strengthened by putting the intensifier *really* in front of them, e.g. *I really can't stand being interrupted.*

B Students spend a few minutes jotting down their ideas in note form. Before they exchange opinions, remind them to use as many of the verbs and expressions from **A** as they can and to use a gerund and not a noun after the verb or

expression, e.g. 'I like listening to heavy metal' not 'I like heavy metal'.
Encourage students to exchange opinions in a more extensive dialogue and to use expressions of agreement and disagreement.

Example

A I hate getting up early.
B Yes, so do I. Especially in winter when it's cold and dark.
A Yes. And on Monday mornings.
B I don't like standing up on the bus.
A Don't you? I don't mind. Sitting down is boring.
 or
A Neither do I. It's awful when the driver brakes suddenly.

Extra activity

Students could finish by reporting their findings in oral or written form, using the following forms: *Both of us enjoy . . . / Neither of us can stand . . .*

5 Use of English

A Always encourage students to read through the text first. It gives them an idea of what the text is about, which will help them to fill the gaps.

ANSWER

Roger Black enjoys spending time at home alone, being with friends (going to the cinema or entertaining in each other's houses) and playing his guitar.

B ANSWERS

1 so	5 as	8 it
2 or	6 a	9 soon
3 at	7 about	10 myself
4 lots		

C ANSWERS

sitting, sorting out, answering (b)
being (a)
partying (b and c)
sitting down, playing (b)

6 Fluency

After students have chosen whether to be A or B, Student As spend a few minutes preparing their roles on their own. Tell them they will have to invent any answers they don't know. Student Bs in pairs or small groups prepare the questions they will ask. These can be checked before the pair activity.

If your students find fluency activities difficult, you could first elicit a demonstration dialogue from the whole class based on Elton John. One half of the class asks the questions, the other half provides the answers, using their imagination when they don't know. Students might like to have another quick look at the reading text. The dialogue which is elicited may look something like this.

B Where do you live?

A I have a house in London and several apartments in the States. I spend a lot of my time on tour so I'm never in one place for very long.

B What do you do in your job?

A I play the piano and I sing. And I write songs.

B What can you do now that you couldn't do before?

A I've got lots of money so I can buy anything I like and go anywhere I want. I've also got more confidence than I used to have for trying out new things.

B What can't you do now that you could do before?

A Go out without being recognized!

B What do you do in your spare time?

A I do exercises and play tennis to keep fit.

B What do you like about your new lifestyle?

A I like being popular. I love performing on stage.

B What don't you like?

A Signing autographs, especially when people haven't got pens on them, and being surrounded by people all the time.

Workbook: Grammar 1, 2 pp 18–19

Exam techniques Student's Book pp 40–41

Use of English: Cloze

Begin by going through the information on Paper 3, Part 2 in the Exam Factfile on page 6 of the Student's Book.

1 Guidelines

Work through the guidelines, following the ideas given in the Introduction on pages 13–14 of this book.

2 Practice

A The aim of this question is to encourage students to read the whole text and to summarize in their heads what it is about before starting to fill in the gaps.

ANSWER _____

2 The price of fame

B The purpose of the questions and clues is to train students to look for and interpret clues as to the type of word required to fill the gap. Students work in pairs or small groups.

ANSWERS _____

1 *than*

2 *as*

3 The word 'year' is a countable noun and must be preceded by an article. 'In +year' indicates that this is a prepositional time phrase. The missing article is *an*.

4 *and*

5 *of*

6 *from*

7 The verb 'be' is missing. 'Be' + the past participle 'paid' forms the passive. The missing word is *are*.

8 *to*

9 *in*

10 *so*

11 *such*

12 *that*

13 The infinitive follows 'to be able'. 'Cope' is a verb. The missing word is *to*.

14 The following word 'brought' is a past participle. The previous verb 'have not been able' is in the present perfect tense. The missing word is *has*.

15 The success of the young stars: *their*

Workbook: Grammar 3 p 19

3

Art for art's sake

Introduction Student's Book p 42

Aim: To introduce students to the topic of the second part of the unit – arts and crafts, and to present related vocabulary.

A Students work on their own or in pairs.

ANSWERS

a pottery: clay	e sewing: cloth
b painting: canvas	f carving: wood
c drawing: charcoal	g sculpture: stone
d knitting: wool	h sculpture: steel, papier-mâché

B Students discuss in pairs, in groups or as a whole class.

Listening Student's Book pp 42–43

1 Think ahead

Aim: To prepare students for the listening by activating the materials vocabulary introduced in the Introduction and making them look closely at the photos they will hear the sculptors talking about.

Students should compare their ideas with a partner but you should not tell them if their answers are right or wrong until they have done 3 Comprehension.

ANSWERS

Sculptures 1 and 3 are by the same sculptor. Sculpture 1 is made of papier-mâché; Sculpture 2 is made of pieces of wood and plaster; Sculpture 3 is made of papier-mâché and steel.

2 Listening

This is a gist listening exercise, which should only be heard once.

ANSWER

Sculpture 3

Tapescript

This one's called 'The Woman'. I tried to give the idea of what a woman is, well, what a woman is for me – tall and proud – that's why it's up on a pedestal. The sculpture's made from papier-mâché with a steel base, which I left uncovered. I used papier-mâché because I like working with it. It's very, very light, so even though the sculpture's so big, it isn't a heavy, solid piece. It can be moved around quite easily. I like the idea of all the weight being at the top, too. Colour is very important to me. My main influence is Africa and colours in

Africa are very strong and powerful, because of the sunlight. I can't make a piece of sculpture without using colour. It's very important for me to express the structure through colour. The colours themselves don't have a special significance. I don't decide that I want pink or blue in a particular place. It's just a feeling I get as I'm working.

3 Comprehension

A Students should read the notes carefully before they listen to the recording. Students answer on their own and then compare answers with a partner. Play the recording again and then check answers. Make sure that students have not written more than five words to complete their answers.

ANSWERS

1 chaos and order
2 (pieces / bits of) wood and plaster
3 a person's brain / the human brain
4 see inside it.

Tapescript

This is one of my earlier pieces. I really like it. I called it 'Chaos and Order'. The sphere as a whole and the bowl that the sphere sits in represents order and the rest of it – all the bit inside – represents chaos. You can see it on various levels – chaos and order inside a person's head, which was my original idea – to represent the human brain and its various workings – emotions and changing moods – contrasted with the more analytical side of the brain. Then again, you can see it on a more global level as representing the world, with order being nature continuing its cycle and chaos being the result of human intervention in nature. Things like the devastation of whole areas of forest in the Amazon and the killing of wild animals for their furs or their horns and tusks. Generally man upsetting the balance of nature. But of course, like any work of art each person decides what it means to them.
It's mostly made of wood but the bowl itself is made of plaster – I made it in a mould. The bits of wood are just glued together any old how. I didn't actually cut the wood up into special sizes or anything like that. They were just bits of wood I found in my workshop, left over from other sculptures. The wood is actually glued to the inside of the plaster mould and, as you can see, they're all twisting and turning everywhere. It looks rather like a ball of string, doesn't it? With everything in a tangle. Some people think it isn't finished and they're quite right but I left it like that intentionally so that you could actually see inside it – see what's going on inside the head. It's supposed to look a bit like a dissected brain.

B Students should read the statements before they listen to the recording. Play the recording twice.

ANSWERS

1 F *Well it's big enough, but I can't see the gentle bit in it.*
2 T *Must be about five metres.*
3 T Woman: *Look at all those lovely colours.*
   Man: *Oh, the colours are all right.*
4 T *It looks like a pile of old junk . . .*
5 F *All right, it's a nice colour . . .*
6 T *At least the giant thing had some sort of shape about it. You can't see anything in this!! There's no woman!*
7 T *That's what art is all about . . . showing beautiful things and beautiful people.*

Tapescript

M = man; W = woman

W   Wow, look at this one over here. It's enormous!
M   Mmm, well, what on earth is it?
W   Oh, I don't really know. Let's have a look in the catalogue. What number is it?
M   It says 43 here, but 43 here is a 'Gentle Giant'.
W   Oh, let's have a look. 'Gentle Giant'? Well, it looks like a giant.
M   Well, it's big enough, that's for sure, but I can't see the gentle bit in it, can you?
W   Well, yes.
M   And what's all that?
W   How tall do you reckon it is? Must be about five metres.
M   Well five, six, something like that, yeah. Perhaps taller.
W   It's nice though. Look at all those lovely colours.
M   Oh, the colours are all right but, um, I can't see any giant there. All you can see is his feet. What's . . . what's the rest supposed to be?
W   Well, if it . . . if it really was a giant you probably wouldn't see anything else other than its feet, would you?
M   Mmm. What's the next one?
W   Well I think the next one is number, is it 43? No, 44. 'Chaos and Order'. What do you think of that?
M   'Chaos and Order.' Well there's plenty of chaos in it, let's face it!
W   Mmm, I like that.
M   It looks just like a pile of old sticks! Where do these bits . . .
W   It doesn't look like a pile of old sticks! It doesn't!
M   Darling, don't argue. Where do these people get their ideas from? It looks like a pile of old junk! It does!
W   It looks like one of those Japanese toys that you can never get back together again.
M   It looks like a load of old junk!
W   Well, I think it's really nice!
M   Well, it's a nice colour. All right, it's a nice colour but that . . . but after you've said that, what've you got? It's just a . . . look . . . just look at it!
W   This one looks quite similar to the 'Giant' . . .

probably by the same artist. Let me have a look.
M   Same colour.
W   Yes, it's by the same artist. 'The Woman'. That's quite an interesting shape as well.
M   Well, if you like ice-cream cones, yes.
W   No. It looks quite majestic, don't you think?
M   No, that's not a woman. That's not a . . . I mean, how can you see a woman in that? At least the giant thing had some sort of shape about it. You could see the feet at least but, I mean, you can't see anything in this! There's no woman!
W   Look – the colours in it are lovely!
M   Well, it's not just a question of colour. It's a question of all kinds of things. You've got to see, well, you've got to see a . . . you've got to see a person in it!
W   You don't have to see a person in it! It depends what it represents to the artist.
M   It's got to look like a person. It's got to look like a woman!
W   You mean it has to have a face and hair?
M   Well, not to that extent, no.
W   Surely, it can just represent what a woman is?
M   Women are supposed to be something beautiful to look at. That's not beautiful! That's just a, just a big blob!
W   So, do you think art has to be beautiful?
M   Well, that's what art is all about, isn't it? Showing, showing beautiful things and beautiful people. That's not beautiful! That's not art!
W   Well, I don't know. I disagree. I don't think art should necessarily be beautiful and I don't think it has to be realistic either.
M   So what's the point of it then?
W   Well, I think it should make you think, or provoke a reaction, or suggest something to you.
M   Well, I have to say, in all honesty, that this doesn't make me think. And it certainly doesn't suggest anything either, except maybe a great big ice-cream cone!

4 Points of view

2   Students work in pairs, small groups or as a class. Students can be asked to think of examples of art treasures which are not kept in their place of origin, e.g. *Greek statues; Egyptian treasures*; where the treasures are kept, e.g. *in museums in major cities like London and Washington*; why they are there, e.g. *they were taken as spoils of war several centuries ago*; what advantages there are of exhibiting them in major cities, e.g. *more people can see them*; why they should be returned, e.g. *they are an important part of that country's history and culture.*

Extra activity
Students write 80–100 words describing a favourite work of art. This could be a sculpture, a painting, a photograph or film, a poster, a piece of music or a song, etc. They should not only describe it, but say why they like it and what it means to them.

This short writing activity could be set for homework.

MODEL
One of my favourite paintings is 'La Baignade' (The Bathers) by the French Impressionist painter Georges Seurat. In this painting a group of men are sitting or lying on the banks of the River Seine. It is obviously a very hot day as they have taken off most of their clothes. Two young men are standing up to their waists in the water. I like the painting because it reminds me of summer. The blues and greens are very relaxing and the whole effect is very restful.

Further activity
Students can bring in their favourite photograph or picture and tell the class why they like it.

Grammar and practice Student's Book p 43

Gerunds and infinitives

Aim: Students revise verbs which can be followed by the infinitive or gerund with no real change of meaning, and verbs where the use of the infinitive or gerund changes the meaning.
This area often seems difficult to students, but since the set of verbs is a closed set it can be useful for students to remember some example sentences such as those given in the Grammar reference on page 202 of their books.

A Change of meaning
Students study the sentences in pairs. They could compare their ideas with other pairs before checking their answers. They could also be referred to section 3 in the Grammar reference on page 202.

ANSWERS

1 a+d+e	b+c+f	3 a+c+f	b+d+e
2 a+d+e	b+c+f	4 a+c+f	b+d+e

B Explanations of all the answers to A are given in the Grammar reference on page 202 of the Student's Book.

C Practice
There are ideas for using grammar exercises in the Introduction on page 11 of this book.

ANSWERS

1 to bring, to buy, to get	5 to discuss
2 to announce	6 offering
3 to open	7 eating / drinking
4 interrupting, doing that	8 leaving

D Fluency
These short speaking activities can be done in pairs, groups or with the whole class.
1 If students have no personal anecdotes to tell, they may be able to talk about something important that someone else forgot to do. Alternatively, they could speak generally about the topic using their imagination. For example: *It's awful if you forget to get someone a birthday present. You feel embarrassed and they feel upset. It would be*

disastrous if a pilot forgot to lower the plane's landing gear before he landed the plane. It would crash.
2 Some ideas are: cheating in an exam; not working harder for exams; doing something illegal; not going to university; getting married so young.

Vocabulary Student's Book pp 44

1 The Arts

A Venues

ANSWERS

a	stage	i	circle
b	curtain	j	gallery
c	orchestra pit	k	stalls
d	conductor	l	screen
e	set	m	drummer
f	footlights	n	guitarist
g	audience	o	microphone
h	aisle	p	loudspeaker

B Use of English

ANSWERS

1 C   2 D   3 B   4 C   5 A   6 D   7 A   8 C   9 B   10 D

Workbook: Vocabulary 2, 3 p 20

Writing Student's Book pp 45–47

Giving an opinion

Aim: This writing section introduces the type of opinion language students will need when writing an article, a report or an opinion composition. It revises the language of opinion used in both formal and informal writing and underlines the importance of the target reader when writing. This writing section should be done before the Exam training section on Articles.

1 Target reader

SUGGESTED ANSWERS

1 teenager	friend	to pass on news
2 local resident	Town Council	to complain
3 newspaper editor	newspaper readers	to comment / give opinion
4 market researcher	Town Council	to give the results of a survey

2 Language of opinion

A ANSWERS

2 *It is a scandal that such events should be allowed to take place. The noise was absolutely deafening!*
3 The entire extract which follows *In our view...*
4 *The noise level was unacceptably high. Concerts of this type should not be held at Eastman Road in the future.*

B ANSWERS

1 *thought* – said (other alternatives would be too formal)
2 *I think* – I feel; In my opinion
3 *In our view* – In our opinion; As we see it; To our way of thinking
4 *felt*; *were of the opinion* – considered; thought

C Formality

Text 4 is the most formal: the opinions are reported; use of the passive *should be held*; percentages are given; the opinion language *were of the opinion* is formal.
Text 3 is fairly formal: use of *In our view*; there are no contractions. (The word *racket*, however, is informal.)
Text 2 is between formal and informal: there are no contractions but there is an exclamation mark; *I think*.
Text 1 is informal: use of contractions; personal questions; direct opinions; informal language, e.g. 'brilliant'.

D Opinions

It wasn't bad. – It was all right / okay; I quite liked it.
It was brilliant... – wonderful / fantastic / great
I'm not very keen on it. – I don't think much of it.
These opinions could be expressed more formally as:
I thought it was quite good.
The concert was excellent. / It was an excellent concert.
I don't like it very much.

Exam training: Articles 1

Aim: This section introduces some of the important features of articles, focusing in particular on the importance and role of the title and opening sentence. (Articles 2 on page 136 looks at opening and concluding paragraphs.) The previous writing section Giving an opinion should be done before this section.

Students can work on their own, or in pairs or groups with class feedback, or the exercises can be done with the whole class.

1 Introduction

Students can read the Introduction or some of the ideas it contains can be elicited from them. Ask students some general questions: what kind of articles they read, what makes them read an article, what styles articles are written in, etc.

2 Titles

A 1 and 2 are essential features of any article. The writer wants people to read his or her article and so must attract their attention and make them want to read it. In magazines and newspapers titles and headlines are usually bigger and bolder than the text of the article to attract people's attention.
4 is advisable, though not essential. Most people like to know what topic the article is about.
3 is not essential. In fact it can be counterproductive. If we know exactly what the article is about we may decide not to read it.
5 is not essential. However, many titles are short, simply because with bigger print they take up a lot of space on the page. Also a short, snappy headline attracts the reader's attention more readily: there is less for the eye to take in.

B
1 To some degree this is a personal choice of answer. Students may say that they wouldn't want to read the articles accompanying d and e. Title d is not specific enough – we have no idea what it is about. Title e sounds rather boring. Students may say they wouldn't want to read c if they think it will be about the scientific processes of recycling, but 'with a difference' may intrigue them enough to at least look at the article. If people are interested in art they will probably want to read a, otherwise they might decide not to. Title b is intriguing and most people would be interested in finding out what the article is about.

2 **SUGGESTED ANSWERS**
   a Paintings and sculptures should be in a gallery, not somewhere else, e.g. in private houses.
   b Modern art made from rubbish? Good and bad modern art?
   c Recycling rubbish in a different way, or for a different purpose.
   d People's opinions.
   e The town's new sculpture.

3 Title a suggests that the article will be serious. Title b suggests that the article will be light-hearted (possibly c, too).

3 Opening sentences

Aim: To emphasize the role of the opening sentence of an article, which is to make a link with the title and to make the reader want to read on. Also, to introduce different kinds of opening sentences.

A Students read the exam question carefully.

B SUGGESTED ANSWERS
   1 A fairly good example. It tells us what we are going to read about and suggests that we are going to hear a variety of very different opinions.
   2 A good example. It is an intriguing question. What's the connection between this and art, we wonder?
   3 A bad example. This doesn't make us want to read on.

C Ask students why the opening sentences of articles frequently contain one or more of these features.

ANSWERS _____
1 a   2 c   3 b

4 Model

Students read the model answer. The missing opening sentence is 2. The word *rubbish* occurs in the title and in the opening sentence. There is also a link with *throw away* in the next line, which is what we normally do with rubbish.

5 Analysis

A The purpose of each paragraph is:
1 To make the reader want to read on and to give the reader an idea of what the article is about.
2 To say what the work of art is, when it appeared and where it is.
3 To describe the sculpture.
4 To give a variety of opinions and conclude the article.

B Informal features
• Several contractions: *you're, don't, wasn't*
• Exclamation marks
• Use of personal pronoun *I*
• Use of inverted commas and quotes
Some examples of a light-hearted style are: *surprisingly; on the pavement, to be precise; No one can see it very well.*
It is appropriate because it fits in with the light-hearted title and opening sentence. A serious and fairly formal style would therefore be inappropriate because of inconsistency. Impress upon students the importance of matching the style of the title and opening sentence with the style of the article.

C The writer uses words like *think* and *say* to preface the opinions. She uses inverted commas to indicate that what is inside them are the actual words used by people.

6 Think, plan, write

A is best done in groups or with the whole class. B could be done in pairs, with ideas elicited from the class. C and D can be started in class and finished at home, or done entirely at home. It is a good idea to ask students to hand in their notes along with their articles, so that you can check that they are actually working out a plan before they start writing.

MODEL
It's certainly different!
No one in Barnton ever has to ask for directions to the accident and emergency hospital. And that's not because the local residents never need hospital treatment, either.
  The reason why is that Barnton's new hospital simply can't be missed. Made from concrete and reflective glass, the fifteen-storey building towers above the elegant nineteenth century buildings on either side of it.
  'It doesn't fit in!' 'It looks out of place.' These are two of the comments most often expressed, in a town which hasn't stopped talking about the new building since it was completed six months ago. Others are more positive, saying for example 'It's a hospital,

not a museum. It should be functional and modern.'
  But will it still look modern and out of place in twenty years' time?

Workbook: Writing p 21

Vocabulary

1 See and watch

A ANSWERS _____
1 watching	4 watch	7 see
2 seen	5 see	8 saw / watched; see
3 saw	6 saw	

B Some general rules of use
We *see* a film (at the cinema); a play (at the theatre); a ballet or exhibition.
We *watch* TV. It is possible to use both *see* and *watch* for programmes on TV. We *see / watch* a film, a comedy programme and the news, but we don't *watch* the weather forecast.
See is commonly used to ask questions about anything on TV, e.g. *Did you see Casablanca last night?*, although *watch* is equally correct.

2 Word building

Noun suffixes

ANSWERS _____
1 admiration (line 93); confidence (line 39); shyness (line 42); popularity (line 24). The corresponding adjectives are admirable / admiring / admired; confident; shy; popular.
2 intelligence, loneliness, education, security, sincerity, darkness

3 Phrasal verbs

ANSWERS _____
A
1 put on	3 put off	5 has put on
2 puts on	4 puts him off	6 was put off

B
1 d get dressed in	4 f distract	
2 c switch on	5 b increase weight	
3 a delay	6 e discourage	

C
1 took off	5 has lost
2 puts off, switches off, turns off	

Workbook: Vocabulary 1, 4 pp 19–20

Your students are now ready to take Unit test 3, which is on page 150 of this book. The key is on page 170.

4 Comparison

Power games

Unit focus Comparatives and superlatives

Topic 1 Television watching habits
Reading
Grammar and practice   Comparative and superlative
                        structures, *The . . . the . . .*, *so*
                        and *such*
Writing   Exam training: Transactional letters 1

Topic 2 Men and women
Listening
Vocabulary   Family relationships, jobs, compound nouns,
              phrasal verbs
Exam techniques   Speaking: Parts 1 and 2
Writing   Describing objects

Introduction   Student's Book p 49

Aim: To introduce the topic of the first part of the unit – television viewing habits.

Before getting students to open their books at the beginning of this new unit, do a brief class survey.
How many hours of TV did students watch the previous day or evening?
How many hours are they going to watch this evening?
What are their favourite programmes?

A Television
Allow students to work through the questions in pairs or groups and then elicit a few answers.

Background information
There are four main channels: BBC1, BBC2, ITV and Channel 4. BBC1 and 2 are non-commercial channels (without adverts), while ITV and Channel 4 are commercial channels (with adverts). A fifth channel will be in operation in the near future. Satellite TV is also available in Britain and the number of homes with this is growing rapidly. Cable TV is available in some cities and towns. The BBC is independent and is not the voice of the government. Certain ITV programmes are regional. British people have to have a TV licence, which costs £86.50 a year for a colour TV and £28.50 for a black and white TV (1995 prices).

B Reading
This semi-authentic TV schedule covers the four main TV channels. The questions are designed to help students study the schedule.

POSSIBLE ANSWERS
1 a BBC 2
   b BBC 1 (or possibly ITV)
   c Channel 4 (7.00 / 12.20)
2 a The Food File (Channel 4 – 8.30)
   b The Late Show (BBC 2 – 11.25); Young Musician of
      the Year (BBC 2 – 7.30)
   c Telly Addicts (BBC 1 – 7.30)
   d 2 point 4 children (BBC 1 – 8.30)
      Spitting Image (ITV – 10.40)
      The Golden Girls (Channel 4 – 10.00)
   e QED: Pisa (BBC1 – 9.30)

C Plan and discuss
Explain the task and ask students to note their individual preferences. The discussions may naturally involve the use of comparison language (the grammar focus of the unit), but do not insist on it at this stage.

Background information
2 point 4 children – a comedy about a family (2.4 is the average number of children per family in Britain.)
Coronation Street – Britain's longest-running TV soap opera
Spitting Image – a satirical comedy programme in which rubber puppets represent famous people, such as the royal family and politicians.
The Golden Girls – an American comedy programme about a group of middle-aged women.

Reading   Student's Book pp 50–51

1 Think ahead

The illustration and the title make it fairly obvious that the text is about which family member controls the choice of TV programmes. The person with their finger on the button is the person in control.
Ask what conclusions students expect the text to reach. Who do they think makes the final decision in most families about what programmes to watch?

2 Reading

Set a limit of four to five minutes for the first reading to encourage students to read for gist.
This reading text is from a general interest magazine and so is written in informal, conversational language. It is a typical example of the way popular journalism presents the results of scientific research to the general public. Though ostensibly about people's TV viewing habits, its real subject is the power relationships between husbands and wives and between parents and children.
The text contextualizes the language of comparison, which is the focus of the Grammar and practice section.

3 Points of view

This point can be discussed in pairs, groups, or as a whole class.

Extra activity

If students find this subject interesting, here are some more points for them to talk about.
1 Which of these statements about the article do you agree with?
- In my experience, the ideas in the article are true to life.
- The families referred to in the article are not like any families I know.
- The article presents a stereotyped, sexist view of the world.
2 The families mentioned in the article had remote control devices to change TV channels. Do you think the results of the survey would have been different if the viewers had not had these devices?

POSSIBLE ANSWER _____

It requires no physical effort to use a remote control, so the laziest person in the family could be the one who decides what everyone else watches. Without a remote control, it might be the most enthusiastic, the most athletic or the strongest member of a family.

4 Comprehension

A Multiple choice

Encourage students to follow the introductory instructions: they should read the questions to find out the information required and then try to find the parts of the article which contain this information.

ANSWERS _____

1 A *part of a bigger power game* (line 19)
2 C *The big decisions . . . are usually joint decisions.* (line 35)
3 A *Women . . . are not as interested in physical control as in emotional control.* (line 75)
4 B *. . .80% of the time it was the man in the house who had his finger on the button.* (line 88)
5 C *. . .they soon realize that the more stubborn they are, the more quickly they get their own way.* (line 108)
6 D *. . .children who had the remote control liked to show off their power. . .* (line 113)

B Vocabulary

ANSWERS _____

1 an argument or struggle between people who have equally strong wishes or opinions
2 the power relationships
3 a decision taken and agreed by two or more people
4 a fight for leadership or the most powerful position
5 communication that does not involve the use of language. Examples of non-verbal communication are facial expressions, gestures, body language.
6 to do or get what you want in spite of opposition

C Reading between the lines

Ideas

1 They are well-off, in employment, probably house-owning, with car and TV and have foreign holidays.
2 Possible alternative explanations: women have got better things to do than watch TV or to care too much about what they watch; women are not prepared to make a lot of fuss just to watch a TV programme; women might be less selfish than men and children about what they watch.

5 Over to you

As students discuss this question in pairs or groups, get them to justify their opinions with examples of specific programmes or types of programmes. Further questions for students to think about:
Do violent programmes encourage people to be violent?
Do people always distinguish between fact (news) and fiction (drama) on TV?
Do political broadcasts change people's opinions?
Does TV advertising work?

Extra activity

Get students to imagine themselves in the following situation.
You are watching TV with two small children who keep changing channels every few minutes while you are trying to watch your favourite programme. In about 60 words, write what you would say to try and persuade them to stop.
Begin by eliciting some of the expressions that might be used in the situation described, for example:
Do you mind (not) + -ing/I wish you'd stop + -ing/I wish you wouldn't + verb
You wouldn't like it if I . . ./How would you like it if I . . .?/Stop doing that or I'll . . .

MODEL

Look, you two, I'm getting fed up with this. I'm trying to watch my favourite programme. It finishes in about ten minutes, so you haven't got long to wait. Then you can watch something else if you want to. How would you like it if I kept interrupting your favourite programme, by changing channels every few minutes? Now just sit still and watch.

Workbook: Reading pp 22–23

Grammar and practice Student's Book pp 52–53

1 Comparisons

This is revision of the basic language of comparison.

ANSWERS _____

2 *much* more serious *than* simply deciding
3 *more* dominant *than* others
4 *most* dominant person
5 have a *greater* need

6 not *as* interested in physical control *as* in mental control

7 far *less* innocent, far *more* knowing

2 Comparative and superlative adjectives

A This list of adjectives contains examples of the different kinds of regular adjectives and some irregular ones.

ANSWERS

bad, worse, the worst (irregular)
common, commoner / more common, the commonest / the most common (two forms)
far, further / farther, the furthest / the farthest (two forms)
friendly, friendlier, the friendliest (-*y* becomes -*i*)
good, better, the best (irregular)
high, higher, the highest (add -*er*/-*est*)
important, more important, the most important (long adjective)
old, older / elder, the oldest / the eldest (two forms)
strange, stranger, the strangest (add -*r*/-*st*)
thin, thinner, the thinnest (double consonant and add -*er*/-*est*)

Further examples of adjectives like those marked with * are listed in the Grammar reference on page 202 of the Student's Book.

B ANSWERS

Far, much and *a lot* are used to compare very different things.
A bit, a little and *slightly* are used to compare slightly different things.
For example:
*Russia is **far** larger than Luxembourg.*
*France is **a bit** larger than Spain.*

C Refer students to the Grammar reference on page 203 of their books.

3 Practice

Elicit ideas from the whole class, or ask students to work in pairs.

A Some ideas for ways of comparing the pairs are given below. Note that comparative, not superlative forms should be used.

1 Height/build/weight/character/intelligence/strength/ facial expression
Hardy is much taller and fatter than Laurel.

2 Intelligence/cleverness/cruelty/size/expression
I think Jerry is far more intelligent than Tom.

B This time comparative and superlative forms can be used. Students should use their imagination for these comparisons.

POSSIBLE ANSWERS

1 Comparing pairs of jobs
• The fisherman has a harder life than the disc jockey.
• The disc jockey has a higher salary than the priest.
• The priest is busier on Sunday than the disc jockey.
• The fisherman has a more dangerous job than the priest.

2 Comparing all three jobs
• The priest probably has the most rewarding job.
• The fisherman is the poorest of the three.
• The disc jockey is the most well-known.

4 Family likenesses

A Students can work out who's who individually and then compare ideas with a partner.

B This can be done orally in pairs or as a whole class, or individually in writing. Remind students to use superlative as well as comparative forms in comparing the family members.

POSSIBLE ANSWERS

Age:
Judy is older than David.
Clive is as old as Jeremy.
Rachel is not as old as Clive.

Build:
Judy is slimmer than Mike.
Paul is the smallest member of the family.

Hair:
Rachel has longer hair than her mother.
Clive's hair is as short as Jeremy's.

Height:
Mike is the tallest member of the family.

C Students compare themselves with other members of their own families. Remind them to use negative (*less*/*least*) as well as positive (*more*/*most*) expressions.
If students know each other's families well, it would be interesting for them to do this exercise orally in pairs or groups, as there would be opportunities for disagreement and discussion. (Friends often see resemblances unnoticed by members of the family themselves.)

Extra written homework
Ask students to do a written comparison between themselves and one other member of their family – maybe one of their parents or a brother or sister. Suggest a limit of about 100 words for this.

Extra activities
1 Do students know any identical twins? How do they tell them apart? This could be for discussion or as a short writing exercise.
2 Students compare members of the class, members of their own family or members of a famous family from their own country.

3 Superlatives quiz

Divide the class into two teams and get them to ask each other questions using superlatives. Questions could be on any subject related to their country, for example, what's the longest river? What's the city with the highest crime rate? Award points for correct answers.

5 *The . . . the . . .*

A Students read through the example sentence and try to work out what it means and how the two parts of the sentence are related to each other.

Answer

The second part is a result of the first.

Work through the seven examples which follow, asking students to supply alternative endings.

B Students practise the use of the structure by making up sequences of sentences to follow those given.

POSSIBLE ANSWERS

1 The later she became, the faster she ran.
  The faster she ran, the tireder she felt.
  The tireder she felt, the more slowly she ran.
  The more slowly she ran, the later she became.
2 The less work he did, the more free time he had.
  The more free time he had, the more relaxed he felt.
  The more relaxed he felt, the easier it was to work.
  The easier it was to work, the more work he did.
3 The more worried he was, the more cigarettes he smoked.
  The more cigarettes he smoked, the less he ate.
  The less he ate, the thinner he got.
  The thinner he got, the iller he felt.
  The iller he felt, the more worried he became.

When students have finished these exercises, ask them to think about and list the various kinds of words that can follow *the*.
Elicit and write their ideas on the board or alternatively get them to check in the Grammar reference on page 203 of their books.

6 *So* and *such*

A Answers

The extracts from the text show that
- *such a* is followed by a singular countable noun (or adjective + noun).
- the clause *so / such a . . . that* is used to express results or consequences.
- *so* is followed by an adjective.

Other words that can follow *so*:
adjectives, adverbs, quantifiers like *much, many, little, few*

Other words that can follow *such*:
a + adjective + singular countable noun *such a hot day*
adjective + plural countable noun *such big eyes*

adjective + uncountable noun *such warm weather*
such a lot of people

B Refer students to the Grammar reference on page 203–204 of their books.

7 Use of English

This is an FCE-type key word transformation exercise, related to the grammar of this part of the unit (comparatives and *so / such*).

ANSWERS

1 Maria is **such a hard worker** that . . .
2 The **hotter it became / got, the** more water. . .
3 Some people have jobs which **are so boring (that)** they can't wait. . .
4 I am not **as interested in history as** I am in . . .
5 Claudia is **the fastest reader in** our class.
6 The **less money you take** with you, the less. . .

Workbook: Grammar 1, 2, 3 p 26

Writing   Student's Book pp 54–55

Exam training: Transactional letters (1)

1 Introduction

If you wish, start by referring students to the Exam Factfile on page 5 of their books and show them where transactional letters appear in Paper 2 (the compulsory question in Part 1). Read through these introductory notes with students to make sure they understand the idea of a transactional letter. Elicit other types of transactional letter.

Ideas
Booking a holiday / Making a complaint / Writing for details of a job / Requesting information / Formal letter of apology / An invitation

2 Sample question and model answer

This presents students with a realistic FCE exam question and model answer. Students can read through the question and plan their own answer. Alternatively, you can get them to use this a reference source and move straight on to 3 Analysis.

A Point out the importance of reading all the information provided in the question very carefully. Then get students to read through the Situation and List of dates and make a list of points they would include in a letter of complaint. You may need to check their understanding of the List of dates, which is written in note form. Check these words and phrases:

CD drawer – the part of the CD player where you put the CD
Recorded cassette – made a recording of a CD on to a cassette (on another part of the stereo system)
Pause button – the button you press to stop the CD temporarily
spare parts – new parts used to replace parts that do not work any more

B Students read the model letter and check how many of their points are mentioned. Check their understanding of the letter.

3 Analysis

This section is intended to focus students' attention on the structure and language of the model letter. Let them work individually or in pairs through the three parts, then elicit their ideas.

ANSWERS

A The purpose of each paragraph

1 is an introduction. The writer says why he/she is writing and explains the nature of the complaint.
2 is a list of important information detailing the exact nature of the problems.
3 explains what the writer did to try to put the problems right.
4 sums up the writer's feelings about the situation and states what he wants the company to do next.
The first sentence lets the reader know the purpose of the letter.
The last sentence states clearly what the writer expects to happen next.

B Key facts

The writer bought the stereo in January. (List)
It started going wrong two days after he bought it. (Situation and List)
The CD drawer went wrong. (List)
The writer recorded a cassette. (List)
The sound quality was poor. (List)
The CD pause button stopped working. (List)
The writer returned the stereo for repair. (Situation and List)
Assistant said it would take a week to repair. (Situation and List)
Nine weeks later the writer collected the stereo. (Situation and List)
The CD player worked. (Date list)
The sound quality was no better. (Date list)

C Formal language

Dear Sir or Madam
I am writing to complain
I returned the stereo to you for repair
I am not satisfied . . . I have received.
I am therefore writing. . . refund
Yours faithfully

4 Practice

A/B Check that students understand this writing task and again get them to read carefully all the information they are given.

MODEL

Dear Sir or Madam,
I am writing to complain about the prize I was sent for winning your recent Travel-n-Learn competition for language learners. There were four different problems relating to the parcel I received.

Firstly the Language pack you sent was for learners of Russian, not English. I clearly remember ticking the box for the <u>English</u> pack. In addition to this, the textbook mentioned in the advertisement was missing and one of the two audio cassettes was broken and impossible to play.

Out of interest, I watched the Russian video and I'm afraid to say that the picture quality was very poor. I hope this is not typical of your videos.

Naturally I am still interested in learning English but I am not prepared to return the Russian pack to you until I have received the correct replacement and checked the contents carefully. I also expect to receive a full refund of the cost of returning the Russian pack to you.
I look forward to hearing from you.
Yours faithfully,

Note: If you set the writing of this letter for homework, remind students of the need to check their work carefully. This may involve rewriting their first draft.

Workbook: Writing p 27

Just for fun

Introduction   Student's Book p 56

Aim: To introduce the topic of the second part of the unit – men's and women's abilities.

The listening which follows compares men's and women's ability to solve mathematical problems. The Introduction gives students two problems to try for themselves. These are intended for fun and interest.

ANSWERS

1 The speaker's birthday is on December 31st, and this statement was made on January 1st.
2 Each of the six friends will be able to listen for 16 minutes.

Listening   Student's Book pp 56–57

1 Think ahead

This discussion can be done in pairs, groups or as a whole class. Keep it brief and light-hearted. After a few minutes, elicit ideas about 'men's' abilities and 'women's' abilities, and note them on the board.

2 Listening

A As students listen to the recording for the first time, they should check to see if their predictions about men's and women's abilities are supported by what the speakers say.

B This may be used as an opportunity for students to comment personally on what they have heard. If they have no strong feelings on this subject, move straight on to the Comprehension exercises.

Tapescript

P = presenter; JT = John Tams; KM = Kathy Manchester

P   Good afternoon. Our first item in today's programme looks at the subject of mathematics and asks 'Who's better at it: boys or girls?' Let's start by asking a teacher. John Tams, you've been a maths teacher for nearly fifteen years now. How would you answer this question?

JT   Well, Jean, in my experience I'd say there isn't as great a difference as people think, but as children get older, boys seem to concentrate harder. Early on, girls have the same ability, but it's still the case that girls tend not to continue with maths after they leave school and go on to polytechnic and university. The unfortunate truth is that people still think of maths as a male subject.

P   Thank you, John. That certainly was my own experience. When I was at school girls were not supposed to be as good at maths as boys. For Kathy Manchester, however, this theory doesn't actually add up. Kathy's a researcher on the popular TV programme *Just for Fun*, where people – just ordinary members of the public – have to solve mathematical problems.

KM   On *Just for Fun* we're trying to bring maths to a non-specialist audience and to counter the common belief that 'maths is impossible and I can't do it' or, worse still, 'I'm not clever enough to do it'. It's very noticeable that the women who come onto the programme seem to have much less confidence than the men, perhaps because they were at schools where girls were not expected to do as well as boys at maths and science. But when it comes to it, women are a lot better at getting the problems right – the programme shows this trend consistently.

P   Yet men show more self-confidence than women?

KM   That's right. They're always ready to jump in and attempt the puzzle, in some cases believing that the women just aren't capable of solving it at all. The strange thing is that, on public display, the macho image begins to crack. The old saying, 'behind every successful man there's a successful woman', may have taken on a new meaning. Maybe it doesn't refer to background support and organization at all, but to actual decisions that are made.

P   So, on the programme, do men and women actually compete directly with each other?

KM   Yes, occasionally – and that's where it all gets very interesting. In the limelight the men become so nervous; blind panic crosses their faces and their minds seem to turn blank. The women, on the other hand, are much calmer; they don't like to take such big risks as the men; they seem to want more time to think about the questions.

P   Two thousand years ago, the Greek philosopher Plato said that even people with no education have an innate mathematical instinct. *Just for Fun* suggests that this is true – and that women have more of it than men. Here's Kathy Manchester with a final word.

KM   What we don't know is whether this ability in women is inherited or whether it comes from years of being the woman behind the man. It's a bit like the tortoise and the hare. Tortoises move more slowly, but they're more consistent – and they cross the finishing line first.

3 Comprehension

A Play the recording again and get students to complete the sentences. (This is the kind of exercise students will have to do in FCE Paper 4 Part 2).

ANSWERS

1 . . .a maths teacher / a teacher of maths.

2 ...concentrate very hard. / concentrate as hard as boys.

3 ...continue with maths.

4 ...a male subject. / ...a boys' subject.

B This is a Paper 4 Part 4 task type. Play the first part of the recording again and get students to answer M or W for each question.

ANSWERS
1 M	2 W	3 M	4 M	5 W	6 W	7 W

4 Vocabulary

A Students work in pairs or as a whole class. Elicit meanings and answers to the extra questions.

ANSWERS

1 *non-specialist audience* = members of the general public who are not trained or expert
   • a specialist / expert / knowledgeable audience

2 *the macho image* = the aggressively masculine image
   to crack = to break up, to weaken
   • typical activities of macho men: chase after women, think they know best, drive cars aggressively

3 *in the limelight* = when a lot of other people are watching them
   • famous people, e.g. politicians, sports personalities, film stars, pop stars
   blind panic = irrational anxiety
   to turn blank = to become empty / to forget everything
   • People's minds turn blank when they are tired or under pressure, e.g. during an exam or an interview.

4 *behind every successful man there's a successful woman* = Many successful men are only successful because of the support and encouragement of a woman (usually their wife).

Elicit students' answers to these two questions. Get them to think of famous couples from history, modern politics, show business, etc.

B ANSWERS
1 at	3 In	5 on
2 In	4 of	6 On

5 Over to you

Let students discuss these questions in pairs or groups. Then one member of each pair or group should report the results of their discussion to the class. In a mixed sex class, do a survey to find out:
• how many students have ever been taught in single-sex classes.
• how many students think that single-sex classes are preferable to mixed classes.

Extra activity

For homework students could write an opinion composition

with the title *What are the advantages and disadvantages of single-sex schools?*

Background information

Research in Britain has produced evidence that girls perform better in single-sex classes or schools than in co-educational situations. The opposite is true for boys.

Vocabulary   Student's Book pp 58–59

1 Family relationships

Remind students about the topic vocabulary list in the Vocabulary reference on pages 215–216 of their books.

ANSWERS

A The answers can be worked out from the family tree.

B a They were *husband* and *wife* (they are now divorced). Mark is Anne's *first husband* (since Anne has remarried). Anne is Mark's *ex-wife*.

b Queen Elizabeth is William's *grandmother*. He is her *grandson*.

c Prince Philip and Princess Diana are *father-in-law* and *daughter-in-law*.

d Princess Diana and Princess Anne are *sisters-in-law*.

e The Queen Mother is Princess Eugenie's *great-grandmother*. Eugenie is her *great-granddaughter*.

C This exercise will come alive if students bring in a few family photographs, but do not insist on this if they are reluctant. Set a time limit of about ten minutes.

2 Jobs

Refer students to the Vocabulary reference on page 216.

ANSWERS

A
1 actor (this can apply to men and women.)
2 miner
3 politician / member of parliament
4 builder
5 dustman / refuse collector
6 civil engineer
7 cook / chef
8 baker
9 butcher
10 lecturer / professor

B
1 electrician	4 musician	7 jeweller
2 lawyer	5 economist	8 civil servant
3 journalist	6 sailor	

3 Word building

A Use of English

This is an FCE Paper 3 vocabulary exercise (Part 5). Remind students that the word in brackets can change its form in any way. They should work out the type of word required (e.g. noun, verb, etc.) and then the likely meaning of the word. To illustrate the importance of this process, take the first line as an example:

1 The word required is a noun. The meaning of the sentence tells us that the word needed is probably the name of a job.

ANSWERS

1 manager	(verb – noun)
2 acquaintances	(verb – plural noun)
3 friendship	(noun – noun)
4 engagement	(verb – noun)
5 relationship	(noun – noun)
6 marriage	(verb – noun)
or	
marrying	(verb – gerund)

B Compound nouns

The use of hyphens to join the parts of compound nouns is problematic in English. Even dictionaries sometimes disagree about when hyphens should be used.

1 **ANSWERS**

1 timetable
2 seatbelt (sometimes hyphenated or two words)
3 rainfall
4 roundabout
5 loudspeaker

2 Allow a few minutes for thought, then elicit suggestions from students.

POSSIBLE ANSWERS

1 back-up, cover-up, follow-up, hold-up, mix-up, rip-off, shake-up, take-off, write-off, break-up, get-away, get-together, lie-in, make-up, pile-up, show-off, slip-up, washing-up
2 half-brother, half-day, half-sister, half-term, half-time
3 Some of the more commonly used words are: self-catering, self-confidence, self-consciousness, self-control, self-defence, self-determination, self-discipline, self-expression, self-government, self-help, self-importance, self-interest, self-pity, self-portrait, self-respect, self-sacrifice, self-satisfaction, self-service

3 **POSSIBLE ANSWERS**

1 **hand**
   handbag, handball, handbook, handkerchief, handwriting
2 **foot**
   football, footpath, footprint, footstep, footwear
3 **day**
   daybreak, daylight, day off, day return, daytime, day-trip
4 **night**
   nightclub, nightfall, nightmare, night shift, night-time
5 **sun**
   sunburn, sunflower, sun-glasses, sunlight, sunrise, sunset, sunshine, suntan
6 **star**
   starfish, starlight
7 **head**
   headband, headlamp, headlight, headmaster, headphones, headquarters, headscarf, head teacher, headway
8 **heart**
   heart attack, heart-beat, heartbreak
9 **water**
   watercolour, waterfall, water-melon, water-skiing, waterworks
10 **air**
   air-conditioning, aircraft, airfield, air force, airline, airliner, airmail, airport

4 Phrasal verbs

Answers

| 1 have taken over | 3 took down | 5 took up |
| 2 took back | 4 took to | 6 takes after |

Workbook: Vocabulary 1, 2, 3, 4 pp 24–25

Exam techniques Student's Book pp 60–61

Speaking: Paper 5 Parts 1 and 2

This section covers the first and second parts of the Speaking test and for this reason has two sets of Guidelines. (Parts 3 and 4 of Paper 5 are covered in the Exam Techniques section of Unit 12 on pages 162–163.) You may like to introduce students to Paper 5 as a whole before working through this section. You could do this by referring to the Exam Factfile on page 8 of the Student's Book.

1 Guidelines for Part 1 – personal information

Work through the guidelines, following the ideas given in the Introduction on pages 13–14 of this book. Stress that it is important for students to keep talking and that fluency is as important as accuracy.

2 Model

Explain that students will hear the first part of a typical Paper 5 Speaking test in which an interviewer (examiner) asks a candidate the kinds of questions students could expect to have to answer themselves. Tell them to think about how they might answer the same questions. Then play the recording once. If you wish, pause briefly after each of the examiner's questions (for about 5 seconds), to allow students to think of their own answers.

Tapescript

I = Interviewer; G = Giorgio	
I	Hello. Come in and sit down, both of you. Could you give me your mark sheets, please? (*Pause*) Thank you. Now, if I could start with you – you're Giorgio, aren't you?
G	Yes, I am.
I	Giorgio, I'd like to begin by asking you a few questions about yourself. All right?
G	Yes.
I	First of all, can you tell me a little bit about your family? Have you got any brothers and sisters?
G	Yes, I've got two brothers and a sister. One of my brothers is called Francesco – he's two years older than me – and I've got a younger brother, Cesare – he's fourteen years old. (*Pause*)
I	What about your sister?
G	Her name's Anna – she's nearly twenty and she's married. She doesn't have any children yet.
I	Right. Now, perhaps you could tell me what you like doing in your spare time?
G	Well, I like swimming – in the summer I often go to the beach with my family – and I like football very much – I play for a local team.
I	Really? And how long have you played football for?
G	Since I was about five years old, I think. I've always enjoyed it – and playing for the team is great, especially when we win!
I	I'm sure. Good. Now I'd like to talk about the future. What are your plans?
G	When I leave university next year I want to travel – I'd really like to spend a few months in another country – maybe the United States . . . or somewhere in Africa. Eventually I hope to go into business.
I	That sounds like a very interesting plan. I hope it all works out.
G	Thanks very much.
I	Good. Now, if I can move on to you, Paola. . .

3 Practice

Check that students understand the role play procedure: from each pair one should take the part of the Interviewer and the other an FCE candidate.

Allow a short time for preparation. Both students in each pair can think of three suitable questions to ask each other. Monitor the role play, without interrupting. Make any general, helpful comments to the whole class after the activity.

4 Guidelines for Part 2 – Talking about photos

Follow the procedure for 1 Guidelines above.

Note: In Part 2, each candidate has a long turn, talking about photos for approximately one minute, after which the other candidate is invited to speak for about 20 seconds on the same photos.

5 Model

Students will hear the same candidate in Part 2 of the Speaking test. Before they listen, elicit their own ideas about the two pictures. This is important preparation as it gives your students a purpose for listening to the recording.

Tapescript

I = Interviewer; G = Giorgio; P = Paola	
I	Right, Giorgio, now I'm going to give you two pictures. They show two different wedding ceremonies. I'd like you to compare and contrast the pictures and say how you feel about them. You have about one minute to do this, so don't worry if I interrupt you. Here are the pictures.
G	Thank you. (*Pause*)
I	You can start whenever you are ready.
G	Well, this one seems to be a very modern wedding – maybe it's in Japan – the people look Japanese. I don't know where they are exactly – it could be a house or a hotel – it doesn't look like a church. Not with that machine making smoke! There don't seem to be many guests. Erm. . . In the second picture, there seem to be more guests – most of them are standing behind the couple, watching. I think this one is in North Africa – Morocco, maybe?
I	You're absolutely right!
G	Yes, in Morocco. Yes. The wedding is not at all like the first one. The clothes they are wearing are obviously different. And this ceremony is taking place outside, isn't it – there are carpets on the ground and it all looks very special, very colourful. There seems to be something official going on – perhaps the couple are getting a marriage certificate? And as I said, everyone is watching – it's a much larger event than the other wedding. (*Pause*) I think if I got married, I would like to have a really big wedding – invite all my friends and lots of family, too, of course. At my sister's wedding last year there were more than a hundred people. Everyone had a great time – good food, dancing, singing . . .
I	It sounds fun. Right, thank you Giorgio. Paola, how do you feel about the weddings shown in the pictures?
P	Well, both of them are very special occasions, aren't they. A wedding has to be special, something you will remember later – have good memories of. I think both of these couples will remember their wedding day.
I	Yes, I agree. Good. Now I want to go on to something else . . .

6 Practice

Students now have the opportunity to role play this part of the Speaking test. Make sure they understand the instructions and know where to find their information and photographs. Allow a few minutes for preparation. Monitor conversations, again without interrupting and saving any general comments until the activity is over.

Extra activity
Ask students to bring in pairs of photographs of their own and repeat the last exercise using these photos. Remind students to move away from the specifics of their photos to the discussion of a related subject.

Writing   Student's Book p 62

Describing objects

1 Theft!

This short newspaper article describes a situation in which descriptions of objects would naturally occur. Students read the article then the three descriptions of missing gifts. This is an opportunity to make sure students are familiar with the kind of vocabulary they will need.

2 What to include in a description

A Students now analyse the language used in the three descriptions and note words and phrases used. Students compare answers in pairs, then check as a whole class.

ANSWERS

	Table lamp	Alarm clock	Candlesticks
Size	medium-sized, about 50 cm tall	small – 8 cm high x 6 cm wide	—
Shape	wide shade	round back	—
Weight	—	—	extremely heavy
Colour	plain blue base dark blue shade with flowery pattern shade	black with clear face, numbers and two hands white, alarm hand black, luminous green tips	silver
Materials	pottery	plastic	(solid) silver
Position of parts	switch below bulb holder, no plug or bulb	knobs on back	stem has three pieces of metal woven together, arms have candle holders at each end
Purpose	to light a room	to wake you up	to hold candles
Price/value	more than £40	about £10	very expensive

B Students could work in pairs to add to these lists. Refer students to the Vocabulary reference on page 216 of their books for ideas.

3 Expanding notes

Students use information in note form to practise producing their own written description of an object. They should use the three descriptions as models.

MODEL
It's an ordinary looking personal stereo, about 14 centimetres long by 8 centimetres wide. It's a lightweight model made of black metal and plastic, and there's a black strap. The buttons are all on the long edge, and there's a microphone socket and the volume control on the short edge. I don't know how much it's worth.

Extra activity
Students work in pairs. Student A describes an everyday object, one phrase or sentence at a time. Student B has to guess what object is being described.

4 Writing

Although the writing itself could be set for homework, encourage students to think and make notes about their object in class. Give help where necessary. Suggest that students write descriptions of about 100 words.
Remind students to check on the rules for the correct order of adjectives in front of nouns in the Grammar reference on page 211 of their books. You may prefer to work through these rules with them.

Your students are now ready to take Unit test 4, which is on page 151 of this book. The key is on page 170.

After they have taken the Unit test, students can do Revision 1, on pages 28–29 of the Workbook. Encourage them to look up anything they have difficulties with. This will help to consolidate their learning, and will prepare them for Progress test 1. Revision 1 could be set for homework.

Your students are now ready to take Progress test 1, which can be found on pages 162–163 of this book. The key is on page 173.

5 Narrative

It happened to me

| Unit focus | Narrating past experiences |

Topic 1 Mishaps
Reading
Grammar and practice   Past tenses
Writing   Exam training: Stories 1

Topic 2 Caving and other dangerous sports
Listening
Grammar and practice   Participle clauses
Vocabulary   Sports, compound adjectives, phrasal verbs
Exam techniques   Reading: Matching headings
                  Use of English: Word formation

Introduction   Student's Book p 63

Aim: To introduce the topic of the first part of the unit – mishaps – through a sequence of related activities.

Students can work in pairs, each having a long turn to talk about one of the photos and to relate them to their own experience. The second student can then speak briefly on the same theme. At the end of the activity, feed in any vocabulary students did not know.
Students in pairs, groups or as a class talk about any similar experiences they (or someone they know) have had. If they have nothing to say at this point, the next activity may give them some ideas.
Students work on their own, in pairs, groups or as a whole class to make a list of things that can go wrong on a journey. This is an opportunity either for dictionary work or for general vocabulary extension.

POSSIBLE ANSWERS

Air
You might be sick / get earache / get food poisoning.
You might miss the plane / take the wrong plane / lose your ticket / forget your passport / lose your luggage.
Your plane might be delayed.
The plane could crash / leave the runway / collide with another plane. The engine could fail / catch fire.
Someone might plant a bomb. The plane might be hijacked.
The company could go bust.

Sea
You might be seasick.
You might have to share a cabin with someone you don't get on with.
The ship could sail without you / hit a rock / capsize / break up / sink.

Rail
You might miss the train / your connection. It might be cancelled / delayed.
The train might crash / come off the rails / break down.

Road
You might get a puncture / run out of petrol / get stuck in a traffic jam / get lost.

The car / bus / coach might not start. It might break down / crash / skid / go off the road / hit a tree / overturn / catch fire. The engine might overheat.

Reading   Student's Book pp 64–65

1 Think ahead

Elicit ideas from students but do not indicate whether or not their predictions are correct.

2 Reading

Students read the text for general comprehension and to check their predictions. Elicit the correct answer.

ANSWER

Because Nigel fell asleep, he didn't get off at London Heathrow, where the plane stopped to let off and pick up passengers before continuing to Rio de Janeiro.

Note: Heathrow Airport, London's main airport, is often referred to simply as Heathrow.

Students are asked to pay attention to the order in which things happen as this will help them to put the missing paragraphs in the correct places in the text.

3 Comprehension

Students work on their own or in pairs or small groups, before comparing answers. In A, students must be able to justify their answers – they can underline or make a note of the relevant content and language links.
The missing paragraphs may have links with the previous paragraph (or paragraphs) or the following paragraph, or both. The links may be grammatical or lexical or there may be a content connection. Because this is a narrative there will also be strong chronological links.

A ANSWERS

1 C *I'd phoned before the plane took off.* (In the previous paragraph he is on the plane). . . . *pick me up at Heathrow Airport* (The next paragraph refers to landing at Heathrow.)

2 B *I sat wondering if we were still on our way down to Heathrow* (This refers back to the previous paragraph.) *I began to realize* connects with *Slowly it began to dawn on me* in the next paragraph.

3 G *What on earth was I going to do?* (This relates back to *felt horrified* in the previous paragraph.)

4 F *We landed at Rio* connects with *The first thing I did was call Georgina* in the next paragraph. (He wasn't able to make a phone call until the plane landed.)

5 A *The driver* connects with *taxi* in the previous paragraph. There is also a connection with *I'd sneaked out* in the next paragraph. (He had done his sightseeing after leaving the airport.)

6 E *Fortunately, there were no problems . . . we landed back at Heathrow* connects back to *I wasn't going to miss that plane* of the previous paragraph.

B Vocabulary
ANSWERS

1 gloomy	3 weirdest	5 a paddle
2 grinning	4 set off	6 frantic with worry

C Reading between the lines
POSSIBLE ANSWERS

1 She had probably got off the plane at Heathrow.
2 Because he had to get into the departure lounge again and he didn't have a ticket.
3 Perhaps because it showed how easy it was to break through their security measures.

Extra activity
Students discuss the following question in pairs or small groups.
If something similar happened to you, would you do the same as Nigel Hughes did? Or would you do something different?
Encourage students to say why they would or would not do a particular thing, and to challenge what other students say.

POSSIBLE ANSWERS
The possible consequences of the actions are in brackets.
• Stay in the departure lounge. If you didn't do what you were told, you could get into trouble. (If you stayed, you would be really bored.)
• Ask the airline staff if you could fly back the next day. If they agreed, you could enjoy yourself without worrying about the consequences of sneaking out illegally. (If they didn't agree, you would have to stay in the airport.)
• Leave the airport but come back at 10 o'clock the next morning, pretending that you hadn't understood what they had said. (You might not be able to get a flight; you might have to pay for your ticket.)

• Do the same as Nigel Hughes but go for a swim and come back to the airport later. You might as well spend as long as possible in Rio.

4 Over to you

The discussion can be done in groups or with the whole class. Here are some questions to help start the discussion: Why do governments have immigration policies and entry controls? What immigration policies / entry controls are in force in your country? What personal experiences have you got? (Have you had to apply for a visa before entering another country? Have you been able to work there? Have you had to study a certain number of hours to be allowed to stay in the country?). How fair are these restrictions? Are they the same for everyone? What would be the benefits and disadvantages of allowing everyone in the world the freedom to live and work in whichever country they wanted?

Grammar and practice

Student's Book pp 66–67

Aim: To revise the verb tenses used to relate past events and related time expressions.

1 The past

Students work on their own (then compare answers), or in pairs.

A Form and use of tenses
ANSWERS

1 Past perfect	a Past perfect
2 Past continuous	b Present perfect
3 Past simple	c Past simple
4 Present perfect	d Past continuous

B Differences in meaning
ANSWERS

1 a Past simple, past simple. Consecutive actions with a cause / effect relationship suggested.
  b Past simple, past perfect. Emma left before Dave arrived.
    You may wish to remind students that the past perfect is often used with time expressions with *by*: *By five o'clock he had finished cleaning the car. Emma had left by the time Dave arrived.*

2 a Present perfect. The decorating is finished.
  b Present perfect continuous. We know the action is recent but we do not know if it is finished or not.

3 a Past continuous, past simple. As the action of crossing the road was taking place, the other action happened.

You may wish to remind students that certain verbs are hardly ever used in the continuous form:
see, hear, want, need, seem
like, love, prefer, hate ('liking' verbs)
know, understand, believe, remember ('knowing' verbs)

b Past simple, past simple. The action of crossing the road happened as a direct result of seeing Michelle. The person may have crossed the road to speak to Michelle or to avoid her.

4 a Past simple. The homework was finished.
  b Past continuous. We know that the action was in progress but we don't know if it was completed or not.

5 a Past simple. He used to play for Arsenal but he doesn't now.
  b Present perfect. He started playing for Arsenal two seasons ago and he still does.

6a Past simple, past simple. Consecutive actions. We waited for them to arrive before starting dinner.
  b Past simple, past perfect. The second action is completed before the first begins. We had already eaten our dinner by the time they arrived.

C Refer students to the Grammar reference on page 204 of their books.

Extra activity
Write the example sentences from the Grammar reference on the board or on a handout with the verbs blanked out. Students fill the gaps with an appropriate verb in an appropriate tense. If there is more than one tense possibility, students must explain the difference in meaning.

2 Practice

A Check students know the meaning of the verbs before they start the exercise.

Background information
A45 – all main roads in Britain are numbered, preceded by the letter M, A or B. M denotes a motorway, A denotes a major road and B denotes a secondary road.
Bury St Edmunds, Colchester, Ipswich and *Clacton-on-Sea* are towns in the south-east of England.
Infirmary is a less common word for hospital, often used in names, e.g. *The Bristol Royal Infirmary*.

ANSWERS

1 happened	5 had been driving
2 was carrying	6 arrived
3 skidded	7 took
4 had braked / braked	8 have charged

B Use of English

ANSWERS
1 He apologized **as soon as he realized** his mistake.
2 Barbara crossed the street **every time she saw Mick** to avoid having to speak to him.
3 I **haven't seen Andy for** a long time.
4 Emily's cousin **has been unemployed for** two years.

5 She didn't **leave until she had locked** up.
6 He added the onions to the soup **when he had peeled** them.

C Background information
King's Cross is the London railway station for trains to the north-east of Britain.

ANSWERS

1	whenever	21	After
2	had just had	22	begged
3	was working	23	offered
4	lived	24	refused
5	As soon as / When	25	agreed
6	heard	26	as / when
7	rushed	27	approached / was approaching
8	then		
9	before	28	held
10	jumped	29	began
11	rang	30	As / When / As soon as
12	was	31	reached
13	told	32	dropped
14	was sitting	33	ran
15	asked	34	saw
16	was going	35	put out
17	replied	36	pulled
18	When / As soon as	37	saw
19	heard	38	said
20	ran	39	missed

3 Pronunciation of regular verbs

Check that students can hear the difference between a voiced sound (when there is vibration of the larynx) and a voiceless sound (no vibration). If students put their fingers in their ears or a hand over their larynx and say the following pairs of phonemes: p / b, t / d, k / g, f / v, s / z, they should note a buzzing noise when they say the second one of each pair.

A / B Students work in pairs. Check answers from the cassette.

ANSWERS

1 /d/	/t/	
lived	worked	
replied	rushed	
begged	jumped	
offered	asked	
refused	approached	
agreed	reached	
pulled	dropped	
	missed	

2 /d/	/t/	/ɪd/
shaved	washed	waited
arrived	brushed	shouted
cooked		
pushed		

C Students work on their own or in pairs. They can read

out their stories to a different partner or the whole class. The class can decide which is the best story.

MODEL

He quickly washed his face, shaved and brushed his teeth. Then he got dressed, grabbed his briefcase and rushed to the bus-stop, where he waited in a queue for the number 47. When the bus arrived, he jumped on, walked to the front and sat down.

The bus was surprisingly empty that morning. He picked up a newspaper someone had left on the seat and started to read it.

Thirty minutes later the bus arrived at his stop. He got off and walked into the building. It was very quiet. He couldn't understand it. By chance he looked down at the newspaper he held in his hand. Sunday, May 8th. No wonder it was quiet!

Extra activities

1 Elicit the above story through mime.
2 Do a gap-fill dictation, snapping your fingers to indicate a missing verb. Pay particular attention to pronunciation of past tense -*ed* endings when checking answers.
3 Do a 'strip story' with the text. Rewrite the text onto strips of paper or card: write one sentence on each strip. Students, working in pairs or threes, have to recreate the text by putting the strips in the correct order.
4 (Groups of 4 students)
• Prepare a pack of cards with the verb stems of both regular and irregular verbs.
• Place the pile of cards face down in the middle of the table.
• Student 1 takes the top card and begins a story in the past tense, using the verb on the card he or she has picked up.
• If the other students think that the form and pronunciation of the verb are correct, Student 1 puts the card face down on the table in front of him or her.
• Student 2 picks up the top card from the pile and must try to incorporate this verb into the next sentence of the story.
• If the sentence is not acceptable to the others (inappropriate, or wrong form or pronunciation), Student 2 must leave the card face up on the table in front of him or her.
• The next player can use this card and / or his or her own card to continue the story.
• The winner is the player with the most cards face down in front of them at the end.

4 Fluency

A Play the recording of Michael's story, pausing the cassette each time you hear a beep. In groups, students predict the next part of the story. Listen to their predictions but don't tell them if they are right or wrong. Let them check for themselves.

Tapescript

> **M = Michael; M2 = Man 2**
> **M** No, it's a true story. It really is. It was when I was a student. I had a holiday job in Germany as a kitchen worker in this really big, super-expensive hotel. Anyway, one day when we had the afternoon off, a few of us decided to go and have a game of football.

> There was this huge field near the hotel, and we used to play there. It wasn't ideal as the grass was a bit long but it was handy. Well, this particular afternoon we played for about an hour and then we went back to the hotel and while we were having our evening meal, someone asked me the time. I looked at my watch to tell him but my watch wasn't there.
> **M2** What do you mean? You'd lost it then?
> **M** Yeah. I realized it must have fallen off while I'd been playing football.
> **M2** So what did you do? (*Tone*)
> **M** We all went back to have a look for it – but the grass was quite long and it was just impossible.
> **M2** So you didn't get it back?
> **M** I'm just getting to that bit. Anyhow, later on that evening I suddenly remembered that the night before I'd been woken up at one o'clock in the morning. I'd set the alarm – the one on the watch – for one o'clock by mistake and I'd forgotten to change it so it was still set for one o'clock.
> **M2** One o'clock in the morning?
> **M** Yeah. So to cut a long story short, I persuaded all my friends to go down to the field at one o'clock with me to have another look. So at about five minutes to one there we all were standing in a big circle in the part where we'd been playing football, waiting and listening in absolute silence. And then someone said it was two minutes past one and we might as well go.
> **M2** Oh no, so, did you?
> **M** No. I remembered that my watch was a bit slow so it probably wouldn't be one o'clock yet. So I asked everyone to be quiet for a couple more minutes. And just then the alarm went off. Now the problem was that my watch alarm only rang for 30 seconds so we didn't have long to find the watch.
> **M2** Did you get it in the end?
> **M** Yeah.
> **M2** Great!
> **M** Well, it wasn't actually.
> **M2** Why not? What happened? (*Tone*)
> **M** Well, unfortunately two days later it stopped working. It'd been lying there for hours in the wet grass and water must have got into it I suppose.
> **M2** After all that! Still it makes a good story. Is it really true?
> **M** Yes it is. People always think I've made it up though.

B Students could be asked to prepare this exercise in advance. Demonstrate by telling a story of your own.

Workbook: Grammar 1, 2 pp 32–33

Writing
Student's Book pp 68–69

Exam training: Stories 1

Aim: The exercises and activities in this section introduce students to some of the important features of narrative writing and prepare them for writing a story about a disastrous holiday. In the exam students who choose to do this question will have to write a story which either begins or ends with certain given words. An example of the latter is given in the model answer. The story which the students write must begin with the words given.

1 Introduction

Ask students what kind of stories they enjoy reading, who their favourite authors are and why. Try to elicit the main features of stories (given in 1 Introduction on page 68 of the Student's Book) and the main differences between novels and short stories, which are more similar to the type of story they will be required to write. (Short story writers have to quickly establish who the characters are and where and when the story happens, and describe what happens in relatively few words).

2 Model

A Students work in pairs to answer questions. Listen to students' ideas but don't confirm whether they are right or wrong. They can check their predictions in B.

3 Analysis

A The purpose of the first paragraph is to set the scene and introduce the characters. The purpose of the last paragraph is to bring the story to an end.

B ANSWERS _____

  1 c   2 f   3 h   4 a   5 g   6 d   7 b   8 e

The writer indicates the order of events through the choice of tenses and the use of sequence words. The main events are told in the past simple in the order in which the events occurred. The past perfect tense indicates the action happened some time before the action related in the past simple. The sequence words also help establish the order of events.

C The three pairs of events are:
1 **As** *she walked* (simple past) . . . *she realized* (simple past)
2 **Just as** *he was disappearing* (past continuous) . . . *a policeman appeared* (past simple).
3 *(Lisa) was walking* (past continuous) *towards the door*. . . **when** *the wind blew* (past simple) *it shut.*

4 Sequence words

1	By the time	4	As soon as
2	While	5	as
3	after	6	just before

5 Think, plan, write

A Students spend five minutes working in pairs using the pictures and their own personal experiences to give them ideas. Elicit feedback from the whole class.

Some ideas
Plane delayed
Hotel not built; hotel overbooked; awful view from hotel window
Bad weather
Dirty or overcrowded beach; polluted sea; dangerous for swimming
Strange food; stomach problems
Insect bites; sunburn / sunstroke
Money / documents lost or stolen

B / C Work through the suggested plan with the students. They could make their notes in class and complete the task for homework.

MODEL
It was the worst holiday Monika had ever had. She had never been to a holiday camp before, but thought that it would be a good place to meet lots of people of her own age.
  The holiday was a disaster from the start. The first thing that went wrong was that she had to share a room with a 75-year-old woman who went to bed at 8 p.m., snored all night, and complained that Monika woke her up when she came back from the disco at 3 a.m. The next problem was that Monika was woken up four hours later by a cheerful voice over an intercom saying, 'Good morning holidaymakers! Time to get up and start the day!' It was impossible to turn over and go back to sleep as the announcement was followed by loud music and repeated every five minutes.
  At the end of the fortnight Monika was exhausted and had not had much fun either. That was the last time she would go to a holiday camp on holiday.

Workbook: Writing p 35

5

A close shave

Introduction   Student's Book p 70

Aim: The short discussion activity introduces the new topic area – sports – and the topic of the listening – caving.

Students discuss the questions in groups or as a whole class. They can use their imagination and the photo to give them ideas.

POSSIBLE ANSWERS

What sort of people go caving?
Adventurous people; people who like danger and taking risks.
What sort of things can go wrong?
The cave could flood; there could be a landslide; the roof could fall in.
You could have an accident (slip or fall) / get lost / be trapped.
What precautions should cavers take?
Check the weather forecast and their equipment.
Have maps of the caves.
Advise people where they are going and when they expect to return.

Listening   Student's Book pp 70–71

1 Think ahead

Allow students enough time to study the diagrams. Elicit the differences between the diagrams if you wish.

2 Listening

As students listen, they have to choose the correct diagram. Don't check that they have the correct answer (b) until they have answered the true / false comprehension questions which follow.

Background information

New Guinea is an island to the north of Australia. One half, *Irian Jaya*, is administered by Indonesia. (The other half is Papua New Guinea.)
Caving – exploring underground systems of caves – is a popular adventure sport in Britain. A related activity is *potholing*, in which *potholers* explore naturally-occurring vertical shafts in rock (*potholes*).

Tapescript

JP = Jeremy Price (Presenter); LM = Leo Marshall

JP   Welcome back. And for the final item in our last *In the News* programme of this series, we trace the lucky escape of members of a four-man British caving expedition in New Guinea two days ago. Team members Mark Williams, Stuart Robinson,

Tony Brett, and Philip Black, who are all highly experienced cavers, were taking part in the exploration of the world's largest underground river, the Baliem River in the Trikora Mountains of Irian Jaya, New Guinea. The mountains, which are situated on the Equator, have an annual rainfall of an incredible 914 centimetres. They are in an area of almost inaccessible tropical rainforest; there are no roads in or around the area at all.
The expedition, which very nearly cost the lives of its four team members, followed a reconnaissance visit to the area last year by the same group. It was during this exploratory expedition that they discovered an entrance to the Baliem River caves – down a deep shaft on a mountain ridge.
I believe we can now go over to Wamena where I hope we have Leo Marshall on the line. Leo, can you hear me?

LM   Yes, I can Jeremy.

JP   Leo. Can you give us more up-to-date details on the incident? I believe all the members of the team are safe and well. Is that right?

LM   Yes, that's right, Jeremy. Everyone's fine. It was a near thing but the team are quite accustomed to such close shaves. Right now, more than anything, they're frustrated at not being able to get on with the job they came to do.

JP   Are any of the team there with you?

LM   No. They've all gone back to the base camp to check their equipment and see what the situation is.

JP   Well can you tell us what happened?

LM   Yes. I spoke to Phil Black yesterday and he gave me all the details. A helicopter dropped the group off at the entrance to the caves on Sunday. The team then proceeded to descend the shaft – which is a considerable way down. Fortunately, as it turned out, they decided that one of them should stay posted near the bottom of the shaft at a sort of U-tube. . .

JP   How do you mean a U-tube?

LM   It's a sort of U-shaped passage that connects the two large caverns. Anyway, Tony Brett stayed there with a radio while the others went on to explore one of the caves.

JP   Were they anticipating any problems?

LM   Well not exactly, but you don't take any chances in this game. They weren't expecting it to rain, certainly – it hadn't, in fact, rained for several weeks and the river had almost dried up, but they knew that if it did there was an obvious risk of flooding.

JP   I believe that Tony was the one who raised the alarm.

LM   Yes, that's right.

JP   Where were the others by this time?

LM   They were about two kilometres from the entrance in one of the large caverns they were exploring.

JP   Can you take us through what happened?

LM   Yes. While they were underground, there was an incredible torrential downpour and the river just flooded. And this is a river that's about 70 metres wide . . . but the water was rising at the rate of about a metre a minute. Tony was alerted when the water reached the far end of the U-tube where he was stationed. He raised the alarm and the others got back just as fast as they could.

JP How long did it take them?

LM It took them all of forty-five minutes – it's not exactly easy going. It's just as well they weren't any further along or that would have been it. As it was they got out with about two minutes to spare.

JP Is it still raining now?

LM No. The rain stopped yesterday afternoon but most of the chambers and galleries have been flooded to the roof.

JP Is the team planning to continue?

LM Yes. Naturally enough, having spent so much time, money, and effort on just getting the expedition under way, they don't want it all to go to waste. So, as I said earlier, they plan to go ahead just as soon as it's at all possible.

JP Any idea when that might be?

LM Well they reckon that if it stays dry, the water level should be back to normal in about ten days' time.

JP Well thank you Leo. And let's hope they do it! And on that note we have to end our programme tonight. We will be back in the New Year with another series of *In the News* but until then this is Jeremy Price saying goodnight.

3 Comprehension

Students listen again and decide whether the statements are true or false. They should be able to give reasons for their answers.

A True or false?

ANSWERS

1 T *They are in an area of almost inaccessible tropical rainforest; there are no roads in or around the area at all.*

2 T *The expedition . . . followed a reconnaissance visit to the area last year by the same group.*

3 F *. . . the team are quite accustomed to such close shaves . . . more than anything, they are frustrated.*

4 F *. . . they decided that one of them should stay posted near the bottom of the shaft at a sort of U-tube.*

5 F *. . . they weren't expecting it to rain.*

6 T *I believe that Tony was the one who raised the alarm. Yes, that's right . . .*

7 T *They plan to go ahead just as soon as it's at all possible.*

B Listening between the lines

POSSIBLE ANSWERS

1 They are very difficult to get to and were only discovered the previous year.

2 The situation the reporter is referring to is the water level in the caves. They probably have radio equipment

at the base camp and can listen in to the weather forecast for the region.

4 Over to you

1 Students discuss as a whole class. If no one has done any of these or any similar sports, go on to 2.

2 Students work in pairs followed by class discussion. If you didn't do 1, the class could talk about what they imagine the risks and thrills of doing dangerous sports such as parachuting, mountaineering and hang-gliding would be.

Possible risks

In all dangerous sports there is a risk of serious injury or even death.

Parachuting:

Your parachute could fail to open.

You could land in a tree, in water, etc.

You could land badly and break your leg.

Mountaineering:

You could get lost / suffer frost-bite / fall.

Hang-gliding:

You could hit an obstacle, e.g. a rock or a tree.

You could lose control of your apparatus.

Possible thrills

In all dangerous sports there is the added thrill of dicing with death and, in many, a sense of achievement.

Parachuting:

Speed during free-fall

Seeing the world from a new perspective

Mountaineering:

Being 'on top of the world'

Hang-gliding:

Sensation of flying

Grammar and practice Student's Book p 71

Participle clauses

Aim: To introduce students to participle clauses as alternatives to clauses of time and reason.

A Form and use

Ask students to identify the type of clause each participle has replaced. Alternatively, write the extracts from the texts on the board and ask students, with their books closed, to rewrite each participle clause in another way. Point out the different forms of the present and perfect participles.

ANSWERS

Sentences 1 and 3 have been reworded using time clauses. Sentences 2 and 4 have been reworded using reason clauses.

The present participle is used in 2 to show that the actions in both clauses happen at the same time. The perfect participle is used in 4 to show that the action in the clause containing the participle took place before the action in the main clause.

B Refer students to the Grammar reference on page 204 of their books.

C Practice

Students work in pairs or alone, then check with a partner.

ANSWERS _____

But, *not recollecting* the man's face immediately, he said nothing. Then, *as he opened* his mouth to ask him what he wanted, Michael realized who the man was. *Not having seen him* for over twenty years, he hadn't recognized him earlier. *Because / Since* his brother had grown a beard, he looked quite different. *Throwing his arms around him*, Michael hugged him tightly.

_____

Students now continue the story in pairs. Encourage them to include some participle and time and reason clauses.

Exam techniques Student's Book p 72–73

Reading: Matching headings

1 Guidelines

Look at pages 13–14 of the Introduction for suggested ways of using the guidelines.

2 Practice

Students should work on their own but will find it useful to compare answers when they have finished. They should be able to justify why they have chosen a particular answer.

A / B Ask students to read the article fairly quickly for general meaning. If you wish, you can set these questions and ask them to find the answers as quickly as possible.
1 Where is the expedition to? (The Himalayas)
2 How many people are interested in going? (11)
3 Why can't they all go? (Because there aren't enough places)
4 Where is the selection procedure taking place? (In Wales)
5 What are the requirements for going on the expedition? (Must be in good physical condition, young and enthusiastic)
6 Name five difficult things they have to do. (10-mile hike; swimming test; climb down a 20-metre rock face; carry someone 2 kilometres on a stretcher in the dark; climb a mountain)
7 How many people are given definite places? (5)

Check their answers to these questions but don't explain any vocabulary or give them any answers they didn't find until after they have matched the missing headings with the text.

Make sure students follow the Guidelines and use the Questions and clues to help them match the headings correctly. Stress that they need to read the headings carefully before reading the article again. Remind them that there is an extra heading which does not fit anywhere.

ANSWERS _____

0 H ***Must** be self-sufficient* is strong advice. What is written on the notice board is a warning. *At risk* means in danger.
1 E *To drop out* means to leave something like a contest or university without finishing. If it is *early* it is likely to be at the beginning of the selection procedure. The first person to drop out is a girl in paragraph 1.
2 F If you *know your limitations* you know what you can and can't do. *A **sensible** young man realizes his swimming is not of the standard required.*
3 B Examples of suffering: *Jo weeps silently; Simon injures his knee; Bobby bruises his spine.* There is no mention of anyone giving up.
4 A The improvement is *the first hot meal in 24 hours.* It doesn't last long as they have to carry someone two kilometres on a stretcher in the dark.
5 D The others distribute the weight of Cathy's pack between them.
6 I People are chosen at the end of the selection procedure. A *few* is not many. Five *are offered unconditional places.*
7 C *Getting everyone back in one piece is the number one priority. Everything else is irrelevant.*

G is the heading which does not fit anywhere in the article. The answers to the clues for G are: *It* refers to the selection procedure. You would use this expression at the end of an unpleasant or difficult experience.

_____

Workbook: Reading pp 30–31

Vocabulary Student's Book pp 74–75

1 Sports

Students can work alone for some of these activities but need to work in pairs or groups for speaking activities A4, C and E.

A Sports and personalities

ANSWERS _____

1 a tennis	f motor racing	j athletics
b cycling	g squash	k weight-lifting
c ice-skating	h basketball	l swimming
d horse-racing	i hockey	m football
e golf		

_____

2 Students should be able to provide plenty of examples of their own. Here are a few ideas.
Roberto Baggio: football, m
Monica Seles: tennis, a
Michael Jordan: basketball, h

Seve Ballesteros: golf, e
Michael Schumacher: Formula One motor racing, f
Colin Jackson: athletics, j
Miguel Indurain: cycling, b
Jahangir Khan: squash, g

3

a tennis player	h basketball player
b cyclist	i hockey player
c ice-skater	j athlete
d jockey	k weight-lifter
e golfer	l swimmer
f racing driver	m footballer / football player
g squash player	

4 This can be a short pair / group / class discussion.

B What do you know?

ANSWERS

1 football: pitch   diving: pool
  tennis: court   gymnastics: gym
  ice-skating: rink   horse-racing: course
2 pitch: rugby, hockey, cricket, baseball
  court: badminton, squash, volleyball, basketball
  rink: ice-hockey, curling
  pool: swimming, synchronized swimming, water polo

C Students discuss in groups followed by class feedback.

D Use of English
This exercise recycles some of the vocabulary in the Vocabulary reference on page 216. Ask students to read the text through first and to summarize what it is about: what you need to do to be good at sport and how professional footballers train.

ANSWERS

1 A   2 D   3 C   4 B   5 B   6 A

E Over to you
Students will need a few minutes' preparation time. Tell them in advance that it is not enough to say that something is boring. They should say why it is boring.

Extra activity
To recycle the vocabulary, play a game of 20 Questions.
• One student / team chooses a sport.
• The other students have to guess the sport by asking questions, e.g. *Is it a team game?*, *Do you play it outside?*
• The answers to the questions may only be 'Yes' or 'No'.

2 Compound adjectives

Demonstrate the formation of compound adjectives by explaining that *an 11-hour flight* is a flight of 11 hours. Point out the word order, the hyphen and the singular noun *hour*. Elicit other examples, or get students to form them from these or similar phrases: *a journey lasting three days, a box of chocolates weighing two pounds*. Students then complete the ten sentences.

ANSWERS

1 three-course meal	6 ten-ton lorry
2 ninety-year-old grandmother	7 one-egg omelette
3 twelve-man jury	8 one-litre bottle of whisky
4 thirty-five-hour week	9 2,000-word essay
5 five-minute walk	10 fifteen piece orchestra

3 Phrasal verbs

ANSWERS

1 took off	4 set off / out
2 look forward to	5 was woken up
3 picks me up	6 threw away / has thrown away

Workbook: Vocabulary 1, 2, 3, 4 pp 33–34

Exam techniques   Student's Book p 76

Use of English: Word formation

1 Guidelines

Work through the Guidelines, following the ideas given in the Introduction on pages 13–14 of this book.

2 Practice

Students work on their own and then compare, or they can work in pairs.

A The questions are designed to get students used to reading the text first for general meaning before starting the exercise.

ANSWERS

Problem: Torquay United football club can't grow grass on their pitch because pigeons are eating the seed.
Solution: They have put cardboard cats on the pitch to frighten away the pigeons.

B Students should use the Guidelines and Questions and clues to help them form the missing words. To encourage them to do this, check the answers to the Questions and clues first.

ANSWERS

The six nouns are: 1, 2, 6, 8, 9, 10. The clues are: definite or indefinite articles (*the / a*) before the missing words and the possessive adjective *their*.
The two adjectives are: 4, which describes the noun *methods*, and 5, which comes before a noun.
The two adverbs are: 3 and 7. They both describe the adjectives which follow.

Don't tell students which words are negative but remind them of typical negative prefixes. There is a list of these on page 102 (Unit 7).

It is more important that students get a feel for word formation than that they get the correct answers at this stage. Refer them to the Common noun and adjective formation boxes and get them to experiment with making nouns and adjectives.

ANSWERS

1	arrival	6	solution
2	variety	7	specially / especially
3	recently	8	concentration
4	unsuccessful	9	presence
5	unacceptable	10	distance

Your students are now ready to take Unit test 5, which is on page 152 of this book. The key is on page 170.

6 Conditions

Cause for concern

Introduction   Student's Book p 77

The Introduction and Reading section which follows focus on the theme of twentieth century problems. If there is currently a problem or an issue of importance which affects your students or their country, start with a brief discussion of this, before getting students to look at the photos.

A Students can work in pairs to match the sentences and the photos. Elicit answers.

ANSWERS

1 e world poverty
2 c serious air pollution
3 b unemployed young people
4 d swan poisoned by pollution
5 a countryside spoiled by new development
6 f city traffic

B This question is intended to start a class discussion, since many of the problems shown in the photos are not exclusively of one type. For example, poverty might seem to be an *economic* problem, but it could be the result of *political* decisions, or *environmental* factors like crop failure due to prolonged drought.

C This question could form a continuation of the discussion started in B. Encourage students to come up with concrete suggestions for dealing with the problems, rather than allowing the discussion to centre too much on negative issues. If you have already spent enough class time on discussion, this could be set as a free writing exercise.

D Allow the class a few minutes to think of additional problems to add to the list.

Possible additions:
Terrorism and crime
Hunger and famine
Diseases and epidemics, e.g. AIDS
Population increase
Hole in the ozone layer
Political instability
Rich / poor divide

Reading   Student's Book pp 78–79

1 Think ahead

In preparation for the article which follows, students are asked three of the questions that British students were asked in a survey into their attitudes and concerns. Your students could compare answers in pairs or small groups. There is no need to widen this into a whole class discussion.

2 Reading

Students should read through the article quickly to find out whether any of the British students share their views. This is a gist reading task to familiarize students with the structure and basic content of the text.
Allow about five minutes for this first reading and then elicit reactions from the class.

3 Points of view

This is an opportunity for students to discuss some of the controversial points raised in the article. They may discuss one or more of the points in pairs, small groups or as a whole class.
Alternatively, you may prefer to move straight on to the Comprehension exercises which follow.

4 Comprehension

A This is a multiple matching reading task of the kind students may meet in Paper 1 Part 4 of FCE. Make sure they understand that they should scan the text for the information they need rather than reading the whole text from beginning to end. Work through the first point with them. If they want to find out *which students are hoping to get a job directly related to the course they are following*, where should they look in the article? Elicit their ideas: in the notes on each of the students which follow their names and in the final section of the text CAREERS.

On this occasion, allow students as long as they need to find the answers, then let them compare and discuss their answers with a partner.

ANSWERS _____

1 T music student / interested in music therapy
2 C Hotel and Catering course / may work at George Hotel
3 J *if I have to pay too much income tax*, etc.
4 T music student / opera
5 R *fewer people out of work*
6 C *Employment is important / Dad redundant*
7 P *Student grants and housing benefits*
8 C *Animal rights . . .*
9 P *The threat to the survival of dolphins . . .*
10 P *I want to be a civil engineer and need to pass the right exams.*
   (Not J, who has no definite plan.)
11 C *I know what I want and that's a job in a hotel . . .*
   (Not J, who says *Ideally, I'd like to run my own business . . .* as this is more like a dream than a definite plan; not T, who says *I haven't decided yet . . . maybe teaching or music therapy . . .* and has therefore not made definite plans.)

B Text references

ANSWERS _____

1 *We* = John and his jazz group
2 *the two* = her two interests – opera and travelling
3 *we* = myself and everyone else in the country
4 *he* = Catherine's father
   it = the fact that her father cannot find work
5 *we* = me and people of my generation
   it = the hole in the ozone layer
6 *they* = animals
7 *they / themselves* = Catherine's Mum and Dad
8 *they* = (the management of) the George Hotel

5 Over to you

This is a short writing exercise preceded by oral discussion between pairs of students.
1 Allow students three or four minutes to compare ideas.
2 Set this as classwork or homework.

Grammar and practice Student's Book p 80

1 Conditional sentences, types 0, 1 and 2

Aim: Revision of zero, first and second conditional structures.

A Elicit ideas about the differences between the three example sentences. Students should describe differences in grammar and in meaning.

POSSIBLE ANSWERS _____

• Sentence 1 is a zero conditional, which refers to a general custom or rule and combines a simple present in the *if*-clause with a simple present in the main clause.
• Sentence 2 is a first conditional, which refers to a possible or likely future event and combines simple present in the *if*-clause and a *will* future in the main clause.
• Sentence 3 is a second conditional, which refers to an unreal or unlikely future event and combines simple past in the *if*-clause with a *would* + infinitive in the main clause.

B ANSWERS _____

a 3 (type 2)   b 1 (type 0)   c 2 (type 1)

Before continuing, make sure students are using the terms type 0, 1 and 2 correctly.

C ANSWERS _____

1 type 0   3 type 2   5 type 2
2 type 0   4 type 1   6 type 1

D Let students discuss the differences in meaning between these pairs of sentences and then elicit their ideas.

ANSWERS _____

1 a The speaker is **sure** he won't be able to afford a reasonable standard of living.
   b The speaker is **uncertain** about the truth of what he is saying.
2 a The speaker thinks it is unlikely that parties will work together, but he is **sure** that if they did there would not be so many problems.
   b The speaker still thinks it is unlikely that parties will work together, but even if they did he is **not sure** whether this would result in fewer problems.
3 a The speaker is **sure** future generations will suffer.
   b The speaker **thinks it is possible** that future generations will suffer.
Note: There are more examples and explanations of the use of modal verbs in conditional sentences in the Grammar reference on page 205 of the Student's Book.

E Point out that the word *unless* means the same as *if not* and is followed by a verb in the affirmative.

ANSWER _____

*Future generations will suffer **unless** we do something about it now.*

F Refer students to the Grammar reference on page 205 of their books.
Note: Third conditionals and mixed conditional sentences are dealt with in the second part of this unit.

2 Practice

A What do you do?
Aim: Practice of zero-conditional sentences.

Elicit suggestions for one of the problems (e.g. headaches) before getting students to discuss the other problems in pairs or groups. Insist on correct conditional sentences.

POSSIBLE ANSWERS _____

1 Go to bed and sleep, take tablets, do some exercise, have a cup of tea
2 Hold your breath (don't breathe), drink water, put your fingers in your ears and swallow hard, drink water out of the far side of a glass, get someone to give you a sudden shock
3 Pinch nose between thumb and forefinger, put a wet cloth on nose, let it bleed till it stops, put something cold and heavy on the back of neck
4 go to bed, take tablets and other medicines, have injections
5 read a boring book, count sheep, get up and work, take sleeping tablets, have a hot drink, have something to eat, close your eyes and relax

B Aim: Practice of first conditional sentences.

POSSIBLE ANSWERS _____

Again, there is scope for students to use their imagination here.
1 you'll get square eyes, or a headache, or become lazy.
2 be tired, you won't get up in time for work, you won't be able to concentrate on your exams.
3 you won't be allowed out next week, you'll have to stay in, I'll deduct £5 from your allowance.

Students could now be asked to think of things parents or teachers say to persuade or warn children, listen for their use of the first conditional and correct them if necessary.

C Elicit more examples of first and second conditional sentences which could be used to bargain or negotiate. You could start by giving students beginnings of sentences to finish, for example
If you give me £10, . . .
If you help me with my homework, . . .
If you lent me your car for the weekend, . . .

D As long as, provided (that), unless
You may wish to draw students' attention to the notes on these alternatives to _if_ in the Grammar reference on page 205 of their books.

1 ANSWERS _____
a – _as long as / provided (that)_ – f
b – _unless_ – d
c – _as long as / provided (that)_ – e

2 Ideas
a . . . we share the driving.
 . . . you don't wake me up in the mornings.
b . . . you apologize for what you said.

 . . . you tell me what I did wrong.
 . . . you give me my money back.
c . . . you promise to pay me back next week.
 . . . you spend it carefully.
 . . . you don't waste it.

3 What would you do if . . . ?

Aim: Practice of second conditional sentences.

Set the scene with specific reference to the room you are in. Students think about how a fire might start, how it might spread, escape routes, etc. Then ask them in pairs or groups to work through the three questions, noting down ideas, and drawing diagrams and plans. Finally get a student from each group to report the group's ideas to the class. Encourage use of the second conditional.

Extra activities
1 Students write a set of instructions telling anyone who comes into the classroom what to do in case of fire. Their instructions will be put up on the wall, so they must be clear enough to be read in under a minute.
2 Get students to imagine what would happen if their town or their home was flooded. How would their everyday life be affected?

Exam techniques   Student's Book p 81

Listening: Note-taking and blank-filling

Notes:
1 Students tried a listening exercise like this in the second part of Unit 4.
2 Before working through the Guidelines, ask students to look at the Exam Factfile on page 7 of their books and read the information about Paper 4 of the FCE. Answer any questions they may have.

1 Guidelines

Work through the Guidelines following the ideas given in the Introduction on pages 13–14 of this book. Stress the importance of students making good use of the time before the recording is played for the first time. They should spend as much time as possible reading through the sentences they have to complete.

2 Practice

Before doing the practice task, you may wish to pre-teach some vocabulary from the recording. Write the following on the board and ask students to match the words with their correct meanings.

1 *dust*   a take air into the lungs and let it out again
2 *asthma*   b part of a port where ships arrive and depart
3 *breathe*   c fine dry powder carried in the air
4 *unload*   d chest illness which causes breathing
                 difficulties
5 *dock*   e fine powder from flowers
6 *pollen*   f remove from a ship what it is carrying

ANSWERS _____

  1 c   2 d   3 a   4 f   5 b   6 e

Explain that students should complete the unfinished
sentences with information from the recording. Allow them
time to read through the sentences and the accompanying
clues, but point out that they will not be given clues like this
in the exam itself.
Play the recording for the first time. Students complete as
many sentences as they can.
Elicit students' answers to the accompanying clues.

SUGGESTED ANSWERS _____

  1 a port on the coast
  2 children, old people, sick people
  3 they might die
  4 a scientific investigation or enquiry / a survey to find
     out the extent of the problem
  5 smoking, infections, poor air quality (pollution)
6/7 people living in the dock area and people living
     elsewhere
  8 to eliminate this as a possible cause of the problem
  9 evidence is analysed, checked, tested, etc.
 10 a time expression (a latest time or date)

Tapescript

> **W = Woman; D = Dr Edwards**
> **W**   For several years now the residents of Wivensea, a
>   small port on the east coast of England, have
>   claimed that dust created by the unloading of
>   cargoes such as grain and fishmeal causes not only a
>   nuisance, but also serious breathing problems.
>   Dozens of new cases of asthma have been recorded
>   since these types of cargo started arriving at
>   Wivensea and what is most worrying is that many
>   of these cases are young children. Feelings are
>   running high in the town – people are saying that
>   it's only a question of time before someone dies
>   from a dust-related attack. Six months ago, at the
>   request of the town council, community medical
>   officer Dr Ralph Edwards carried out a small survey
>   which seemed to suggest a link between periods of
>   unloading and increased health problems. This
>   encouraged the council to commission a more
>   detailed survey at a cost of several thousand
>   pounds. Dr Edwards takes up the story.
> **D**   What we're trying to do with this survey is to find
>   out whether the complaints of damage to people's
>   health are actually justified. To prove the resident's
>   case and force the port authorities to take action,

there will have to be very strong evidence. The
problem is that breathing difficulties can have many
causes. Smoking, for example, and the common
cold. There are two forms of evidence, however,
that would be very strong. The first would be if,
over a very long period of time, we were able to
follow two groups of people, one living near to the
port itself and the other living in the north part of
the town. That's what we're actually doing here in
Wivensea. If it is found that the people in the port
area always get their symptoms when the ships are
unloading, but at no other times, and if a similar
pattern is not visible in the group living in the other
area, then this will provide us with strong evidence
that it is in fact the dock that is responsible for the
problem.

W   Yes, I see. And did you say there was another form
of evidence that might be used?

D   Yes, indeed. The other type of evidence would be
positive proof that the breathing problems were
caused by a reaction to particular types of dust. If
the tests showed that people were allergic to the
dusts coming from the dock area, but not to other
kinds of dust, for example, grass pollen, then again
that would be strong evidence that it was the dock
that was actually the cause of the problem.

W   So how long will it be before the anxious residents
of Wivensea know whether their complaints are
justified and whether something can be done about
the problem?

D   Well, quite obviously, evidence has got to be
collected, enquiries have to be made and then the
results have to be analysed. Personally, I'm
optimistic that by the end of the year there will be
sufficient evidence for us to advise the town council
about the next step that should be taken.

Play the recording again, so that students can check
sentences they have already completed and complete the
remaining ones. Since this is a practice exercise, you may
wish to play the recording for a third time. Elicit or give
answers.

ANSWERS _____

  1 the port area / the unloading of cargoes / ships being
     unloaded
  2 young children
  3 die (from breathing problems)
  4 a small survey
  5 smoking and colds / smoking and the common cold
  6 groups of people
  7 parts / areas of the town
  8 responsible for the problem /causing the problem / to
     blame for the problem
  9 to be analysed
 10 the end of the year

Writing
Student's Book pp 82–83

Exam training: Reports 1

1 Introduction

Read through this introductory paragraph with students, making sure they understand what reports are and how they differ in style from other types of writing (e.g. letters, articles, etc.). Check students' understanding of these words: *factual / layout / title / sub-heading*.
Don't spend too long on this, as a model report follows immediately.

2 Sample question and model answer

A Read through the sample question, checking students' understanding. If they show any interest in the subject, ask for their views about zoos.

B As students read the model report, they pick out the sub-heading which is written in an unsuitable style.

ANSWER
What people really hate – too informal, too personal.

C A more suitable sub-heading might be 'Dislikes' or 'Negative responses'.

3 Analysis

This section allows students to look in much more detail at how the model report is structured and written.

SUGGESTED ANSWERS
A
1 The sub-headings tell the reader what the sections which follow are about.
2 Paragraph 2
   Have you been to / visited the zoo in the last year?
   What is you (main) reason for going to / visiting the zoo?
   What do you think / consider the main function of a zoo is / should be?
   Paragraph 3
   What do you dislike about zoos? / What do you find annoying about zoos?
   Paragraph 4
   Do you think the zoo should stay open at public expense? / Do you think the public should pay for the zoo to stay open?
3 A factual and impersonal style is achieved by the inclusion of:
   • facts and figures
   • precise references
   • clear, unambiguous sentences.
   Note: Brief comments may appear, but the writer's opinions should not be apparent in the main body of the report.

B Number phrases
over 200 people / A total of 62 per cent / Half / only about 10 per cent / 88 per cent thought / Just under 10 per cent / a large majority, 70 per cent

C Report language
   • to introduce
     The aim of this report
   • to generalize
     On the whole . . .
   • to comment on a fact
     Interestingly . . .
     Not surprisingly . . .
   • to conclude or summarize
     To sum up . . .

4 Practice

A Students read the extra paragraph and suggest suitable sub-headings.

Suggestions
Main attractions / Favourite animals / Popular animals

B Students now try to rewrite the paragraph using about 40 words.

Possible rewriting
Apes and monkeys are often thought to be the main attractions at zoos, but in the survey one-third of those questioned chose lions and tigers. Apes and monkeys were chosen by 23%. Other attractions included penguins, elephants, and pandas. (40 words)

5 Think, plan, write

This task is similar in many ways to the one used as a model.

A Read through the question with the class, making sure they understand what to do.

B This preparation stage is very important. It can be done, as suggested here, by students working in pairs or groups, or by individuals. If you have the time and opportunity to conduct a real survey, this is well worthwhile as a class project.

Additional possible questions
   • What do you like most about owning a pet?
   • Is there anything you dislike about owning a pet?
   • If you could have a second pet what kind would you choose?
   • Who feeds and looks after your pet?

C Remind students of the need to plan their writing carefully, and emphasize the importance of a title and sub-headings.

D Students could be asked to write the report for homework.

See next page for Model.

MODEL

THE GROWTH IN POPULARITY OF DOMESTIC PETS

<u>Introduction</u>
The purpose of this report is to summarize the results of a survey about pets. It is based on the answers of 100 students.

<u>The number and kind of pets</u>
Over 70 per cent of those questioned had a least one pet. Surprisingly, five per cent had three or more pets. A large majority of owners had a dog or a cat. Ten per cent owned birds, mice or hamsters. Just under half had had their pets for less than one year.

<u>Reasons for owning pets</u>
Students found it difficult to say why they owned pets, but the most common reasons were: interest and 'love of animals'. Only ten per cent said their pets had a special purpose. Some dogs, for example, were used to guard apartments.

<u>Looking after pets</u>
Most of the students claimed that they looked after their pets themselves, but some admitted that their parents took over when they were at school.

<u>Conclusion</u>
To conclude, it is clear that pets are becoming increasingly popular among young people. What is unclear is exactly why this is happening.

> Workbook: Writing p 41

6 Conditions

If only . . .

Introduction   Student's Book p 84

Aim: To introduce the second topic of the unit – lying.

The questions and discussion points should encourage students to think about their own attitude to truth and honesty. Let them talk about the questions in pairs or groups and then discuss their ideas with the whole class. The four quotations about lying are the words of these people:

a Hilaire Belloc – British writer and poet 1870–1953
b Michel de Montaigne – French essayist 1533–1592
c Adolf Hitler – German dictator 1889–1945
d Robert Louis Stevenson – Scottish author 1850–1894

Introduce *white lie*, a harmless lie told to avoid hurting someone.

Listening   Student's Book pp 84–85

1 Think ahead

Allow students two to three minutes to discuss these questions. Elicit their stories.

2 Listening

A This is a gist listening task which gives students a first chance to listen to the recording. They could compare reactions after listening, but there is no need to broaden this into a class discussion.

Tapescript

> 1   I was round at my boyfriend's house a couple of weeks ago, and his mother asked me if I'd like to stay for lunch. I said I was expected home, but it was a complete lie – I'd actually told my parents I'd be out all day, and not to expect me home before the evening. The thing is I'd eaten there before and the food was terrible, but you can't tell the truth in situations like that, can you?
>
> 2   I'm not really keen on lying, but I was in town the other day and I bumped into one of my neighbours – she's a well-known local busybody. She said she'd heard that my sister and her husband had split up, and she wanted to know if it was true. I kept an absolutely straight face and said I'd no idea. It was a blatant lie, of course – I mean I'd known for ages – but I wasn't going to give family secrets away in the street. The trouble is, she'd have wanted to know all the details and everyone would have known by the weekend.
>
> 3   I have to admit, my life would have been pretty dull if I hadn't told a few lies from time to time. Not wicked ones, you know, just white lies that don't

hurt anyone. I remember once I was at a party and I got stuck with this really boring boy – all he could talk about was football. Anyway, after about half an hour, I was really fed up so I told him that my cousin used to play for England – his eyes nearly popped out of his head. He wanted to know my cousin's name, and could I introduce him to him and everything. When I said it was Paul Gascoigne, I thought he was going to pass out with excitement.

4   The other day the phone rang and my brother asked me to answer it. He thought it was probably his friend Barbara and for some reason he didn't want to speak to her. He asked me to say he wasn't in. As it turned out, it wasn't Barbara – it was another friend of his – Annie. Anyway, I didn't know the difference, so I just said he was out. When I told him who it was afterwards, he was absolutely furious. I remember the exact words he used. He said, "If I'd known it was Annie, I'd have spoken to her." But then that's one of the problems about lying for someone else, isn't it? Anyway, it taught me a lesson – I'm not going to lie for him again – probably not for anybody else either.

5   It was when my sister was away on holiday last summer – and she was expecting her exam results – towards the end of August. She'd asked me to open all her letters and telephone her with the results as soon as they arrived. The thing is, she'd only been away about a week when the letter came – I was so excited, I just ripped the letter open without thinking. I couldn't believe it when I saw that she'd failed. I didn't know what to do – I couldn't bring myself to tell her. She rang a couple of days later and I said the letter hadn't come. I mean, if I'd told her the result, it would have ruined her holiday.

B   Now explain the main listening task and give students enough time to read through the six reasons, before playing the recording again. Check that they understand these expressions:
do someone a favour / offend / spoilt / privacy
Play the recording a second time. Exam-length pauses are included on the tape.
Elicit or check answers but **do not explain the answers** at this stage. If you do so, you will make the comprehension questions which follow too easy.

ANSWERS
Speaker 1 – Reason C – she didn't want to offend her boyfriend's mother
Speaker 2 – Reason E – she was trying to protect her sister's privacy
Speaker 3 – Reason F – she found it exciting to tell lies
Speaker 4 – Reason B – the speaker answered the phone for his brother
Speaker 5 – Reason D – the speaker didn't want to spoil her sister's holiday by telling her that she had failed an exam.

3 Comprehension

A   Multiple choice
Notice that there are only three choices of answer for each of these questions.
Allow students time to read through the questions and then play the recording again.

ANSWERS
1   C *I'd eaten there before and the food was terrible*
2   B *everyone would have known by the weekend*
3   A *I was really fed up, so . . .*
     his eyes nearly popped out of his head – this reaction obviously pleased the speaker
4   A *'If I'd known it was Annie, I'd have spoken to her.'*
5   B *it would have ruined her holiday.*

B   Vocabulary
ANSWERS
1 e   2 h   3 b   4 c   5 g   6 a   7 d   8 f

5 Over to you
Allow five to ten minutes for this fluency exercise.
A compulsive liar is someone who cannot prevent themself from lying.

Grammar and practice   Student's Book p 86

This completes the revision of the main conditional forms.

1 Conditional sentences type 3

A   Form and Use
1   Elicit answers. The standard form of the third conditional is
     If + past perfect . . . would have + past participle
2   Allow students time to discuss the differences between these four sentences and then ask for answers. Type 3 conditional sentences differ fundamentally from types 0, 1 and 2 in that they refer to a past situation which is impossible to change. They are used for speculating about imaginary situations.
     Type 0: The speaker regularly tells lies.
     Type 1: The speaker will probably tell lies in the future.
     Type 2: The speaker regularly tells lies now, and is likely to tell lies in the future.
     Type 3: The speaker has already told lies (and is saying how different life would have been if she hadn't told lies.)

B   Ask students to read through the Grammar reference notes on page 205 of their books.

C   Making excuses
This is an FCE-type key word transformation exercise, limited to third conditional sentences. Students should work

through the exercise individually and then compare answers in pairs.

ANSWERS _____

1 If I **had known it was you**, . . .
2 . . . **if I had known** you were back . . .
3 . . . postcard **because she didn't have / she hadn't got** my address . . .
4 He wouldn't **have been late if** he hadn't forgotten . . .
5 . . . you a present **if I hadn't forgotten / if I had remembered** when your birthday was.
6 . . . so late, **we would have come** to your party.

2 Moments of decision

Students read the first text, then discuss what they would have done in Jill Frame's situation. Elicit as many ideas as possible.

Students read and discuss the second story. Monitor, listening for the correct use of the third conditional. Don't interrupt the flow of discussions, but deal with errors later. Students should be encouraged to use some of these expressions:
1 If I'd been in X's situation . . .
2 If it'd be me . . .
3 If I'd been X . . .

Ideas
Motorway nightmare:
I'd have waited until the road was clear, then I'd have crossed the motorway and phoned for help.
I wouldn't have left my car. I'd have locked all the doors and waited until a police patrol car arrived.

Supermarket Mum:
I'd have asked the manager to phone for an ambulance.
I'd have left my shopping in the trolley, walked to the car park and driven myself to the hospital.

3 On the spot

Set this writing task for homework. Remind students to use the third conditional and to follow the suggested paragraph plan. As preparation allow students five or ten minutes classroom time to exchange experiences with each other in pairs.

4 Mixed conditionals

Work through the introductory example and explanation of a mixed conditional sentence, then elicit students' suggestions for possible continuations of the first sentence of the exercise. Once students seem to have understood the idea, allow them to continue the exercise orally in pairs, or in writing individually.

POSSIBLE ANSWERS _____

1 . . . I wouldn't be able to do my job now.
. . . I wouldn't be able to enjoy newspapers or novels.
2 . . . I wouldn't be at work today.
. . . I would be relaxing in a luxury hotel somewhere.

3 . . . I'd be able to afford to go on holiday this year.
. . . I would be very rich.
4 . . . I wouldn't be doing such an interesting, well-paid job now.
. . . I'd be stuck in a boring dead-end job.
5 . . . I wouldn't need to work for a living.
. . . I'd probably be bored and miserable.
6 . . . I wouldn't be me.
. . . I'd be someone else.

Workbook: Grammar 1, 2, 3 pp 38–39

Vocabulary   Student's Book p 87

1 Body language

A Reactions

POSSIBLE ANSWERS _____

1 they turn pale, they sweat, they shiver, their eyes open wide
2 they shiver, their teeth chatter, they get goose-pimples, they go blue
3 they shake, they go red in the face, they shout, they stamp their feet
4 they go red (blush), they look at the ground, they stutter when they speak, they laugh or giggle

Extra activity
Get students to think about how people react when they are nervous, confident, proud of themselves, bored.

B Parts of the body

ANSWERS _____

The parts of the body in the photos are:

1	forehead	6	neck	11	toe	16	shoulder
2	eyelash(es)	7	palm	12	ankle	17	elbow
3	cheek	8	chest	13	knee	18	wrist
4	jaw	9	stomach	14	calf	19	waist
5	chin	10	shin	15	thigh	20	hip

The words missing from the sentences are:

1	shoulders (*shrug* = raise)	5	wrist
2	toe (*stub* = knock accidentally)	6	hips
3	palms	7	knees
4	eyelashes (*flutter* = move lightly and quickly)	8	elbows

2 Compound adjectives

Make sure students understand how these compound adjectives are formed before moving on to A.
Ask students questions like these:
• How would you describe baby with a round face?
• What would you call a man with dark hair?
• And a girl with blue eyes?
• A dog with thin legs?

Students work in pairs to think of famous people with these characteristics. Point out the pronunciation of these two:
long-legged – /legɪd/
left-handed – /hændɪd/

Extra activity
Students use similar compounds to describe someone they know well. Monitor descriptions and discussions, correcting any errors in the formation of compound adjectives.

Workbook: Vocabulary 1 p 39

Exam techniques   Student's Book pp 88–89

Reading: Gapped text (missing paragraphs)

Note: Before working through the Guidelines and Practice, remind students that they have already dealt with texts from which sentences are missing (Unit 2, page 26). How many of the Guidelines can they remember? Elicit these and write on the board. Get them to think about whether any of these guidelines are also applicable to texts with missing paragraphs.
If students cannot remember any of the guidelines from Unit 2, move straight on to these new guidelines.

1 Guidelines

Work through the guidelines, following the ideas given in the Introduction on pages 13–14 of this book.
Stress the importance of looking for textual progression and language connections.

2 Practice

A Students read through the main text, thinking about what kind of information may be missing. There are clue questions to help them. After this first reading, elicit students' answers to the clues only.

POSSIBLE ANSWERS
1 They could be children, but are more likely to be animals of some kind, since they are obviously eating raw potatoes.
   They could be animals who are behaving rather like humans. What kind of animals could dig and scream?
2 Instinctive behaviour involves no thought or decision-making.
   Other kinds of behaviour: voluntary, thoughtful, deliberate.
3 There may be other tricks to follow.
4 Research in the field / real-life research / Research based on observation of nature.

5 It is probably deliberate, not instinctive behaviour.
6 Apes can behave in deliberately deceptive ways.

B Students now read the missing paragraphs and make a first attempt to fit them into the gaps in the text. Make sure they realize that there is one paragraph that doesn't fit anywhere.

C Students could work through the language connection questions in pairs or as a whole class. Elicit ideas.

ANSWERS
Language connections
Paragraph A *another* tactic suggests that one tactic has already been mentioned.
Paragraph B *such* intelligence suggests that an example of intelligence has already been mentioned. (This is the extra paragraph).
Paragraph C *this* probably refers to an experience or a story that has just been told.
Paragraph D The expression *Taking all the evidence into account, . . .* would normally be used to summarize before concluding.
Paragraph E *another* way to decide suggests that there has already been mention of one or more ways to decide.
Paragraph F *So* means as a result of, or bearing in mind something that has already been established.
Paragraph G *however* suggests a contradiction to or a contrast with what has gone before.
Gaps
1 C 2 G 3 A 4 F 5 E 6 D
Paragraph B is not needed.

Workbook: Reading pp 36–37

Vocabulary   Student's Book p 90

1 Word combinations

Say, speak, talk, tell
Do not attempt to explain the differences between these four verbs. Students should think of these expressions as collocations to be learnt. Elicit answers.

ANSWERS
say a prayer, hello and goodbye, 'yes' and 'no', your name
speak your mind, a language
talk sense, nonsense, rubbish
tell someone's fortune, a lie, a story, the truth, a joke, the time (tell someone the time)

Find out if students know any other expressions using these four verbs.

2 Colours and their associations

A Possible associations of colours

Note: These often differ from culture to culture.

black	death / negative / exotic / mysterious / magical / good luck, bad luck
blue	unhappiness / royalty / pornography / the unexpected
green	envy / immaturity / environmental / approval / permission
red	anger / prohibition / stop / love / socialist / important / blood / embarrassment / heat
white	illness / death / purity / weddings / cleanliness

B This text contains eight common colour idioms. Let students work through it, filling as many gaps as they can, before eliciting or providing answers. Make sure students understand the idioms.

ANSWERS

1 *I could feel myself going* **red** *with embarrassment* = blushing
2 *. . . gave me really* **black** *looks* = angry or evil looks
3 *. . . quite out of the* **blue** = unexpectedly
4 *They're probably* **green** *with envy.* = very envious / jealous
5 *. . . my grandfather stopped talking and went as* **white** *as a sheet* = turned very pale
6 *You've had a* **black** *mark against your name, . . .* = a record of misconduct or failure
7 *Suddenly I saw* **red**. = I became very angry.
8 *. . . he only rings me once in a* **blue** *moon . . .* = very infrequently

Extra activity

Here are some more colour idioms. Can students guess what they mean?

- to be on a *black list* = be on a list of people considered dangerous or undesirable for some reason
- to be the *black sheep* of the family = a person whose conduct is considered unacceptable by other members of a family or group
- to have *green fingers* = to be good at gardening
- to be in the *red* = to owe money to the bank / be in debt
- a *red letter day* = a very important day
- *red tape* = official, bureaucratic formalities or procedures

3 Phrasal verbs

This section focuses on nouns associated with phrasal verbs.

A Students work through the exercise. Check answers.

ANSWERS

1 held up	4 broke out
2 turned out	5 let (you) down
3 gave away	

B ANSWERS

1 important discovery
2 adults – people who have *grown up*
3 a meal that you buy in a restaurant and eat at home
4 something so badly damaged to be not worth repairing
5 where you pay for goods in a supermarket
6 period of physical exercise or training
7 the sudden appearance or start of something unpleasant, like an illness
8 medical examination

Workbook: Vocabulary 2, 3 pp 39–40

Your students are now ready to take Unit test 6, which is on page 153 of this book. The key is on pages 170–171.

7 Description

A woman's place

Unit focus **Describing people's character and appearance**

Topic 1   Jobs people do
Reading
Grammar and practice   Relative clauses
Writing   Exam training: Applications 1

Topic 2   Appearance and character
Listening
Vocabulary   People, negative prefixes, phrasal verbs
Exam techniques   Use of English: Error correction
Listening   Multiple matching
Writing   Describing people

Introduction   Student's Book p 91

Aim: To introduce the topic of the first part of the unit – jobs.

The vocabulary exercises focus on the qualities people need to do particular jobs well.
Students can work on their own or in pairs for A and B. C is a paired discussion.

A ANSWERS

1 judge	3 firefighter	5 nurse
2 reporter	4 hairdresser	6 teacher

B ANSWERS

b energetic	g brave	k fit
c creative	h sociable	l enthusiastic
d strong	i fair	m hard-working
e patient	j organized	n cheerful
f caring		

Reading   Student's Book pp 92–93

1 Picture discussion

Students in pairs study the photos and decide what they think Kate Adie does for a living. Don't tell students the answer as they will be checking their predictions themselves.

2 Reading

This article contextualizes the grammar focus of the unit, relative clauses. It comes from a magazine, and is written in a style typical of that genre: sentences begin with 'and' or 'but', there are many contracted forms, and examples of informal language such as:
frilly (line 52) – decorative, only interested in superficial things

a buzz (line 70) – a feeling of excitement
chicken (line 72) – coward.

Background information

Kate Adie is Chief Correspondent for the BBC and often works as a war reporter, both of which have traditionally been seen as men's jobs. In Britain, although more and more women are moving into jobs previously done almost exclusively by men, it is still seen as an achievement and something a little out of the ordinary. Despite legislation which provides for equal job opportunities for women, women still find barriers to reaching the top in many fields of employment.

ANSWER

She's a TV reporter (a reporter for the BBC).

3 Points of view

Pairwork or whole class response. Don't spend more than a few minutes on this activity.

Possible back-up arguments:

In support of emergency service workers – they save lives; firefighters risk their lives to save the lives of others. Front-line TV reporters are only observers of tragedy.
In support of front-line reporters – they draw our attention to the horrors of war and famine; their reports have an immediate impact and are often influential in getting something done.

Extra discussion point

Why do you think some people see the job of war reporter as an exclusively male job? Do you think they are right?

4 Comprehension

A ANSWERS

1 C *it's her cool, objective reporting that people most praise.* (line 17)
2 D *admits that her job rules her life. She's never off duty. ..it would be a very tolerant man who would stay at home while Kate rushed off on an assignment.* (line 27; 35)

3 C . . . *she was terrified that the camera crew would think she was a 'silly frilly girl'. That's the reason why she crammed everything she needed into a tiny bag.* (line 51)

4 A *Now she knows that it's her appearance as well as her words that matter. So she decided to a include a pair of curling tongs.* (line 58; 62)

5 A *. . . despite all the drawbacks, she wouldn't change her life for the world.* (line 80)

6 C *It wasn't just me. Don't forget the camera crew. It's unusual to find this attitude these days but typical of Kate Adie.* (line 20)

B Reading between the lines
ANSWERS

1 Her job is very important to her. *(She) admits that her job rules her life (line 27); she wouldn't change her life for the world (line 81).*

2 Her boss at the BBC. 'Get down to Brixton quickly! A riot's broken out.'

3 She may never get married because it would be difficult to combine marriage with the kind of life she leads. Her job also constantly intrudes on her private life.

5 Over to you

This group discussion could be preceded by a class brainstorm of disasters and tragedies students have seen on television. Possible topics are famine, war, pollution, earthquake, fire, plane crashes. Be aware that this may be a sensitive subject for some students.

Students should answer the questions for themselves, then form groups with others who share their opinions. After a few minutes sharing ideas, divide the class into groups containing people of opposing views.

POSSIBLE ANSWERS

Agree: Difficult for people to imagine disasters from a written report. When people see effects of disasters they may donate money or pressurize governments into taking action, e.g. the Live Aid concert in 1985.

Disagree: People are becoming immune to human suffering (it seems like a film, not real life). Events are often exploited for sensational effect, e.g. plane crashes.

Grammar and practice Student's Book pp 94–95

Aim: To focus on the form and use of the relative pronouns *who, which, that, whose* (and no relative pronoun, Ø) in defining and non-defining clauses, and the relative pronouns *where, why, when*.

Although relative clauses are rarely used in conversation, students need to know how to use them in their writing.

1 Relative clauses

Form and use
Aim: To check what students already know.

In pairs students fill in the gaps and then check their answers from the reading text. Confirm any other possibilities but don't tell them why answers are wrong at this point. (See 2C.)

ANSWERS

The pronoun most likely to be used is given first.
1 whose
2 who, that
3 that, Ø, which

2 Defining and non-defining clauses

A Difference in meaning
Aim: To focus on the importance of commas in relative clauses.

Students discuss the sentences in pairs or as a whole class.

ANSWERS

In sentence 1, I have more than one sister. In sentence 2, I have only one sister.

B Practice

Students work alone or in pairs. Before they do this practice activity, check that they understand the difference between defining and non-defining clauses. You can demonstrate the difference using the sentences in A. The relative clause in 1 is defining; it makes clear which of my sisters I am talking about. The relative clause in 2 is non-defining; it simply gives extra information on where she lives.

ANSWERS

The wedding context presupposes a situation where only one couple is getting married at a time. Where alternative pronouns are possible, these are given.
1 Defining; that.
2 Non–defining; *The groom, who is Erica's cousin, is much older than the bride.*
3 Non–defining; *The bride, whose family is quite well-off, has just celebrated her 21st birthday.*
4 Defining; that.
5 Non–defining; *The reception, which will be held at the Crown Hotel, is for invited guests only.*

C/D Students work on their own, compare answers with a partner and finally check their answers in the Grammar reference on page 206 of their books.

ANSWERS

. . . it's her cool, objective reporting that (Ø, which) people most praise. (line 17)
. . . into a tiny bag which (that) would fit underneath her plane seat. (line 54)
. . . a holdall that (Ø, which) she now takes everywhere . (line 64)

. . . places Ø (that, which) you'd never dream of going to.
(line 83)

3 Relative pronouns and prepositions

A ANSWERS

1 Mr Walker, who I have worked closely with for years, is an excellent colleague.
2 The man (Ø) I complained to was extremely rude.
You can leave out the pronoun in 2.

4 Other relative pronouns

A ANSWERS

1 when   2 where   3 why
The relative pronoun can be omitted in 1 and 3. (See Grammar reference 4 on page 206.)

B ANSWERS

We visited the house Shakespeare was born in.
that Shakespeare was born in.
which Shakespeare was born in.
in which Shakespeare was born.

C Refer students to the Grammar reference on page 206 of their books.

5 Practice

ANSWERS

1 who, that
2 Ø, that, which
3 why, Ø
4 which (add a comma after *concert*)
5 that, which
6 where (*that, which* and Ø are only possible when the preposition *in* follows the verb *live*.)
7 whose (add commas after *Irons* and *Venice*)
8 whose
9 Ø, that, which
10 when (add a comma after *winter*)

6 Relative clauses and prepositions

Students should spend a few minutes in pairs studying the sentences and answering the questions. Elicit any ideas they have before referring them to section 5 of the Grammar reference on page 207 of their books.

ANSWERS

In each case, sentence a is in formal English and sentence b is in informal English.

In formal English, prepositions usually come before the relative pronoun. In informal English they usually come at the end of the relative clause.

In formal English, the relative pronoun *whom* follows the preposition in both defining and non-defining clauses. In informal English, *who* is used instead of *whom* in non-defining clauses, and no relative pronoun is used in defining clauses.

7 Use of English

ANSWERS

1	for	5	what	8	her
2	whose	6	not	9	about
3	all	7	whom	10	of
4	to				

8 Expanding a text

SUGGESTED ANSWER

However, Stephen's manager, *who controls his finances*, puts most of his earnings straight into the bank. Stephen, *whose earnings were over £500, 000 last year*, started playing snooker when he was 12. World champion at the early age of 21, Stephen, *who comes from South Queensferry in Scotland*, says his success lies in his killer instinct, *without which he believes he would be just another good player*.
Note: *killer instinct* = a ruthless, competitive determination to get what you want.

Workbook: Grammar 1, 2 p 44

Writing   Student's Book pp 96–97

Exam training: Applications 1

Aim: The exercises in this section introduce students to some of the main features of letters of application, which is one of the question types in Paper 2, Part 2. They focus on the presentation of relevant personal information and how to begin and end a formal letter applying for a job. Applications 2 on page 182 covers letters of application for scholarships or grants.

Students work on their own and then compare answers, or in pairs for all the activities.

1 Introduction

Students read through the information in their books. Ask them if they have ever written a letter of application either in English or in their own language. What was it for? Was it successful? What kinds of letters of application do they think they may write in the future?

2 Model

Note: In a real letter of application you would need to include your address (but not your name) in the top right-hand corner of the page, and the name (if known), position and address of the person you are writing to on the left-hand side of the page. There are several slightly different conventions for this. You would also include the date under your address. In the exam, however, students are not required to do this.

ANSWER

The applicant is likely to be successful for the following reasons:

1 She fulfils the requirements:
   She is the right age; a non-smoker; and expects to have a driving licence soon. She is available to go to the USA for a year and is interested in going there and finding out about life in the States. She is keen on sports. (She is good at swimming and likes horse-riding). She has some experience of looking after children.
2 She sounds like a responsible and honest person.
3 Her letter of application is well written.

3 Analysis

ANSWERS

1 The purpose of paragraph 1 is to give the reason for writing. If you are writing in answer to an advertisement, it is usual to say where (and when) you saw the advertisement.
   The purpose of paragraphs 2 and 3 is to give relevant personal information in support of the application.
   The purpose of paragraph 4 is to conclude the letter.
2 She begins the letter *Dear Sir or Madam* because this is a formal letter and she does not know the name of the person she is writing to. She finishes the letter *Yours faithfully* because it is the convention to sign off in this way when you begin *Dear Sir or Madam*. See the summary box at the end of Applications 1 for more information about the conventions of beginning and ending formal letters in English.
3 Some examples of formal language (informal equivalents are in brackets) are:
   The beginning and ending of the letter
   I would like (want)
   to continue my studies at university (to go to university)
   I am a non-smoker (I don't smoke)
   an ideal opportunity (fantastic)
   Although ... (I haven't got any experience ... but I have)
   The whole of paragraph 4.

4 Think, plan, write

A and **B** can be done in pairs or with the whole class. Once students have some ideas they can plan and write their applications at home.

MODEL

Dear Sir or Madam,
I am writing in reply to your advertisement in last Friday's edition of the Daily News. I am interested in working as a summer camp helper and believe that I meet the necessary requirements.

I am 22 years old and will be finishing university this summer. I would be able to take up employment on June 15, and could work until the end of September. Although I am French, I speak English well and have some experience of working with children. In my last year at school I accompanied groups of boys aged 12–14 on several weekend camping trips. I helped the teacher in charge to look after the group and also organized competitions and songs around the camp-fire in the evenings. I can play the guitar quite well.

I am fit and healthy and keen on sports. I play football and am in the university basketball team. I also have a life-saving certificate. I hope you will be interested in my application. Looking forward to receiving your reply,
Yours faithfully,
Pierre Marcelle

Workbook: Writing p 47

7 Only skin deep

The title comes from the saying 'Beauty is only skin deep', which means that physical beauty does not guarantee good character and, conversely, a lack of beauty does not necessarily show a lack of good personal qualities.

Introduction   Student's Book p 98

Aim: To introduce the topic of the second part of the unit – appearance and character, and how descriptions change according to purpose and context.

Students spend a few minutes in pairs answering the questions. Check their ideas.

POSSIBLE ANSWERS _____

1 Their character or personality, their job and interests.
2 How we feel about the person.
  Who we are talking or writing to.
  Why we are giving the description.

Listening   Student's Book pp 98–99

1 Think ahead

Students working in pairs can compare ideas on the women's character / personality / job / interests. Elicit a selection of ideas.
Before students do 2 Listening they could compare what the women look like and say what the main differences are. Feed in any vocabulary students ask for.

2 Listening

Play the recording and check that students have the correct answer.

ANSWER _____

Diana Jacobs is number 2. She is not wearing jeans, and has chin-length hair and a fringe.

Tapescript

First description

Oh, thanks a million. I know it's an inconvenient time. I really appreciate it. I hope you don't mind too much. *(Pause)* Yes, well, apologize for me, will you? You know I'd go myself, only with my leg in plaster, it's impossible to drive. *(Pause)* Well, it's supposed to touch down at half-past midnight, but they're often a bit late, aren't they? And by the time she's waited for her luggage and been through customs . . . *(Pause)* Yes, yes, I know. And there's

nothing you can do about it, is there? *(Pause)* Yes, that's right. Okay, have you got a pen handy? Right? Well, she's slightly shorter than me, about an inch, so she's about five foot five. She's slim. *(Pause)* No, she's a bit slimmer than me. She's got short, well, shortish – well sort of chin-length hair, dark-brown. It's really straight. And she's got a fringe. *(Pause)* I've no idea. She usually dresses quite casually, but smart. *((Pause)* No, I don't think she'll be wearing jeans. *(Pause)* Yeah, I know, but I can't think of anything else. Look, if you're worried, just hold up a card with her name on it. *(Pause)* It's Jacobs – J-A-C-O-B-S, Diana Jacobs. Have you got that? *(Pause)* Right, it's flight BA 527 Washington to London. Oh, and it's Heathrow not Gatwick.

3 Comprehension

A Play the recording again and check the answers.

ANSWERS _____

A friend; a family member; a private conversation.

B Students now listen to two more descriptions of Diana Jacobs and follow the same procedure as for A. Play each description twice.   •

ANSWERS _____

Someone who fancies her; a friend; a casual chat.
A potential employer; a colleague; a discussion at work.

Tapescript

Second description

G = Gary; M = Mick

G Hi, Mick. How're things? What happened on Saturday? Did you go to *Charlie's* in the end?
M Yeah, I got there about twelve.
G Who else went?
M Just Dave.
G Was the band any good?
M Mmm. Not bad. But it was incredibly crowded. I've never seen it so busy.
G Did you meet anyone interesting?
M Yeah, I did actually.
G Don't tell me. She's tall, blonde . . .
M She's not, actually.
G Well, that makes a change. Well, go on then. What's she like?
M Well, she's called Di. She's nice-looking, long legs, quite classy, friendly. She's got a nice smile.
G Mmm. So are you seeing her again?
M Yeah, maybe. I said I'd give her a ring sometime.
G Can I get you another drink?
M Yeah, cheers. Same again.
G Two pints of bitter, please.

Third description

W = Woman; M = Man

W No, I agree. He's rather inexperienced. What about this one? Diana Jacobs. She's 27 years old, she's been working for McKenzie, Brennan and McKenzie for the last six years, since she graduated from, let's see, Newcastle.

M They're quite a good firm, aren't they?

W Yes.

M What sort of experience has she had with them?

W Mainly general legal matters. She seems to be particularly interested in getting more into company law.

M Well, that would suit us. We're getting more call for that sort of thing these days.

W Yes, you're right.

M Have we got any character references for her?

W Yes. There's one from her present employer. He says she's very efficient, extremely reliable, works well under pressure and can work equally well on her own and in a team. I think she'd fit in pretty well. What do you think? Shall we get her in?

M Yes. Let's do that. Now, are there any more to look at?

W Uh. We've got one here from a Michael Summers but I don't really think he'd be very suitable. But see what you think.

4 Missing person

Play the recording twice and allow students time to fill in the form. Check that they understand what *distinguishing features* are. See the Vocabulary reference on page 217 for examples.

ANSWERS

Name:	James Durie
Reported missing by:	Mother
Address:	64, Priory Road
Phone number:	41709
Age:	16
Height:	5'8"
Build:	Slim
Hair:	Brown, short, straight
Distinguishing features:	None
Clothes:	Blue jeans, white trainers, plain black T-shirt
Last seen by:	One of his friends
Time last seen:	9.30 p.m.
Place last seen:	Bus Station, Bridge Street

Tapescript

Missing person

PO = Police officer; W = Woman

PO Yes, how can I help you, madam?

W It's my son, Jamie. I know I probably shouldn't worry but he didn't come home last night.

PO I see. Can I have the name, please?

W Yes, It's Durie, James Durie.

PO Can you spell that please?

W Yes, it's D-U-R-I-E.

PO And the address, Mrs Durie?

W 64, Priory Road. That's P-R-I-O-R-Y.

PO How old is your son, Mrs Durie?

W He's 15, no 16. It was his birthday last month.

PO And has this ever happened before?

W No, never. That's why I'm worried. It's just not like him.

PO So, when was the last time you saw him?

W Well, yesterday evening, about six. He, um, went straight out after he'd had his tea.

PO Did he say where he was going?

W No, just 'out'. Well, that's what they all say, isn't it?

PO And when did you realize he hadn't come home?

W Not till half seven, this morning, when I went to get him up.

PO Have you telephoned any of his friends to see if he stayed the night with them?

W Yes, but they don't know where he is either.

PO So they didn't see him last night, then?

W Yes, one of them did. He said he'd seen him at the bus station in Bridge Street.

PO What time was that?

W About half-past nine.

PO So that was the last time anyone saw him?

W As far as I know, yes.

PO OK, the first thing we'll do is get a detailed description of your son. I'd like you to describe him in as much detail as you can. All right? Now, how tall is he?

W He's fairly tall for his age. About five eight.

PO Five feet, eight inches. And build? Is he slim, well-built?

W Slim.

PO Fine. And what's his hair like?

W Well, it's quite ordinary, really. It's hard to say.

PO Colour?

W It's brown. Sort of mousy.

PO And is it wavy, straight?

W No, it's straight. And it's short.

PO Fine. And has he got any other distinguishing features, you know, scars, that sort of thing?

W No, none that I can think of.

PO OK. And can you tell me what he was wearing when you last saw him?

W Yes. He was wearing blue jeans, trainers, that's white trainers, and a black T-shirt.

PO A plain T-shirt?

W Yes.

PO OK. Well, thanks, Mrs Durie. I'm sure there's nothing to worry about but we'll get this description circulated and see what comes up. Have you got a phone number we can contact you at in case we hear anything?

W Yes. 41709.

PO 41709. I would suggest you go home now, Mrs Durie. And try not to worry. There's a very good chance he'll just turn up none the worse. They usually do.

5 Appearances

Give students a few minutes to read the five incomplete sentences. Remind them that they should only write a word or short phrase to complete their answers. They should not need to write more than five words. Elicit any ideas students have about what they will hear and the type of information which could fit in the gaps.

ANSWERS

1 the blonde woman / the woman with blonde hair / the other woman
2 find them attractive / are attracted to them / like them
3 like them or dislike them
4 clothes / clothing / what they wear
5 their appearance / what they look like

Tapescript

W = Woman

W   Can you judge someone by what they look like? Is it a good idea, in fact, to even try? A few years ago, a friend of mine who is a television reporter had to fly off at short notice to interview an important politician. The office had booked her a two-seater plane to fly her to wherever it was he was speaking, but when she turned up at the airport – it was a small, local airport – there was no sign of a pilot anywhere. After half an hour, he still hadn't appeared, so she asked a young woman with blonde hair, who was also hanging around, if she had any idea where the pilot was. Then the penny dropped. 'Oh no,' said the woman, 'Are you the reporter?' 'Oh no,' said my friend, 'Are you the pilot?' The answer was yes to both questions. My friend felt pretty stupid, but judging someone by their appearance, and jumping to conclusions about people is human nature. We all tend to make quick decisions about someone the moment we see them. We glance at a stranger in the street and within seconds calculate their age, decide what sort of person they are and, microseconds later, decide whether or not we find them attractive. We jump to conclusions about people simply on the basis of what they look like. If we meet someone who resembles a friend, we are ready to like them. If they look like someone we can't stand, we are inclined to dislike them. But first impressions are not always correct and most of us have been proved wrong about someone at some time in our lives. So why do we do keep on doing it? The main reason is that it is practical to do so. We just don't have the time to find out what the hundreds of people we come into contact with every day are really like. People are not cardboard characters; they are complex individuals each with their own life history and personality. It takes time to discover this. The result? Everybody jumps to conclusions about everybody else. Faces and clothes offer clues, of course, but sometimes these are deliberately misleading. Our clothes are often chosen for the person we would like to be and not the person that we are. Everyone can exploit their appearance though women have more choices than men, with a greater range of clothes, hairstyles and cosmetics to choose from. But everyone can create their own image. Everyone can disguise their real self if that is what they want to do.

Exam techniques   Student's Book p 100

Use of English: Error correction

1 Guidelines

See pages 13–14 in the Introduction of this book for ideas on how to use this section.

2 Practice

Ask students to read the text through quickly and to say briefly what it's about: a description of someone's (probably a girl's) brother. Then ask them to follow the guidelines and use the error checklist to help them find the extra words.
Students work on their own but compare answers before making their final choices. It may help them to identify the four correct sentences first. When checking answers try to elicit why the words are wrong.

ANSWERS

The correct sentences are: 5, 9, 10 and 12.
The extra words are:
1   *the*   no article before measurements or weights
2   *that*   no 'that' after how + adjective constructions, e.g. 'I'd forgotten how expensive it was.'
3   *like*   look like = to resemble a person e.g. 'He looks like his father.' Look = appear; seem to be, e.g. 'She looks friendly.' / 'You look fat in those trousers.'
4   *of*   *in spite of* but *despite* (Ø)
6   *has*   Past simple tense with 'ago'
7   *since*   It is not possible to have 'since' and 'ago' in the same sentence.
8   *a*   'Hair' can be a countable or a countable noun, e.g. 'Waiter there's a hair in my soup!' / 'She's got lovely hair.'
11   *the*   no definite article when talking about the whole class i.e. all girls.
13   *it*   It is incorrect to include a pronoun which refers to a noun in the same sentence.

14 *to* to help someone (to) do something
15 *got* The infinitive form is *to have*. 'Have got' is generally only used in the present tense.

Workbook: Grammar 3 p 45

Vocabulary   Student's Book pp 101–102

1 Describing people

A Students work in groups. Give groups five minutes to write down as many words as they can under the descriptive headings. Write suggestions on the board. Point out that general words are required under age and height.

B Find someone who . . .
Students should work in pairs.

ANSWERS

going grey 10	curly hair 3, 9
petite 4	dyed hair 9
plump 6	freckles 12
skinny 2	a parting 3, 10
slim 3, 4	a pony-tail 13
stocky 5	a scar 13
tanned 10	spiky hair 11
well-built 1, 5	shoulder-length hair 7
a beard 10	a spotty complexion 7

C Modifying adjectives and adverbs

Ask students in pairs to list the modifiers in three groups – most intense, medium intensity, least intense – but not to grade within each group. As the relative intensity of each modifier depends to a great extent on stress and intonation, absolute grading is impossible.

ANSWERS

1 Most intense: *incredibly*, extremely, really*, very*
Medium intensity: *rather, quite, fairly*
Least intense: *a bit**
Pretty* can replace *very* and any of the modifiers in 1.
Other words like *incredibly* are *terribly*, amazingly**.
* = informal English
2 Other modifiers like *fairly* are *quite* and *rather*. The Grammar reference on page 207 has examples of these.

Extra activity

Writing and speaking practice: dictate the exercise, or write it out.
Fill the gaps in the following dialogue with the most appropriate adjective from those given. Use each adjective once only.
long reasonable uncomfortable boring good awful
Sue: What did you think of the film?
Liz: Well it was quite (1) I suppose, but a bit (2).
Sue: Yes, it was rather. They could have cut it by at least half an hour and Tom Cruise wasn't wonderful, was he?

Liz: He certainly wasn't. I thought he was really (3). Mind you, I think he's very overrated. I haven't thought much of him in anything I've seen so far.
Sue: He is good-looking, though. But the middle part was a bit weak. I kind of lost interest there.
Liz: Yes, it was rather (4).
Sue: And those seats are terribly (5).
Liz: Mmm, they are a bit hard, aren't they?
Sue: Still, what can you expect for £3 nowadays?
Liz: Yes, it is very (6).

ANSWERS

1 good	3 awful	5 uncomfortable
2 long	4 boring	6 reasonable

Now have a similar dialogue with your partner. Choose one of these topics:
• a film you've both seen
• a TV programme you both watch
• a record you've both heard
• a singer, actor, politician, etc. you both know
• a kind of food (e.g. Chinese) you've both tried
Try to use as many different modifiers as you can and give reasons for your opinions.

2 Use of English

Students should not do this exercise until they have studied the vocabulary in the Vocabulary reference on page 217 of their books.
Ask students to read the text quickly and say what it's about: a description of a young man called Mark.

ANSWERS

1 C   2 A   3 D   4 B   5 D

Extra activity

A selection of magazine photos of famous or ordinary people could be brought in. Students, in pairs, choose one and write a physical description of the person in the photo. Set a time limit. Put the photographs on the board, number them, and read out the descriptions. Students note down the number of the person they think is being described. Don't check answers until the end. This activity could be done at a later date to recycle vocabulary.

3 Word building

ANSWERS

uncaring	impatient
inconvenient	impolite
unenthusiastic	disorganized
unfair	irresponsible
unfit	insecure
illogical	unsociable

Ask students if they know any other examples, e.g. untidy / unadventurous / unambitious / impractical / unpopular / unpleasant / disloyal

4 Phrasal verbs

ANSWERS

1 Turn down	4 turn down	6 turn up
2 turned up	5 turn it over	7 (had) turned into
3 turns out		

Workbook: Vocabulary pp 45–46

Writing   Student's Book p 103

Describing people

Aim: To encourage students to use a few simple strategies for making their descriptions more interesting.

1 Bringing descriptions to life

A Text 1 contains more physical description than text 2 and gives the writer's opinion at the end. Text 2 starts with the writer's opinion, contains only one physical detail (wrinkled face) but has more descriptive detail.

While text 1 is not a bad example of descriptive writing, students will hopefully recognize text 2 as a better example. Text 1 gives rather too much detail to take in. The person described in text 2, however, seems more real because of the examples and selective detail that is given.

B Text 1 begins with a rather ordinary fact, the man's age. A lot of descriptive details are given, rather too many, and there are no comparisons. There are no examples either. Text 2 begins with an interesting opinion and the writer is selective in the descriptive details given (miserable character and wrinkled face). His face is compared to a prune. Examples are given of what he complains about.

C ANSWERS

1 clever	5 nervous
2 ambitious	6 sentimental
3 reserved	7 shy
4 affectionate	

Alternative activity

If time is short and students do not have time to make examples with the remaining words, the following could be used (possibly dictated) as gapped sentences. Students then provide the missing words in brackets.

1 Jason thinks he's wonderful. He's so _____ (big-headed)
2 Cindy never offers to pay when we go out. She's very _____ (mean)
3 If Rick has promised to take you to the airport, he will. He's extremely _____ (reliable)
4 Stuart is always shouting and getting angry. He's very _____ (bad-tempered)

2 Think, plan, write

Elicit some ideas from students and set the writing for homework.

MODEL

My favourite person is also my best friend, Louis. We have been friends ever since we first met ten years ago.

Louis is in his late thirties, tall and well-built. His black hair is now going grey and, much to his disgust, receding fast. He must have spent a small fortune on 'miracle' hair lotions before he finally accepted he could do nothing about it.

Like everyone else, he has his good and bad points. He is hard-working and intelligent, loyal and generous, but can also be extremely stubborn.

I suppose that what I most admire about him is his love of life and his endless optimism, even when nothing is going right.

Exam techniques   Student's Book p 104

Listening: Multiple matching

1 Guidelines

Pages 13–14 in the Introduction give some suggestions for using this section.

2 Practice

A Spend only a few minutes on this, as a class discussion. It is simply a warm up to the theme of the listening. Ideas will depend on the country and the types of employment available.

B Students should read options A–F carefully and spend a few minutes answering the clue questions under the options. These are the sorts of questions students should be asking themselves while they are waiting to hear the recording. Elicit ideas from the class but don't supply any. Before students listen, remind them that there is an extra option.

POSSIBLE ANSWERS TO CLUE QUESTIONS

A To solve a problem; to create something
B Because they don't want to hurt someone. Because they will get into trouble if they tell the truth.
C Pain
D Stealing money from a company; unprofessional conduct
E Holiday camp organizer
F When they do something they shouldn't have done.

Ask students to say what helped them to decide their final choice of answers.

ANSWERS

1 F *She told me I'd be in serious trouble if it ever happened again.*

2 B *I said 'Okay' when actually I was hopeless at it.*
3 E *We did everything from polishing the floors to serving the meals and washing up.*
4 C *I felt a really sharp pain in my hand. I had to have a couple of stitches.*
5 A *If I pile them up on one side I can pack them in my own time. I thought the supervisor was going to be really impressed.*

Tapescript

1 Woman

I was working on an adventure scheme in Sheffield. You know the sort of thing they organize for kids during the school holidays. And one day I was left in charge at lunch-time. And everything was fine until one boy shouted something at another and the next minute there were plates and food flying everywhere. Anyway, without really thinking I grabbed hold of the boy who'd started it by the shoulders and was just about to shake him when the supervisor walked in. Well, I knew I was in for it because you're not allowed to lay a finger on the children. And I was right. She took me to one side and told me I'd be in serious trouble if it ever happened again.

2 Man

It was my own fault really because when the employment agency asked me what my maths was like I said 'Okay', when actually I was hopeless at it. Anyway on the Monday morning when I arrived at the bakery I was put in the office and given the job of working out the bills. And I was given about 50 sheets of paper with about 60 items to calculate on each page. They didn't have calculators then and I had till lunch-time to do it. By 12 I was only halfway down the first page, because they were impossible calculations like the cost of 144 bread rolls at 3.75 pence each! People kept saying 'All right?' and I said 'Yes, fine' when I was anything but. I found out later on that there was a book you could use with all the answers in. I suppose you could say it served me right.

3 Woman

I didn't really get on with the woman who owned the hotel and the other two girls who were working there weren't terribly friendly, so it certainly wasn't the nicest summer job I'd had. In fact I probably worked harder in that job than in any of the others. We were on from 7 in the morning till 9 at night if there were a lot of guests staying, so it was a long day and we did everything really from polishing the floors to serving the meals and washing up. The worst thing was cleaning out the guests' bedrooms, especially if it was a family with kids, because the hotel was next to the beach and the sand ended up absolutely everywhere.

4 Man

I worked as a postman one Christmas but once was enough. The worst thing that happened to me was when I was delivering a small package to a house. I rang the bell but no one came and I couldn't be bothered carrying it round with me the rest of the morning, so I decided to shove it through the letter-box. Anyway, it got stuck and as I was trying to push it through I heard this deep growl from behind the door and then I felt a really sharp pain in my hand. I let go of the package and pulled my hand out as fast as I could. It could have been a lot worse but fortunately, I'd been wearing gloves. As it was, I still had to have a couple of stitches.

5 Woman

I was working in a large bakery in Glasgow on the cakes section. I had to stand at the end of a conveyor belt and pack these small chocolate cakes six at a time in a cardboard box. Anyway, the cakes used to come along the conveyor belt in hundreds and I was rushed off my feet for about 20 minutes and then for some unknown reason had nothing to do for 20 minutes. Then, one day I thought, this is daft. If I pile them up on one side I can pack them in my own time. I thought the supervisor was going to be really impressed. Then he picked up one of the cakes on the top of the pile and all the rest came with it. They'd all stuck together and they all had to be thrown out.

Your students are now ready to take Unit test 7, which is on page 154 of this book. The key is on page 171.

8 Points of view

A burning issue

| Unit focus | Expressing and reporting opinions |

Unit focus   Expressing and reporting opinions

Topic 1   Smoking
Listening
Grammar and practice   Reported speech
Exam techniques   Reading: Multiple matching

Topic 2   Crime and punishment
Reading
Writing   Presenting an argument
              Exam training: Compositions 1
Vocabulary   Crime, phrasal verbs, noun suffixes

Introduction   Student's Book p 105

Aim: To introduce the topic of the first part of the unit – smoking.

Students discuss the questions in small groups of three or four and then give feedback on their opinions to the rest of the class.

A Answers require a personal response.

B POSSIBLE ANSWERS

Passive smoking is breathing in other people's smoke. Recent research suggests that it is harmful to health.

C POSSIBLE ANSWERS

Research seems to indicate that cancer and other serious diseases of the lungs like bronchitis can be caused by smoking. It also appears to indicate a connection between smoking and heart disease and stomach ulcers. If you smoke, your breath smells and the nicotine stains your teeth and fingers. In some countries smoking is an expensive habit.

Listening   Student's Book pp 106–107

1 Think ahead

Students discuss their ideas in groups or as a whole class.

ANSWERS

Most answers require a personal response, but some ideas follow.
Many people go to watch sporting events or see them on television so advertisements on hoardings at, for example, sports grounds are seen by a large number of people. Cigarette advertising has been banned on television in many countries so this is an indirect way of advertising their product legally. Cigarette companies want to give their product a clean, healthy image by associating it with sport.

2 Listening

Play the recording once and check which ideas students heard. These may include: sponsorship of Formula One Grand Prix racing; similar restrictions on advertising. Don't correct any wrong information students provide or supply any information to them. They are tested on their understanding of the listening in 3A.

Tapescript

Part 1
W = Woman (Presenter)
W   Good afternoon and welcome to *Burning Issues*, the weekly programme where you, the listener, give your views on items in the news. This week we look at cigarette advertising.
The European Commission has recently proposed a total ban on all advertising and promotion of tobacco. But, while most European countries support the ban, the British government has just made a new voluntary agreement with the tobacco industry which merely limits advertising. So what is the present situation in Britain?
Since 1965 there has been a ban on cigarette advertising on TV and since 1971 there's been a series of voluntary agreements negotiated between the government and the tobacco industry. The current agreement says that ads must contain health warnings; they must not appeal to the young or encourage them to smoke; and they must be approved by the Advertising Standards Authority. They also restrict advertising in magazines for young women and children – these are not allowed to carry tobacco advertising if young women (aged 15 to 24) account for a quarter or more of their readers – and they restrict advertising on shop fronts and on posters which are near schools or can be seen from childrens' playgrounds.
There is a separate agreement which restricts sports sponsorship: in 1977, tobacco companies agreed not to sponsor sports where most participants are under 18. It was because of the ban on cigarette advertising on TV in 1965 that the tobacco

companies decided to move into sports sponsorship. And it has proved to be a very successful way of advertising their product. For example, during a recent Formula One Grand Prix series on BBC television, their names and logos were visible on television pictures for eight minutes of every hour of screen time, which is more time than the commercial TV stations give over to all advertising. The government sees no need to abandon these agreements and put a total ban on advertising. Instead it claims that there are more effective ways to cut the number of smokers. These methods include high taxes, warnings on cigarette packets, health education and smoking restrictions in public places and at work.

So what are the facts and figures about smokers and smoking? Fewer than a third of British adults smoke, but that's still 13.8 million people. Numbers have been dropping steadily for 20 years, though the drop among women has been less dramatic. The number of teenage girls smoking has actually gone up. About one in ten children aged 11 to 15 smokes regularly, slightly more girls than boys.

Although tobacco sales in Britain have been falling for ten years, world-wide they have increased by one to two percent each year. The tobacco industry has shifted its attention to countries in South America, Africa, Asia and Eastern Europe.

And a final point of information. The British tobacco industry spends more than £113 million a year on advertising.

Now, over to you. We've had hundreds of calls from listeners, who phoned in to give their opinion of the question we asked you last week, which was 'Do you think the government should support a ban on cigarette advertising?' Here's a representative selection.

3 Comprehension

A Sentence completion
Before students hear the recording again they should read the incomplete sentences carefully and think about the kind of information that goes in the gaps. Elicit a few ideas. Remind students that they should only use a word or short phrase to complete the gaps. They are not expected to write more than five words.

ANSWERS

1	items in the news	6	sports sponsorship
2	cigarette advertising	7	cut / reduce the number of smokers
3	over 24	8	more men (fewer women)
4	children's playgrounds	9	women (men)
5	people under 18	10	sells less tobacco

B Matching speakers to topics
1 Before students listen to Part 2 of the recording they should list as many arguments as they can for and against the banning of cigarette advertising in general, for example on billboards, in magazines, at cinemas, on television. This brainstorming activity can be done in pairs, groups or with the whole class. Ideas should be noted on the board or in students' notebooks as they have to tick off their ideas if they are mentioned.

Suggested arguments
*mentioned in the recording
For a ban:
1 Advertising persuades people to buy a product. People are being encouraged to take up what could be a life-long and fatal addiction.
2 *Advertisements make smoking look fashionable and socially acceptable.
3 Smoking is one of the main causes of death in adults.
4 *The government spends a lot of money on health care for smokers.
5 A large number of working days are lost through smoking-related illnesses. This affects the economy.
Against a ban:
1 Smoking helps you relax and can reduce stress.
2 *Smoking brings in a lot of money in taxes.
3 People will still buy a product whether it is advertised or not, e.g. drugs.
4 *A ban on advertising a product which is not illegal goes against basic democratic values (freedom of speech; freedom of choice).

ANSWERS

Speaker 1	C	And even though there's a notice up in all the shops which says they aren't allowed to sell you cigarettes if you're under 16. . . there are no questions asked. They're making it easier for kids to start.
Speaker 2	F	Smoking on the train.
Speaker 3	A	They must be spending just as much on hospital treatment for people with cancer and the like.
Speaker 4	D	Peer pressure. It's difficult not to smoke if your mates all smoke. And if your parents smoke as well you're much more likely to start.
Speaker 5	B	It should be up to me to decide whether I want to smoke or not, not somebody else.

Tapescript

Part 2
Speaker 1
Hello. My name's Chris Mitchell and I'm 18. I think cigarette advertising should be banned. I don't think the government is doing enough to stop young people taking up smoking in the first place either. I started smoking when I was eight. It's really easy for kids to get hold of cigarettes if they want to. And even though nowadays there's a big notice up in all the shops which says they aren't allowed to sell you cigarettes if you're under 16, you usually only need to say they're for your dad and there're no

questions asked. I don't think that's right. They're breaking the law and they're making it easier for kids to start. They're adults and they should know better.

Speaker 2

Hi! My name's Katie Braithwaite and I'm 17. I think smoking's awful. I have to travel to school by train and when we get on the train it's packed and there are just the smoking sections left. And they're disgusting! The floor's covered in cigarette butts and it's really smokey. You go in there and the smell nearly knocks you over. And when you get out your clothes all stink of it too. And it sets a bad example. The young kids see adults smoking and they think it must be all right. One or two of my younger brother's friends smoke because they think it makes them look big. I know it's really stupid. But they're not old enough to know that.

Speaker 3

Hello. I'm Dave Snow and I'm phoning from Plymouth. I think there should be a total ban on tobacco advertising, not this partial ban that there is at the moment. It seems stupid to ban cigarette advertising on television but allow tobacco companies to sponsor sports events, which you can see on television. It makes smoking seem acceptable, fashionable. . . healthy even. I know the government gets billions of pounds in taxes from the sale of tobacco but they must be spending just as much money on hospital treatment for people with cancer and the like as they are getting in taxes. It just doesn't make economic sense. Why doesn't the government just put a stop to the sale of tobacco altogether?

Speaker 4

My name's Wendy Johnson. I support a ban on tobacco advertising, though I'm not convinced it will change people's attitudes towards smoking. I don't think people start smoking because they've seen an advert and want to associate themselves with the person in that advert. I think adverts just influence which brand of cigarettes people smoke. I think the main reason why people start smoking is peer pressure. When you're young, it's very difficult not to smoke if your friends all smoke. It's really hard to be the only one that doesn't smoke. You feel like an outcast. You aren't one of the group. So you end up smoking. And if your parents smoke as well you're much more likely to start. You grow up seeing them doing it and it seems quite a normal thing to do.

Speaker 5

My name's Gordon Jackson and I'm phoning from Leeds. I'd just like to say that I'm getting absolutely sick to death of people telling me what to do and what not to do. I'm 65 years old and I'm still fit and healthy. I've been smoking since I was 14 and I haven't had a day off work from ill health in my life! It should be up to me to decide whether I want to smoke or not, not somebody else. It's my body after all and I should be allowed to do what the hell I like with it. This whole anti-smoking thing makes me so angry. And this ban on advertising cigarettes is just another example of people poking their noses into things that have nothing whatsoever to do with them.

4 Vocabulary

ANSWERS

1 has been decreasing gradually and regularly
2 children; to buy
3 ends
4 smell strongly
5 important
6 product made by a particular company.

Note: *Brand* is used for food, cigarettes and small household goods, e.g. coffee, washing powder. *Make* is used for machines, equipment and cars.

7 strong influence placed on someone by people of the same age
8 someone who has been rejected by their friends, society, etc.
9 my choice / decision
10 interfering in things which are not their concern.

5 Over to you

This should be a short class or group discussion.

Extra activity
Roleplay: students can act out these situations in pairs.

Situation 1– Student A
Student B, who is your parent, is quite a heavy smoker. You think that smoking is an unhealthy habit. Try to persuade Student B to give up.

Situation 1– Student B
You are Student A's parent. You are quite a heavy smoker. You have never really worried about the effects of smoking on your health, but you think it would be very difficult to give up.

Situation 2 – Student A
You are the boss of a small company which employs 10 people. Nine employees are smokers and would be angry if you introduced a no-smoking policy at work. One of your best employees has a problem. Try to find a solution.

Situation 2 – Student B
You are the only non-smoker in the office where you work. You find the situation intolerable. You are thinking of changing jobs unless your boss introduces a no-smoking policy at work. Explain your situation to him or her.

Extra activity

Use of English Cloze: Ask students to fill the gaps in this text with an appropriate word. You could dictate the text to them, making clear where the gaps occur.

In my opinion, people should be allowed to choose (1) ___ or not they want to smoke. Even if (2) ___ is true that smoking causes lung cancer, and it has not been proved (3) ___ it does, there is no ban on drinking alcohol, (4) ___ is said to cause heart and liver disease. So why should smoking (5) ___ treated differently?

If the government were (6) ___ ban tobacco advertising altogether, it would (7) ___ make smoking more attractive. This would result in more rather than (8) ___ young people taking up the habit.

ANSWERS _____

1 whether	5 be
2 it	6 to
3 that	7 only; just; simply
4 which	8 fewer

Grammar and practice Student's Book pp 108–109

Aim: To revise the grammar and use of the range of reported speech features required at this level.

1 Reported speech

A Give students, working in pairs, a few minutes to discuss the questions, then check their answers.

Verb tenses 'go back one', e.g. the present continuous becomes the past continuous. Write the verb tenses on the board: present simple, past simple, etc. (for a list see section 3 in the Grammar reference on page 207) and ask pairs to write down the verb changes for reported speech.

We might need to change the pronoun references. In this sentence *I* changes to *he* . Although there are no examples in the sentence given, students may also mention that time and place references may have to change, as well as word order in reported questions. These come in later sections.

B Refer students to the Grammar reference on page 207 of their books.

C Practice

ANSWERS _____

1 Katie Braithwaite said (that) she had to travel to school by train and that when she got on the train it was packed.
2 Katie Braithwaite said (that) one or two of her younger brother's friends smoked because they thought it made them look big.
3 Wendy Pearson said (that) she supported a ban on tobacco advertising, though she was not convinced it would change people's attitudes towards smoking.
4 Gordon Jackson said (that) it was his body and (that) he should be allowed to do what he liked with it.

2 Reported questions

A/B Students can check their answers in the Grammar reference after a few minutes' discussion. Don't tell them the answers until they have checked for themselves.

ANSWERS _____

We need to remove question marks and change the form of the original question into a statement. This may involve omitting auxiliary verbs or changing word order. We need to use an appropriate reporting verb, e.g. *ask* or *want to know*.
We use *if* when the original question does not begin with a *Wh-* word (*why, how, who, what, where, which, when*). We could use *whether* instead of *if*.

C Practice

ANSWERS _____

1 The girl asked him if he had a light. (We do not usually say *had got* in the past tense.)
2 Val asked Rob if he smoked.
3 Nick asked me how long Chris had been smoking.
4 Rachel asked Sharon why she had started smoking.
5 Julie asked Tim if he would like to give up.
In sentences 1, 2 and 5 *if* can be replaced by *whether*.

3 Changing references

A Time references

We need to change the time reference if what we are reporting was said at a different time from when we report it. (In this case on a different day.) Otherwise, we don't change it.

ANSWERS _____

The time references would be reported as follows:
last week	the previous week, the week before
next month	the following month
next week	the following week
three days ago	three days before, three days earlier
today	that day
tomorrow	the next day, the following day
yesterday	the previous day, the day before

B Other references

Determiners like *this, that, these, those* may change to *the*. We may need to change place words like *here* to *there*. Ask students in what circumstances you could keep the place reference *here*. (When you are reporting the question in the same place as it was originally asked). Try to elicit other words that may have to change, e.g. the verb *come* may change to *go*.

C Ask students to check their understanding of changing references in the Grammar reference on page 208.

D Practice

ANSWERS _____

1 Marsha asked Mr Hunt if the work had to be finished that day.

2 Mr Gilbert asked if there had been any phone calls for him the previous day / the day before.
3 The police officer informed Ian that the car had been used in a robbery two weeks before / earlier.
4 Dorothy said that she had written to her the previous week / the week before and (had) phoned that morning.
5 Matthew said that he had arranged to meet them after lunch the next / following day.

E No change in tense

Students can check their ideas in the Grammar reference on page 207 or you can check their ideas.

ANSWER

If the reporting verb is in the present tense, there is no tense change. If the reporting verb is in the past tense and you want to emphasize that what is reported is still true, you can keep the same tense. This is only done for emphasis, so students will not need to do it in the First Certificate exam.

4 Reported functions

A Sentence 2 is a reported statement whereas sentence 3 is a reported command. If students can't see the difference between the two sentences, ask them to give you the words in direct speech. ('I'm leaving tomorrow', 'Leave me alone!')

Sentence 4 is a reported question whereas sentence 5 is a reported request. Follow the same procedure as above. ('Why did you do it?', 'Could you leave your keys, please?')

The verbs *advise* and *warn* are followed by the object pronoun + infinitive. *Suggest* is followed by the gerund or (*that*) + subject pronoun + *should*. *Suggest* + past tense is also possible.

B SUGGESTED ANSWERS

1 'Why don't we talk it over?'
2 'I'm leaving tomorrow.'
3 'Leave me alone!'
4 'Why did you do that?'
5 'Can you leave your keys?'
6 'Don't (you dare to) try and get in touch!'
7 'If I were you, I'd try and forget her.'

Before students go on to the practice exercise, ask them to read section 5 in the Grammar reference on page 208.

C Use of English

ANSWERS

1 The man **warned us not to swim** (**warned us about / against swimming**) there because it was dangerous.
2 Laura **advised Pete not to buy** (**advised Pete against buying**) Dave a book.
3 The teacher **told Claire to take** the chewing gum out of her mouth.
4 Marie **asked John if / whether he could** speak Spanish.

5 Jason **offered to pick Tracy up** from work.
6 Mike **said (that) he would see** Angie after class.

5 Fluency

Students should spend a few minutes preparing their roles. The members of the public should think about how they will explain their situation. They can jot down a few notes if they like. The police officers should think of the questions they will ask. They can jot down a few ideas but these should be in note form, not complete sentences. During the role-play the police officers must take notes, as they will need these to write up their reports. These can be written after both situations have been acted out or set for homework.

Before students write anything, take a couple of examples from the class and go through them on the board, converting both question and answer from direct to reported speech. Once students understand what is expected of them, allow them to write their own reports. Police officers could also be asked to report back orally to the class at the end of the role-play.

Extra situations

1 A child has dropped something for sale into your shopping bag. As you leave the shop, an alarm sounds and you are stopped by a security guard. You are accused of shoplifting and the police are called.
2 You have found a wallet containing £200 in £10 notes. You decide to keep the money but when you try to buy something with it in a shop, you are told that the notes are forgeries. The police are called.

Workbook: Grammar 1, 2, 3 pp 50–51

Exam techniques Student's Book pp 110–111

Reading: Multiple matching

1 Guidelines

The Introduction on pages 13–14 of this book contains some suggestions on how to use this section.

2 Practice

Go through some of the guidelines again with students checking their ideas at each stage.

Check that they know what the collection of short texts is about: people talking about their smoking habits. Explain the title if necessary: in this context, weed is a rather old-fashioned, informal and jocular way of referring to tobacco and cigarettes. *Evil* has two meanings; wicked and harmful.

Check that students have underlined relevant words in the questions, e.g. *has never tried to stop smoking*.

Students should answer the clues alongside the questions

before beginning to read the texts. The clues reflect the types of question that they should be asking themselves as they look for the answers. Check students' ideas before they continue but don't say whether their ideas are correct or not, or supply any information.

POSSIBLE ANSWERS TO CLUES

0; 1; 2	give up; quit
3	lung cancer; bronchitis
4	the medical profession (doctors; nurses)
5	upset
6	someone in the family dying
7	a parent; teacher
8; 9; 10	lung cancer; bronchitis; stomach ulcer; cough; shortness of breath
11; 12	university
13; 14	bad temper; depression; anxiety; withdrawal symptoms
15	acupuncture; hypnosis; nicotine pills or patches

Allow students approximately eight minutes to find the answers to the questions. Remind them that they will not need to read everything. A good approach is to scan the texts quickly looking for key words, and then to re-read the parts that seem relevant in more detail. After eight minutes, ask students to compare answers and give them another few minutes to look at the texts again if they have different answers. They should be able to justify their choice of answer to one another and to you by quoting relevant parts from the texts.

ANSWERS

Note: Where there is more then one answer to a question these can be in any order.

- 0 B There is no mention of trying to stop.
- 1 D *I've never tried to give up.*
- 2 E *. . . I've never tried.*
- 3 A *There's nothing to prove that passive smoking causes cancer.*
- 4 G *Most doctors don't smoke. There are only about 8% of us who still do . . .*
- 5 C *. . . had died of lung cancer. . . . it was someone I knew.*
- 6 F *When my husband died last year, I would have been utterly lost without cigarettes.*
- 7 H *Two weeks after I'd quit . . . I was suspended from school . . .*
- 8 A *I was wheezy and short of breath . . .*
- 9 F *. . . chest problems . . .*
- 10 H *. . . short of breath; have chest pains . . .*
- 11 B *I started when I was at university.*
- 12 G *It all started when I was at university.*
- 13 F *I've tried to give up . . . but I'm not happy with my personality as a non-smoker.*
- 14 H *I've tried to give up, but gained weight and became so bad-tempered that I started again.*
- 15 A *I tried to stop once . . . I had electric shock treatment . . .*

Workbook: Reading pp 48–49

An eye for an eye

Introduction   Student's Book p 112

Aim: To introduce the second topic of the unit – crime and punishment.

The poster is trying to get across the message that the death penalty is barbaric and should be abolished. Don't ask students whether they agree with this message, as it will come up again in 3 Points of view.

Reading   Student's Book pp 112–113

1 Think ahead

Students brainstorm the topic in groups or as a class. Check that students know what capital punishment is. Ask them if they can name any countries which have the death penalty and any which don't. If in groups, students can make a list of arguments for and against the use of capital punishment, or you can elicit ideas from the whole class and write them on the board. Either supply students with any vocabulary they require or pre-teach vocabulary you think they will need. Students can give their own personal opinions here or in 3 Points of view.

ANSWERS

- Capital punishment is the execution of a human being for crimes which can range from political offences to robbery. The most common methods of execution are hanging and the electric chair.
- Some of the countries which have capital punishment are the USA, Japan, Nigeria, South Africa, Iran, Iraq, Thailand.
- Some of the countries which don't have capital punishment are Austria, Denmark, Ecuador, France. Some countries, e.g. Britain, Spain and Greece, have capital punishment for treason only. Their reasons for not having capital punishment appear in the article.

2 Reading

Students check their ideas from Think ahead on their own as they read the text. If you want to go over their answers, do so after they have done the comprehension exercises. The text comes from a British newspaper for young people. While pretending to inform, it is meant to persuade. The short sentences, some of which are not real sentences at all, are typical of an attention-grabbing journalistic style. The longer, more complex sentences in the second part of the text are intended to give a serious and profound tone to the writer's argument.

3 Points of view

Students exchange views with a partner, in groups or as a class.

4 Comprehension

A Remind students to look for lexical, grammatical and content clues, which will help them to locate the missing paragraphs correctly. Ask them to justify their choices to their partner and to you.

ANSWERS

1 D *Nowadays* contrasts with *over the centuries* in the previous paragraph. *Methods* and *crimes* is repeated.

2 A *By contrast, in Britain* contrasts with *In the USA*. The previous paragraph talks about public opinion in the USA. This paragraph talks about public opinion in Britain.

3 F There is a chronological link with paragraph A, which talks about opinion in the 1950s. This paragraph mentions 1965. *Despite this change of opinion* relates back to *public opinion began to turn against the use of capital punishment* also in paragraph A.

4 B *The next argument* follows on from the first argument of the previous paragraph. *Bringing back capital punishment* also links with *the reintroduction of capital punishment* also in the previous paragraph.

5 E *The fourth and last* links with *the other two arguments* (only one of which is given) of the previous paragraph.

6 G The previous paragraph outlines the first main argument against the death penalty. This paragraph begins *The second main argument against reintroducing capital punishment*.

B Reading between the lines

POSSIBLE ANSWERS

1 The electric chair. He is shocked because someone could suffer for as long as 20 minutes before they died.

2 A majority of politicians are against it though there are obviously enough who are very much in favour of bringing it back to have tried 14 times.

C Vocabulary

ANSWERS

1 B 2 A 3 C 4 A

5 Over to you

This could be a group discussion followed by group feedback and possibly further discussion with the whole class. The discussion will be livelier if there is more than one opinion within the group. A quick test of opinion would be to ask students their answers to question 1. This will enable students with different opinions to be put together.

Vocabulary Student's Book p 114

1 Crime

A Breaking the law

ANSWERS

1 b 2 d 3 e 4 a 5 c

B Name the criminal

ANSWERS

| 1 SHOPLIFTER | 3 MURDERER |
| 2 MUGGER | 4 HOOLIGAN |

Extra activity

Students could think of more topic words and play 'Hangman' in pairs, taking turns to guess the answers. There are useful lists in the Vocabulary reference on page 217.

C Rob and steal

ANSWERS

1 You *rob* a person, a bank, and a shop.
  You *steal* money, a car, and a wallet.

2 1 has been robbed / was stolen   5 are robbed
  2 being stolen   6 stole
  3 've been robbed   7 was robbed
  4 stealing

Note: to *steal* something *from* a person, place or organization; to *rob* a person, institution or organization *of* something.

2 Word building

A ANSWERS

-tion	-ence
population, populate	deterrence, deter
injections, inject	sentence, sentence
reintroduction, reintroduce	occurrence, occur
retribution, (no verb)	consequences, (no verb)
executions, execute	conscience, (no verb)
reduction, reduce	
-ness	-ity
forgiveness, forgive	security, secure
-ment	
punishment, punish	
arguments, argue	
Parliament, (no verb)	

B ANSWERS

1 occurrence	4 action
2 accommodation	5 preference
3 disagreement	6 movement

Workbook: Vocabulary 1 p 51

Writing Student's Book pp 115–117

Presenting an argument

Aim: This section prepares students for writing the discursive composition (pages 116–117). It examines the different functions of some of the discourse markers used in presenting arguments and focuses on how to present and back up arguments and opinions.

Students can do all the sections on their own and then compare answers, or in pairs. Check answers section by section.

1 Discourse markers

A Introduce the topic of the model answer. Check that students know what a jury is and if necessary pre-teach the following vocabulary, most of which is in the Vocabulary reference on page 217: *offence, verdict, judge, corruption, political interference, threat, bribe, guilty, costly, serve on a jury, trial, lawyer.*

Background information
In England and Wales, a jury is made up of 12 men and women aged between 18 and 65. After they have heard all the evidence, they decide whether they think the accused is innocent or guilty. It is not always necessary for the verdict to be unanimous. Sometimes a majority verdict with only two people disagreeing is enough.

Elicit one or two advantages and disadvantages of the jury system. Students can check their ideas as they read for the first time.

ANSWERS

1 On the one hand	4 In addition
2 Another advantage is	5 Another disadvantage is that
3 On the other hand	6 On balance

The discourse markers which do not fit anywhere in the text are *in contrast* and *instead*. *In contrast*, which is used to introduce contrasting information, comes in the next exercise. *Instead* introduces an alternative e.g. *Instead of* one person deciding the verdict, the verdict is decided by 12 people.

B ANSWERS

1 to introduce additional information:
   apart from that
   as well as (that)
   besides (this)
   what is more

2 to introduce contrasting information:
   however
   on the contrary
   nevertheless
   in contrast

3 to summarize or conclude:
   in short
   on the whole
   to summarize
   in conclusion
   to sum up
   on balance
   to conclude

2 Arguing your point

A There are four main points in total.
2 *No one person can be blamed or made to feel guilty for a wrong verdict.*
3 *The jury system is very costly in terms of time and money.*
4 *It is relatively easy for skilled lawyers to influence the opinions of the members of the jury.*

B The other parts of the text support the main arguments by giving additional information. This may be factual information or opinion or both.

C Practice
Suggested additional information:
1 In fact, these programmes should begin with primary school children, who are the most at risk.
2 They are carried out when people see a chance – an unlocked car, or a door or window of a house left open.
3 Drink-driving is one example. Football hooliganism is also linked to drink.
4 There are so many false alarms that many people's reaction is to assume that every alarm is a false alarm, which defeats the main purpose of having one.

Exam training: Compositions 1

Aim: This section introduces discursive writing and looks at two types of composition: presenting a balanced argument and presenting an opinion. The differences between the two types of writing are highlighted in the model answers and the analysis section. There is a special focus on discourse markers and opinion language. It is important that this writing section is done after Writing: Presenting an argument (page 115).

1 Introduction

Read through the Introduction with students.

2 Model answers

A Check that students understand what community service is: instead of being sent to prison or a detention centre, offenders can be ordered to do a certain number of hours of community service. They can be asked to do anything from cleaning up ponds to decorating a pensioner's house. Students read the first question and spend a few minutes thinking of their own arguments for and against community service as an alternative to prison. They can discuss their ideas briefly in groups or as a class. They then read Composition 1 to check how many of their ideas are mentioned.

B Follow the same procedure as for **A**. This time students think of arguments disagreeing with the statement. Ask students whether they can add any more arguments to the two that were given in Composition 1 (community service is not a deterrent; not all young offenders are first offenders). After they have read Composition 2, elicit any of their ideas which are not included in the composition.

3 Analysis

1 The purpose of the opening paragraph is to introduce the topic and to indicate the type of composition the writer is going to write.
In Composition 1 the writer makes a general statement about the topic under discussion. In the second sentence she makes it clear that she is going to consider the pros and cons of the system.
In Composition 2 the writer begins with a personal opinion disagreeing with the statement but with some reservations.
The purpose of the closing paragraph is to summarize the arguments and make a concluding statement. In Composition 1 the writer makes a general statement in which she concludes that there are as many advantages as disadvantages. In Composition 2 the writer sums up his argument with a strong reassertion of opinion.
2 There are five main arguments in Composition 1 and two main arguments in Composition 2.

ANSWERS
Composition 1:
1 Community service may help integrate people into society while prison may educate them in crime.
2 Community service is cheaper than prison.
3 Through community service the offender gives something back to the community.
4 Prison is a deterrent; community service is not.
5 Community service would be regarded by many as a soft option.
Composition 2:
1 People should be punished for the crimes they commit.
2 Community service does not act as a deterrent whereas the thought of facing a prison sentence does.

3 Point out to students that in compositions of this length there is more room for back-up arguments in the opinion type than in the advantages and disadvantages type.

ANSWERS
The additional arguments are:
Composition 1:
In the first part of the composition the fact that young offenders are often first offenders. In the second part of the composition the fact that not all young offenders are first offenders; some are already hardened criminals.

Composition 2:
Prison punishes offenders but community service doesn't and people need to be taught that crime doesn't pay. Community service should only be used as an alternative when the crime committed is minor and is a first offence. Crime victims wish to see the people pay the price for the suffering they have caused.

4 Language study

ANSWERS
1 a In the first place; The main disadvantage is; First of all
 b Another advantage is; Besides; Also; Another reason
 c In contrast; But, while
 d To sum up; To conclude
2 I do not agree; I believe; In my opinion; I am against; In my view.
Note: See page 43 in this book for more words and phrases (Unit 3 Writing: Giving an opinion).

5 Think, plan, write

Students brainstorm ideas in groups or as a class and make notes. The planning and writing sections can be set for homework.

MODEL
Pupil behaviour is a growing problem in British schools. One form of discipline used by teachers in Britain is to ask pupils to write 'lines'. As a form of discipline it has both advantages and disadvantages.
 The main advantage from the teacher's point of view is that it is easy to administer and doesn't involve the teacher in extra marking. Students find it boring and hate having to do it so it is also quite an effective deterrent.
 Nevertheless, it does not deter very badly-behaved pupils from misbehaving. They regard it as a 'soft' form of punishment and some simply refuse to do it. In cases like this, the teacher would have to use an alternative method of punishment.
 To sum up, asking pupils to write lines is a fairly effective form of discipline except for problem pupils. However, it could be argued that for these children no form of discipline is effective.

Workbook: Writing p 53

Vocabulary   Student's Book p 118

1 Use of English

ANSWERS

1	C	6	A
2	C	7	C
3	B	8	B
4	A	9	C
5	D	10	A

2 Phrasal verbs

ANSWERS _____

1 had gone out	4 doesn't go with
2 goes off	5 went over
3 went off	6 go out

Workbook: Vocabulary 2, 3 pp 51–52

Your students are now ready to take Unit test 8, which is on page 155 of this book. The key is on page 171.

After they have taken the Unit test, students can do Revision 2, on pages 54–55 of the Workbook. Encourage them to look up anything they have difficulties with. This will help to consolidate their learning, and will prepare them for Progress test 2. Revision 2 could be set for homework.

Your students are now ready to take Progress test 2, which can be found on pages 164–165 of this book. The key is on page 173.

9 Interaction

Hooked

Unit focus Suggesting, advising and warning

Topic 1 Computer games and other addictions
Listening
Grammar and practice
 Suggestions, advice and warnings (*ought to*, *should*, *could*)
 Regrets and criticisms
 Contrasting conjunctions and other linking words

Topic 2 Holidays and travel
Reading
Vocabulary Travel, holidays, colloquial language, word building, phrasal verbs
Writing Exam training: Transactional letters 2
Exam techniques Use of English: Vocabulary cloze

Introduction   Student's Book p 119

Aim: To introduce the first topic of the unit – computer games.

As a possible lead-in activity before students look at this page, ask general questions like:
What crazes (obsessions) have there been among young people in recent years? Why do certain things suddenly become popular among young people?

A Draw attention to the questions and ask students to read the three short texts to find the answers. Allow about three to four minutes for this before checking answers.

Background information
Barbie   a well-known doll for young girls
Pitfighter, *Streetfighter*, etc.   computer games
Gameboy   one of the world's most popular hand-held games computers (see photo on page 120)

ANSWERS
The texts are all about computer games.
Sources:
A lost childhood   letter to a women's magazine
Universal monsters   advertisement for a new game
Toys for boys . . .   newspaper article
Universal monsters matches the illustration.

B–D Allow as much or as little time as you wish for these three questions. They could be discussed in pairs or groups, or by the whole class.

Listening   Student's Book pp 120–121

1 Think ahead

A Allow four to five minutes for students to work individually on the gap filling task, then check answers.

ANSWERS
1 addicts
2 screens

3 intended
4 fingers, compensation (*numbness* = lack of feeling, *tingling* = pricking feeling)
5 advisers (*queries* = questions / enquiries)

B ANSWERS
Possible physical effects:
- pains in fingers, wrists, arms caused by repetitive movements
- damage to eyesight, headaches
- exhaustion from playing too long
- back pains from sitting in a tense position
- epileptic fits (there are cases of these resulting in death)
Possible mental effects:
- mood changes
- antisocial behaviour
- irritation, bad temper, anger

2 Listening

A Check that students understand what a radio phone-in programme is (a programme in which members of the public phone to ask a question or express a point of view). Allow students a few minutes to read through the unfinished sentences, then play the first part of the recording. Check answers.

ANSWERS
1 children's physical and mental health
2 child psychologist
3 (secondary school) headteacher
4 London

Tapescript

Part 1
P = Presenter
P   This week on 'Call the Experts' we're dealing with a question more and more of you seem to be asking: 'Are video and computer games harmful to our

children's mental or physical health?' Here in the studio, we've got Helena Brook, a child psychologist, Jim Edwards, a secondary school headteacher and Oliver Newton, a university lecturer currently doing research into the effects of the latest generation of computer games. They'll be answering your questions on this subject. Our first caller this morning is Marion Jeffries from London.

B As students listen to Part 2, they should listen for any of the harmful effects they listed previously.

ANSWERS

Harmful effects mentioned in the programme:
Caller (Marion Jeffries):
• aggressive and bad-tempered
• tired and uncommunicative
• rude and abusive
• screams and shouts
• violent
• changed personality
Expert (Jim Edwards):
• overtiredness
• difficulty in concentrating
• children get into arguments and fights
• possible damage to eyes and brain
Expert (Oliver Newton) mentions only possible good effects:
• improved powers of observation and reaction
• improved reading speed

Tapescript

Part 2
P = Presenter; MJ = Marion Jeffries; HB = Helena Brook; JE = Jim Edwards; ON = Oliver Newton

P Our first caller this morning is Marion Jeffries from London. Hello, Marion. What's your question to the experts?

MJ Thank you. Good morning.

HB, JE, ON Hello Marion / Good morning / Hi.

MJ Hello, erm. . . It's my son Adam – he's just 11 – and we bought him one of those hand-held computer games for his birthday last month, you know. Well, the thing is, he's hardly put it down since he got it. He gets so involved in the games, I ask him to stop but he doesn't even hear me. If I shout to get his attention, he loses his temper and gets aggressive. Then, when he's finished playing, he's absolutely exhausted and completely uncommunicative. He can also be very rude, even abusive, especially if he's been playing a difficult game. I shouldn't have bought it for him, I realize that now.

P That's very worrying, Marion, I can understand your concern. What exactly would you like to ask the panel?

MJ I suppose I need some advice really – I'd like to know what your panel thinks I should do about Adam's obsession?

P Helena Brook, you're a child psychologist – what would you advise Marion Jeffries to do?

HB Marion, when you say your son has hardly put the game down since his birthday, what exactly do you mean? How many hours a day has he been playing for? On average?

MJ I'd say about five or six – more at weekends.

HB And you say he gets aggressive if you try to stop him. What does he do exactly?

MJ He screams and shouts at me, you know, like a two-year-old having a temper tantrum. Last week, he got so annoyed that he actually threw his computer at me. Oh, and yesterday he kicked his little sister who'd gone to tell him his lunch was ready. Sometimes he just refuses to stop playing. It seems to be changing his whole personality.

HB Well, Marion, you really ought to stop worrying. There's no evidence that computer games are harmful in any way. Don't forget, most boys of Adam's age are naturally aggressive – it's part of becoming an adult. Obsessions like this are a passing phase – it's pretty certain that in a month or two, your son will get bored and move on to something else. One last thought, Marion. You could try ignoring Adam altogether – it might just do the trick.

P Jim Edwards, would you agree with that?

JE No I'm afraid I wouldn't. I'm a teacher and I'm all too familiar with the effects of computer games on kids in the classroom: they become overtired, unable to concentrate, and they often get into arguments or fights with other children – even teachers sometimes. If I were you, Marion, I'd point out to Adam that he could do permanent damage to his eyes or his brain if he continues to play for hours on end.

MJ What about taking the game away from him?

JE No, no, I wouldn't do that. I think that'd be an over-reaction – you'd be asking for trouble, but you could persuade Adam to cut his playing time down. And above all, encourage him not to abandon other activities, otherwise he could lose all his friends. Just try and show him that there's more to life than computer games.

P Oliver Newton, you've taken a scientific look at some of these games. Have you been able to reach any firm conclusions?

ON Not yet. My research is still in the early stages. At the moment the evidence is inconclusive, but what I can say is that these games affect different people in different ways. Certainly, they make some people behave more aggressively, but it is likely that if they didn't play computer games, they would have to find another outlet for their aggression.

P So, the games bring out this behaviour rather than cause it?

ON That's right. Another rather unexpected finding from my research is that children who play these games very intensively develop improved powers of observation and reaction. There are significant improvements for example in their normal reading speed.

P That's very interesting Oliver. So in the light of your research, how would you respond to Marion Jeffries' question?

ON Well, Marion, don't stop your son from playing altogether or you might make the situation worse. It could make him resentful and depressed. No, I think I agree with Jim's advice – try and get him to play less and encourage him to develop other related interests. Why don't you tell him he's got a flair for computers and suggest that he learns basic computer programming. After all, it's pretty certain that computers are the key to our future, one way or another.

3 Points of view

This discussion will be particularly interesting if students themselves have played the kinds of games referred to in the recording. Get them to back up their opinions with evidence and examples.

4 Comprehension

A Before playing the recording again, get students to read through the seven statements and attempt to answer them. This will ensure that they listen carefully to the recording. Play the cassette and check answers.

ANSWERS

1 T . . . *he's hardly put it down since he got it.*
2 F not mentioned
3 F *Marion, you really ought to stop worrying. There's no evidence that computer games are harmful in any way.*
4 T *Obsessions like this are a passing phase – it's pretty certain that in a month or two, your son will get bored and move on to something else.*
5 F He doesn't say they do badly. He simply says *they become overtired, unable to concentrate.*
6 F *I wouldn't do that* (take the game away). *I think that'd be an over-reaction – you'd be asking for trouble.*
7 F . . . *what I can say is that these games affect different people in different ways.*

B Listening between the lines

It shouldn't be necessary to play the recording again for this exercise. If students work in pairs or groups, allow four to five minutes for discussion of the questions.

POSSIBLE ANSWERS

1 In general, the opposites of the qualities mentioned by the boy's mother, i.e. good-tempered, communicative, polite, nice to his little sister, obedient.
2 She may think his behaviour is worse because his parents are reacting in a shocked way, or that he is seeking attention.
3 A means of releasing or expressing pent-up feelings of hostility or anger.

Other outlets for aggression could include
- hard physical sports, e.g. football, boxing, squash, running
- driving fast cars (adults)
- competitive games, e.g. chess

C ANSWERS

1 c (opposite *keep your temper*)
2 h 3 b 4 g 5 e 6 d 7 a 8 f 9 i

5 Use of English

This is the kind of word formation exercise students will meet in Paper 3 of the FCE exam. Before they work out the answers, go through the text with the whole class, eliciting the type of words that are missing:

1 adverb	6	adjective
2 noun	7	adjective
3 adjective	8	noun
4 noun	9	noun
5 plural noun	10	adjective

Students may work out the answers individually or in pairs.

ANSWERS

1 increasingly	6	scientific
2 addiction	7	dangerous
3 harmful	8	difficulty
4 personality	9	equipment
5 arguments	10	expensive

6 Over to you

Start by eliciting addictions from the whole class. Examples: alcohol, cigarettes (tobacco / nicotine), drugs (heroin, cocaine, cannabis, etc.), drinks containing caffeine (coffee, tea, cola), chocolate, work, gambling, fitness training. Once you have built up a list of addictions, get students to rank them in order of seriousness.

Grammar and practice Student's Book pp 122–123

1 Suggestions, advice and warnings

It is less important that students know the functional names for this language than that they are aware of the relative strengths of the expressions.

A Students work out their own order of strength, and then compare with a partner. Elicit answers.

ANSWERS

You could try . . . (least strong)
You really ought . . .
Don't stop your son . . . (strongest)
3 is a suggestion.
1 is a piece of advice.
2 is a warning.

B ANSWERS

1 advice 2 advice 3 warning 4 suggestion

C Advice and suggestion phrases

Elicit these from the whole class.

ANSWERS

1 *If I were* in your position / place / shoes
2 *What about* telling him he's got a flair for computers?
  You could tell him / *try* telling him he's got a . . .
  How about telling him he's got a . . . ?

D ANSWER

Here *shouldn't have* is used for regret – 'retrospective advice' to oneself. She wishes she hadn't bought him the game.

E Refer students to the Grammar reference on page 208 of their books.

Note: You may wish to draw attention to the following additional points.

1 *Should* and *ought to* are often used with the emphasizing adverb *really*. Note its position before the modal:
  You really shouldn't drink so much.
  You really ought to go on a diet.
2 *Ought to* tends to be used for stronger advice than *should*, and often suggests that the speaker is expressing a moralistic viewpoint:
  You ought to listen to what your parents say, you know.
3 Advice beginning *You'd better* . . . contains an implied warning: '. . . or X will happen'.
4 The expression *Whatever you do* . . . introduces very strong advice, with the meaning 'this is the one important thing'.
5 A common way of asking for advice is with the question *What would you do if you were me? / if you were in my position?*
6 Because *If I were you* is a conditional clause, it is usually followed by a comma.

2 Practice

A Students could do this exercise individually in writing and then compare sentences with a partner. Alternatively, they could work in pairs from the beginning and then write down their agreed answers.

POSSIBLE ANSWERS

1 *Suggestions*
  You could get a job in a supermarket.
  What about delivering newspapers or letters?
  Advice
  If I were you, I'd advertise in the newspaper.
  You really ought to phone up as many companies as you can.
2 *Suggestions*
  How about making a timetable for yourself?
  Why don't you do one subject a night?

Advice
  You should work for three hours every evening.
  If I were in your shoes, I'd find a friend to revise with.
3 *Suggestions*
  You could ask them to explain the problem to you.
  What about making it clear that you think they're behaving childishly?
  Advice
  I'd threaten to leave home.
  If I were in your position, I'd tell my parents to grow up.

B POSSIBLE ANSWERS

1 Don't drive so fast, or you might have a serious accident.
  Drive more carefully, otherwise you might kill someone.
2 If you always drink so much at parties, people will stop inviting you.
  You really ought to stop drinking so much at parties, otherwise you'll get a bad reputation.
3 Stop taking things from shops, or you'll be prosecuted.
  You should stop shoplifting, otherwise you'll be arrested.
  If you don't stop stealing, one of these days you'll get caught.

C POSSIBLE ANSWERS

He shouldn't have fallen asleep.
He shouldn't have lain down to rest.
He should have stayed on his feet / standing up.
He shouldn't have been working so many hours a week.
He shouldn't have cried for help. He should (just) have waited until the plane arrived back home and pretended that nothing had happened.
He should have refused to pay the bill for £298.
He should have claimed compensation from his employers.

3 Conversation

This exercise recycles some of the language of suggestion and advice. Get pairs of students to work through the conversation orally. Monitor and then elicit missing words.

ANSWERS

1	couldn't	7	will (would)
2	don't	8	more
3	would	9	were
4	about	10	isn't
5	could	11	what
6	can (could)	12	can / could

4 Regrets and criticisms

Work through the explanation and examples of *should / shouldn't* to express regrets and criticisms. If students find this terminology confusing, you could describe *I shouldn't* have as a 'self-criticism' rather than a regret.

Make it clear that for each of the sentences in the exercise they should think of a criticism (*You shouldn't have . . .*) and a regret (*I shouldn't have. . .*). Allow students a few minutes to work out their answers and then elicit their ideas.

Ideas

2 You shouldn't have spent so long talking to your friends.
   I shouldn't have let my friends use the phone.
3 You shouldn't have gone out every evening during the exams.
   I shouldn't have expected the exams to be easy.
4 You shouldn't have believed the weather forecast.
   I shouldn't have gone out without my umbrella.
5 You shouldn't have said you'd wait till he arrived.
   I shouldn't have agreed to meet him in the town centre.
6 You shouldn't have eaten so much.
   I shouldn't have danced so soon after I'd eaten.

5 Fluency

A Work through the instructions with the class. Set a time limit of four to five minutes for students to think about the problems individually.

B Students now present their problems to the rest of their group. Monitor the discussions, listening for advice and suggestion language.

Extra activity

If the fluency exercise is successful, students could discuss one of their own problems.

6 Linking ideas

Aim: To get students to think about the relationships between parts of sentences and to revise knowledge and use of conjunctions and other linking phrases – in particular those which link contrasting ideas.

A Students work through the sentences on their own.

ANSWERS _____

1 (1) The boys and their friends have pasty faces *and* (2) they have become aggressive and irritable.
2 (1) Since Nintendo's Gameboy hit the British market in 1988, it has been a toy for the boys. *Despite this*, (2) there are no plans to bring out a Gamegirl.
3 (1) Girls don't mind joining in male pursuits, *but* (2) it never works the other way round.
4 (1) Don't let him give up his other hobbies, *otherwise* (2) he'll lose all his friends.
5 *Although* (1) the children who play these games behave more aggressively, (2) they also develop improved powers of observation.

B Students now work in pairs or groups on questions 1–3.

ANSWERS _____

1 1 a   2 b   3 b   4 c   5 b
2 *Despite this, But, Although*

3 *though, even though, in spite of (this), despite the + noun, in spite of the fact that + clause, however, nevertheless, whereas*

Extra activity

Ask students to rephrase extracts 2, 3 and 5 using different contrasting linking expressions.

POSSIBLE ANSWERS _____

2 *In spite of the fact that* Nintendo's Gameboy has been a toy for the boys since it hit the British market in 1988, there are no plans to bring out a Gamegirl.
3 *Whereas* girls don't mind joining in male pursuits, it never works the other way round.
5 The children who play these games behave more aggressively. *However*, they also develop improved powers of observation.

C Refer students to the Grammar reference on page 209 of their books. Check particularly that they know how to use *despite* and *in spite of* correctly.

You may wish to point out these common uses of commas in sentences which contain connectors.

• Between two clauses where one of the clauses begins with a conjunction:
  Whereas girls don't mind joining in male pursuits, it never works the other way round.
  (Commas are not usually used before the conjunction *and*.)
• To separate *however* from the rest of a sentence:
  Girls, however, don't mind joining in male pursuits.
  However, girls don't mind joining in male pursuits.
• Before a clause starting with *otherwise*:
  Don't let him give up his hobbies, otherwise he'll lose all his friends.

7 Practice

Stress that there are several ways of linking these pairs of contrasting sentences.

POSSIBLE ANSWERS _____

1 Although / Even though John does a lot of exercise, he's very fat.
   Despite the fact that he does a lot of exercise, John's very fat.
2 Even though we've got three television sets at home, I never watch TV.
   I never watch TV, but we've got three television sets at home.
3 Despite the fact that coffee keeps me awake, I drink three cups of coffee every night.
   I drink three cups of coffee every night, even though coffee keeps me awake.
4 Although I had a terrible cold, I went to work as usual yesterday.
   I had a terrible cold. Nevertheless, I went to work as usual yesterday.
5 Even though he is very well qualified, my brother can't find a job.

My brother's very well qualified. Despite this, he can't find a job.

6 My sister never does any revision. However, she always gets good marks in exams.

In spite of never doing any revision, my sister always gets good marks in exams.

Workbook: Grammar 1, 2, 3, 4 pp 58–59

On the right track

Introduction Student's Book p 124

Aim: To introduce the second topic of the unit – holidays and travel. Pairs or groups could discuss these questions for about five minutes. List the holiday types and methods of transport on the board.

Reading Student's Book pp 124–125

1 Think ahead

This pre-reading activity is a continuation of the Introduction discussion and is probably best done as a whole-class brainstorming session.

Possible problems:
Finding a place to sleep / deciding how much luggage to take / deciding how many places to visit / having money stolen / running out of money / being ill / being attacked.

Next, elicit the precautions students would take before going on a journey like this. Precautions could be linked to problems.

Possible precautions:
Take a sleeping bag / only take essentials / plan route / keep money in different places / take travellers' cheques / take a first aid kit / have injections / take maps / take telephone numbers of friends / make sure someone knows where you are.

2 Reading

Students read the Eurorailing leaflet for the first time, underlining any problems and precautions that they mentioned in Think ahead.

Vocabulary notes

the Greenest	the most environmentally-friendly
a ringside seat	a seat with a good view (the best seats at a boxing match)
Universal plug	one that can be used in any type of electrical socket
Swiss army penknife	a pocket knife with many blades and mini-tools
con man	someone who tries to deceive people, often cheating them out of money

Extra activity
After this first reading, students might spend a few minutes discussing the best way for a visitor without a car to travel round their country visiting places of interest.

3 Comprehension

A Having already read the leaflet once, students should find this multiple matching reading task quite quick and straightforward to do.

ANSWERS

Beware of criminals 7
Fill your time NOT NEEDED
Planning a sensible schedule 6
Take care but enjoy yourself 8
Calling all students 1
Money matters 3
Packing the essentials 4
Minor irritations 5
Trains! They're the best 2

B Remind students about the guidelines for answering multiple choice reading questions on page 14 of their books.

ANSWERS

1 C This a global question, which depends on students' understanding of the text as a whole.
2 B *It's sensible to take some cash, but you should take most of your money in traveller's cheques.* (paragraph 3)
3 C *. . . put out everything you want to take – then halve it.* (paragraph 4)
4 D *. . . these frustrations (which make the best stories afterwards, anyway!) . . .* (paragraph 5)
5 B *. . . try to vary your route, mixing visits to cities with relaxing spells . . .* (paragraph 6)
6 A *The best way to prevent this is to carry them with you at all times . . .* (paragraph 7)

4 Over to you

This fluency exercise is best done in groups of three or four students. Their 'most interesting journeys' could be their best, worst, longest, etc. Allow thinking time, then ask each student to talk for about one minute to their group. Monitor discreetly.

Extra activity

Students write about an interesting journey: their own, or one of those they have just heard about from a partner. Suggest the following plan:
Paragraph 1: Mention a few interesting journeys you remember, then say why you have chosen this particular journey to write about.
Paragraph 2: Describe the beginning of the journey.
Paragraph 3: Describe the incident(s) that made the journey interesting.
Paragraph 4: Describe your feelings immediately after the journey, and how you feel now, looking back.

> Workbook: Reading pp 56–57

Vocabulary Student's Book p 126

1 Travel and holidays

Correctly completed tables for A and B could be useful for future reference. Answers for A below are in italics.

A Modes of transport

ANSWERS

1	car	to *drive* (*a car*)	to go by road
2	*train*	to travel on a train	to go by *rail*
3	ship	to *sail* (*on a ship*)	*to go by sea*
4	(*aero*)*plane*	to fly	to go by *air*

B Noun-verb collocations

ANSWERS

Vehicles	car	bicycle	boat / ship	bus	motorbike	plane	taxi	train
Verbs catch / miss			✓	✓		✓		✓
get into / get out of	✓			✓			✓	✓
get on / get off		✓	✓	✓	✓	✓		✓
ride		✓			✓			
take	✓			✓			✓	✓
drive	✓			✓			✓	✓

1 you *get into* or *out of* a small boat (e.g. a canoe), but you *get on* and *off* a large boat (e.g. a liner)
2 *get into / out of* a train is less common than *get on / off*
3 *take the car* is possible, as in *he took the car to the office.*

C ANSWERS

1 journey (a journey is one way. The emphasis is on the travelling, not on the purpose. 'A travel' is not possible.)
2 tour (a journey to several places, often for pleasure – but, also, *a fact-finding tour, a tour of the war zone*)
3 trip (a two-way journey)
4 excursion (a short journey for pleasure, usually with a group of people)
5 trip (*expedition* could also be used here)

2 Colloquial language

Students match colloquialisms from the Eurorailing leaflet with their meanings.

ANSWERS

1 d 2 e 3 g 4 f 5 b 6 a 7 h 8 c

> Workbook: Vocabulary 2 p 59

Writing
Student's Book p 127

Exam training: Transactional letters 2

Students were introduced to transactional letters in Unit 4, so start by finding out how much they remember. Elicit examples of commonly written transactional letters and if necessary, get them to read through the Summary box on page 55 of the Student's Book. Remind them that this forms Part 1 of Paper 2 and is a compulsory question.

1 Sample question

Give students time to read through all the information provided in the sample question. Check that they understand these words:
Student **representative** / **brief** information / local **reputation**.

2 Think, plan, write

A Think

1 It is important that students imagine or visualize the Welcome party they are going to write about. Get them to brainstorm ideas as a whole class or in groups. If ideas are slow in coming, ask if anyone has ever been to an event like this, either as a guest or a host. (What were the good and bad points? How could the party have been improved? etc.)

2 If students are working in groups, get them to write note-form answers to these questions. If you are conducting a class discussion, note their answers on the board for future reference.

B Plan

1 Students should now work individually writing brief notes for each of the four paragraphs suggested.

2 Make sure students realize that this letter should be informal but polite. Some short forms of verbs would be appropriate, but slang and very colloquial expressions would not.
Finally, you might like to elicit some useful expressions from the class. Examples:
I am writing, on behalf of the Central High School, to invite you to our Welcome Evening.
I hope you will all be able to come.
I am enclosing a map which shows . . .
We look forward to welcoming you to the school.

C Write

Set the writing task for homework. Remind students to check their grammar, spelling and punctuation carefully.

MODEL

Dear Tom,
 I am writing, on behalf of the school, to invite your group to our Welcome Evening in the Main Hall on 6th June. I hope that you'll all be able to come.

The Central High School has about 650 students between the ages of 12 and 18 and is well-known locally for two main reasons. Firstly, most students pass their exams with high grades, and secondly we've got a reputation for being a friendly place to study.
 The Welcome Evening will start with drinks at 8.30. There's an entertainment programme, including a folk dance display and a concert by the senior jazz band. At 9 o'clock the director is going to make a short speech and then there's a disco until 11 o'clock. That should give us a chance to get to know each other better.
 The school is about two kilometres from the city centre. I am enclosing a sketch map – it's very easy to find. We look forward to welcoming you to the school and hope the evening is a great success.

Best wishes,

Workbook: Writing p 61

Exam techniques
Student's Book pp 128–129

Use of English: Vocabulary cloze

Note: Part 1 of Paper 3 is intended to test students' knowledge of vocabulary rather than grammar.

1 Guidelines

Work through the guidelines, following the ideas given in the Introduction on pages 13–14 of this book.

2 Practice

A Students work through a typical passage, following the guidelines. Items 1–7 are accompanied by question clues which may help them in their choice of answers. These clues represent the kind of questions students should be asking themselves in this type of exam task.
If you wish, work through 1–7 with the whole class.

ANSWERS _____
  1 D goes
  2 A between
  3 C idea
  4 A artificial(the use of the article *an* makes B impossible)
  5 B bottom(*bed* is used in the phrase *on the sea-bed*)
  6 A two (*both these schemes*)
  7 C broke

B Students should work on their own for items 8–15.

ANSWERS _____
  8 B 9 C 10 A 11 B 12 C 13 D 14 A 15 B

Extra activity
If students find the text about the Channel Tunnel interesting, they could discuss these questions.

1 What do you think British people will gain and lose from being connected to the mainland of Europe?
2 If you could choose, would you want to be closer to or further away from neighbouring countries?

Vocabulary Student's Book p 130

1 Use of English

This vocabulary cloze exercise practises holiday vocabulary. Remind students about the guidelines in the Exam techniques section on page 128 of this unit.

ANSWERS

1 C 2 B 3 B 4 A 5 B 6 A 7 B

2 Word building

Roots

Knowing what the root of a word is can often help with understanding its meaning. This is also good practice for the word formation task (Paper 3, Part 5) of the FCE exam.

ANSWERS

1 *observation*   observe (verb)
  reaction   react (verb)
  amusement   amuse (verb)
  valuables   value (noun and verb)
2 *addictive*   addict (noun)
  resentful   resent (verb)
  unrivalled   rival (noun and verb)
  unlucky   luck (noun)
  glamorous   glamour (noun)
3 *honestly*   honest (adjective)
  enviably   envy (noun and verb)
  especially   special (adjective)

Extra activity

Make up tables like this for students to complete.

verb root	noun	adjective	adjective with opposite meaning
satisfy			
receive			
communicate			
compete			
succeed			
attract			

ANSWERS

verb root	noun	adjective	adjective with opposite meaning
satisfy	*satisfaction*	*satisfactory satisfied*	*unsatisfactory unsatisfied*
receive	*reception receipt*	*receptive*	*unreceptive*
communicate	*communication*	*communicative*	*uncommunicative*
compete	*competition competitor*	*competitive*	*uncompetitive*
succeed	*success*	*successful*	*unsuccessful*
attract	*attraction*	*attractive*	*unattractive*

3 Phrasal verbs

ANSWERS

1 brought *in* (to bring in a law / regulation)
2 was brought *up* (to bring up a child)
3 brought *on*
4 (has brought *back* / will bring *back* (to bring back memories)
5 bring him *round* (a doctor brings a patient round, the patient comes round)

Workbook: Vocabulary 1, 3, 4 pp 59–60

Your students are now ready to take Unit test 9, which is on page 156 of this book. The key is on page 171.

10 Restrictions

Within limits

Introduction   Student's Book p 131

Aim: To introduce the main language themes of the unit – obligation, necessity and permission, and the first topic – rules and restrictions.

A Students discuss questions 1–3 in pairs, in groups or as a class. There are no right or wrong answers – encourage them to express their opinions. In their discussion of question 3, students may use some of the modal verbs focused on in this unit (but do not insist on this). Examples: *Guards can't smile. Doctors have to work long hours.* Students now talk about the restrictions on each of the groups of people in the photos.

B Brainstorm this question with the whole class. Ideas: prisoners, film stars, royalty, pop stars, sports personalities, blind people, old people, babies.

Listening   Student's Book pp 132–133

1 Think ahead

Because of its rather personal nature, students may prefer just to think about this question and not discuss it in pairs or groups.
Whole class pre-listening discussions on a similar topic might be:
• Do you know anyone who has more than one image?
• Can you think of a famous personality whose private and public images are very different?

2 Listening

A Because this is a general understanding task, play the recording once only. Students match the names of the speakers with their jobs or positions. Check answers.

ANSWERS _____
1 Suzy   E schoolgirl *pupils / school*
2 Jenny   F parent (this person talks about buying shoes for a boy)

3 Becky   D fashion designer *creations / materials / colours / styles / collection*
4 Sheila   B unknown actress . . .*I'd probably have had a more successful film career*
5 Mary   A model *I'm paid to wear the kind of clothes. . .*

B Make sure students understand this second listening task, and then play the recording again. Check answers.

ANSWERS _____
A 4 Sheila   D 1 Suzy
B 5 Mary   E (extra subject)
C 3 Becky   F 2 Jenny

Tapescript

1 Suzy

It's not what you'd call trendy, but at least you don't have to worry about what to put on in the mornings. Some of the rules are incredible though – you just wouldn't believe it. Listen to this one: 'Pupils must wear ties at all times.' or this: 'Boys must not wear earrings while at school.' There was a row here recently when they sent a boy home and told him to get his hair cut. And I think the rule about not letting boys wear earrings is very unfair. Some of the girls wear skirts which are much shorter than the regulation length. In the end, it's all part of going to school – I mean, it's something to rebel against, isn't it?

2 Jenny

It's a constant battle. So far I've simply refused to pay more than £25 for trainers, but Adriano's desperate for a pair of Nike-Airs – and the cheapest I've found is £35. He says he wants them because they're more comfortable than other makes, and apparently they're lighter and better designed than the ones he's got at the moment. The truth is his friends at school have all got these Nike-Air ones, and they make fun of him because he hasn't . He's just so persistent – I'll probably give in eventually.

3 Becky

I've always based my creations on what's happening out there on the streets. Recently, most of my inspiration has come from teenagers who go down to the second-hand shops with a fiver in their pocket and spend several hours choosing original combinations of materials, colours and styles. Let's say I *borrow* their creativity and turn it into something softer, less harsh, the kind of thing that wouldn't look out of place at a royal dinner party or a high-class wedding. The thing is my stuff is so expensive that only a few lucky people can afford it. Anyway, look, you must come and see my new collection – it opens next week.

4 Sheila

If I were prettier, I'd probably have had a more successful film career – but you have to admit it – it's easier if you're Michelle Pfeiffer or Julia Roberts, isn't it? A pretty girl once said to me 'You don't know what prejudice there is against beautiful women.' I think I could put up with that kind of prejudice. Actually, most of the time I dress for comfort – I'm afraid most of my clothes are pretty messy. I don't wear anything sleeveless any more, though – my arms are too fat for that now.

5 Mary

Basically, it's a wonderful life. Quite apart from the money, there's the glamour, the fame, the travel. And on top of all that I'm paid to wear the kind of clothes most women would kill for. From that point of view, it's brilliant, but of course there is a downside. In my situation, if you've got a busy schedule, it can be absolutely exhausting, especially if I'm not eating much because I have to lose a couple of kilos for the next job. And whatever you do, you mustn't let the press attention go to your head. I know that if I want to stay sane, I've got to have a break from time to time. I need to get right away from the business, even if it's just for a day or two.

3 Points of view

These questions could be discussed in pairs, in groups or as a whole class. If your students do not have to wear school uniform, ask them how they would feel about having to. You could elicit lists of pros and cons of school uniforms.

4 Comprehension

Students have now heard the recording twice, so should be familiar with the general idea of what each speaker says. This exercise consists of one question for each of the five extracts. Allow students time to read through the questions and alternative answers before playing the recording. Check answers.

ANSWERS

1 B *to get his hair cut*
2 B *The truth is his friends at school have all got these. . .*
3 C *my stuff is so expensive that only a few lucky people can afford it.*
4 C *most of the time I dress for comfort*
5 A *I've got to have a break from time to time*

5 Vocabulary

ANSWERS

1 a flatly (absolutely, definitely)
  b flat (hitting his face on the ground)
2 a free (without paying)
  b freely (without restrictions)
3 a hard (industriously)
  b hardly (scarcely)
4 a lately (recently)
  b late (after the correct time)
5 a widely (among many people)
  b wide (fully open)
6 a near (close to)
  b nearly (almost)

6 Over to you

This brief discussion / writing activity rounds off the topic of fashion and image. Spend a few minutes discussing the two photos of Claudia Schiffer and then set the writing task either as classwork or homework.

MODEL

Whatever she's wearing Claudia Schiffer looks beautiful, but personally, I prefer the photo of her in her normal everyday clothes. I think that's because she looks much more natural and friendly in blue denim. She looks like an ordinary person, like someone you could talk to and be friendly with. In my opinion, when she's wearing expensive designer clothes she looks cold and unfriendly. Maybe it's also because I don't really like that kind of clothes.

Grammar and practice Student's Book pp 134–135

1 Modal verbs

A Obligation and necessity

Aim: To focus on the difference in meaning between *must*, *have to* and *need to*.

Before students do these inductive grammar exercises, check that they understand the functional terms obligation and necessity. Give a few clear examples.

• obligations: going to school, national laws, rules of a game
• necessities: eating, sleeping, qualifications needed for a job

Set the first task and check answers.

ANSWERS

1 don't have to	a 7
2 must	b 4 (invitation) / 6 (advice)
3 must not	c 2 (rule or law) / 3 (prohibition)
4 must	d 5
5 have to	e 1
6 mustn't	
7 need	

Must is followed by the infinitive without *to*; *need* and *have* are followed by *to* + infinitive.

Note: You may also wish to point out or remind students that
a) a speaker may use *I must . . .* to express a strong feeling that he / she should do something, e.g. *I must go now or I'll miss my train.*
b) *You must . . .* is often used when the speaker is angry with someone, e.g. *You must be more careful in future!*
c) *must* has no past simple form – *had to* is used instead.

B In this exercise, students have to distinguish between the negative forms *shouldn't, mustn't, needn't, don't have to.* The meaning of *mustn't* in the example sentence is 'it's necessary *not* to do something'.

POSSIBLE ANSWERS

2 It's advisable not to sunbathe for too long.
  I don't think it's a good idea for you to sunbathe . . .
3 British people aren't obliged to / don't have to vote . . .
  British people can choose whether to vote . . .
4 Soldiers aren't obliged to wear uniforms . . .
  There is no regulation which forces soldiers to wear uniforms . . .
  It isn't compulsory for soldiers to wear uniforms . . .
5 (Please) don't worry about me.
  I don't want you to worry about me.
  (*Mustn't* here is like a negative imperative, with the meaning 'Don't.')

C/D These exercises draw attention to the difference in meaning between *didn't need to* and *needn't have.*

C ANSWERS

1 The speaker didn't hurry – he or she knew there was plenty of time.
2 The speaker did hurry. He or she didn't know until later that there was plenty of time.

D ANSWERS

1 needn't have driven	4 needn't have taken
2 didn't need to go	5 didn't need to
3 didn't need to wash	6 needn't have gone

E Refer students to the Grammar reference on page 209 of their books.

2 Practice

A ANSWERS

1 must	4 don't have to
2 must	5 will need to / should / must
3 should	6 must not

B Students should read the whole text before filling the gaps. Remind them of when to use the three modals in this kind of context.
• *must* for legal obligations
• *should* for advice
• *need* for physical necessities

ANSWERS

1 shouldn't	5 need to
2 must	6 must not
3 should / need to	7 should
4 must not	

Extra activity
Ask students to write guidelines for foreign motorists planning to drive in their country. They should use the motorway text as a model.

3 Permission

A This exercise provides controlled practice of the language of permission.
Allow students time to make up sentences using *are allowed to / can* and *aren't allowed to / can't*, then elicit answers.
Note: Both verbs are possible in each case.

B Refer students to the Grammar reference on page 210 of their books. (Or you may wish to do this before they write sentences in A.)

C Students could work in pairs to compile their own chart like the one in their books. If students are from different countries, they could interview each other and produce a chart about their partner's country.
Finally, the class might like to discuss some of the more controversial age restrictions. For example, British people can join the army when they are 16, but they can't vote in an election until they are 18.

4 Fluency

This unlikely situation is meant to provide enjoyable fluency practice. Student A objects to certain restrictions, and Student B is an authority figure defending them. Allow pairs a few minutes to prepare roles before they begin. Monitor, but do not interrupt. Students may use obligation and permission language, but don't insist on this.

Extra activity
Students should be asked to imagine they are in a position of political power in their country and then to write a public notice listing new laws they would introduce.
Elicit a few suggestions from students, then get them

working individually or in pairs to write the notice. Because the context is legal obligations, most of the laws could include the words *must* or *must not*.

Some ideas are:
- People must not let their dogs roam the streets after ten o'clock at night.
- Everyone over the age of 18 must vote in local elections.
- People must not mow their lawns on Sundays.
- All young people must have at least one day a week with no homework.
- From the beginning of next year, children do not have to start school until the age of eight.
- Cyclists should wear crash helmets at all times.

Notices could be displayed on the classroom walls and some of the more provocative new laws could be discussed.

> Workbook: Grammar 1, 3 pp 64–65

Writing   Student's Book p 136–137

Exam training: Articles 2

Students were introduced to writing articles in Unit 3. Before starting this section try to elicit the main features of articles already covered.
- The importance of the title in introducing the topic and attracting the reader's attention.
- The opening sentence should be connected with the title, and make the reader want to read the rest of the article.
- The style can be serious or light-hearted but should be consistent throughout the article.

If you wish, refer students back to the Summary box on page 47.

1 Model

A Read through the sample exam question with the whole class and elicit students' ideas on the two questions in the YOU WRITE – WE PRINT box. You could list these ideas on the board.

B Now ask students to read the model answer, drawing attention to the questions about the first and last paragraphs. Elicit students' ideas.

POSSIBLE ANSWERS
- The opening sentence is a direct question to the reader. The readers will probably think of an answer automatically. The reader may want to continue just to find out why the writer was wearing torn jeans.
- The last paragraph is meant to be provocative. It suggests that everyone everywhere reacts in the same way as everyone else. The reader may agree or disagree with this, or may need some time to think about the idea.

Extra activity
If students find the text interesting, spend a few minutes discussing the ideas in it and how far they agree with the writer.

2 Analysis

A/B Let students work individually through these two tasks and then elicit their answers.

ANSWERS
A 1   The writer gives an example from personal experience
 3   The writer asks the reader a personal question
B Students could argue for 2 or 3. The last paragraph could be a genuine personal opinion or it could be a deliberately provocative point intended to leave the reader thinking.

Extra activity
You might also get students to think about these questions:
- What ideas are introduced in the second and third paragraphs?
- How are the four paragraphs linked to each other?

ANSWERS
- In paragraph 2, the writer explains her own ideas about children's choice of clothes and parents' reactions to this choice. In paragraph 3, the writer adds a sociological aspect to the discussion.
- Paragraph 2 provides the answer to the question posed by paragraph 1. The phrase *In my case*, makes it clear that this is a personal answer. Paragraph 3 opens with *In addition to this*, . . . making it clear that this is providing a further opinion on the subject of clothes.

3 Practice

Students now have to match the beginnings and endings of three more articles loosely related to the subject of fashion.

A ANSWERS

Beginning	Ending
1	B
2	C
3	A

For **B** and **C** below, refer students back to the lists in 2 Analysis on page 136.

B First paragraph techniques
1   3 and 1 – the writer asks the reader a question and gives a personal example to illustrate the topic.
2   4 – the writer expresses a strong opinion.
3   2 and 5 – the writer describes an unusual scene; the writer describes a puzzle which needs an answer.

C Purpose of last paragraph
Note: Because we have not read the middle paragraphs of these three articles, we cannot tell whether any of them summarize the main points of their articles.

A 4 – this rounds off an article about the popularity of jeans.

B 4 and 2 – this rounds off the article, but it also leaves the reader with something to think about. (Will trainers come back into fashion? What else may come back into fashion in the future?)

C 3 – this final paragraph is mainly the expression of a personal opinion.

4 Think, plan, write

Students are given a similar question to think and write about.

A Think

Students read through the sample exam question and then discuss questions 1–3.

You may like to add a fourth question to the list if students are short of ideas:

Can you tell what jobs people do just by looking at the clothes they are wearing?

Elicit their answers to the third (and fourth) question, about hairstyles (and clothes) and list any particularly strong or interesting opinions on the board.

B Plan

Students should work individually through the six points, making notes.

Notes

1 Less imaginative students could be asked to write an article for readers of their own age. They could follow the style of the model.

2 Titles could be made up before or after the article is written.

3 Check that students go through this essential planning process. It need only involve writing a few words about each of three to five paragraphs.

4 Refer students back to the list of points in 2A.

5 Remind students of the importance of linking paragraphs thematically and with a linking phrase.

6 Refer students back to the list of points in 2B.

C Write

1 Students should write their first paragraph in class to enable them to test it out on a partner. You could also offer to give an opinion on their writing.

2 The final version of the first paragraph and the rest of the article can be set as homework, in the normal way. As usual remind students to check their grammar, spelling and punctuation.

MODEL

Appearances can be deceptive

My grandmother once opened her front door and saw a smart young man in a dark suit and with short hair standing there. He said he was from the bank, so she let him in and gave him tea. Twenty minutes later the man left with her life savings. My grandmother spent a week in hospital recovering from the robbery.

This story shows that you cannot tell what a person is really like from their appearance. Of course people in some jobs have to look smart and tidy, like bank managers, but this does not prove that they are all honest.

Unfortunately some older people think that all young people in worn-out clothes and with long untidy hair must be dishonest. In fact, many people who look like this are students or nurses in training.

What you look like is your own decision, but other people have their own opinion about you. Next time you look in the mirror, imagine what you would think if you opened your front door and saw yourself standing there.

Workbook: Writing p 67

10

Space

Introduction Student's Book p 138

The second part of the unit continues the theme of restrictions, this time related to the physical situation of an astronaut in a spaceship.

Students should discuss questions A, B and C in pairs, in groups or as a whole class.

When you elicit their ideas, stress the idea of astronauts having to live a restricted life. Examples:

You'd have to stay in the same position for long periods of time.
You wouldn't be able to move very much.
You'd have to eat your food in the form of pills.
You might get very bored and depressed.
You'd probably feel very lonely and you'd miss your friends and family.

Reading Student's Book pp 138–139

1 Think ahead

This is a continuation of the introductory discussion which leads directly into the article. Elicit students' ideas of the mental and physical qualities needed by astronauts and list them on the board. Examples:

Possible mental qualities: intelligence, good education, patience, mental stability, tolerance of others, imagination, calm.

Possible physical qualities: fitness, strength, stamina, good digestive system, good circulation, strong heart, good eyesight and hearing.

2 Reading

During the first reading students should read quickly to find out whether the qualities they thought of are mentioned in the article. Set a strict time limit of three to four minutes for this first reading. Students should not attempt to fill the gaps yet.

ANSWERS

Qualities mentioned in the article:
well-educated / intelligent – *scientifically trained, speak foreign languages*
calm – *deal with difficult situations without panicking*
Note: *a strong digestive system* is also mentioned in one of the missing sentences.

3 Comprehension

This type of reading task was introduced in the Exam techniques section of Unit 2. If your students find these exercises difficult, give them a few minutes to read through the guidelines on page 26 of their books before doing this task. Remind them of the importance of looking for definite

thematic and linguistic clues to help them fit the missing sentences into the gaps, rather than relying on instinct or guesswork.

A Students should work individually in the first instance. Allow them plenty of time for this. Then let them compare answers in pairs, changing their answers if appropriate. Finally elicit answers, together with reasons.

ANSWERS

1 H The text before 1 lists the qualities needed; the text after describes exactly how suitable Helen Sharman was.

2 G The text after 2 describes why a strong digestive system is vital. The word *also* shows that this additional to qualities already listed.

3 B The phrase to *do this* in the sentence after 3 refers to *simulate weightlessness* in the missing sentence. Missing sentence D does not fit here because of the word *also*.

4 F The use of *the* in the phrase *When the plane* in missing sentence F refers back to *huge freighter aircraft* in the text before 4.

5 A This is a thematic link.

6 E *Up there* in the sentence following 6 refers to *the Mir Space Station* in missing sentence E. This sentence also describes the next stage of Helen Sharman's experience.

7 C *The results* that were *brought back* were those of the experiments referred to in the text before 7.

Sentence D does not fit anywhere.

B Reading between the lines

Remind students that there are no definite correct answers to these questions. Allow them to work individually in pairs for about five minutes and then elicit their ideas.

POSSIBLE ANSWERS

1 Being an astronaut is something very different and exciting.
It's a once-in-a-lifetime opportunity.
Space is one of the few unexplored places to visit.
Living in space is a challenge, mentally and physically.

2 There are many potentially stressful situations that could occur in space. If astronauts were not able to stay calm they could turn a difficult situation into a catastrophe.
Situations could include: mechanical breakdown / loss of communication with Earth / fire / illness / the need to do work on the outside of the spacecraft – requiring a spacewalk.

3 It's exciting / interesting / rewarding.
Scientific research is necessary for the future well-being of the world.
Not enough people are doing this vital work.

Workbook: Reading pp 62–63

Grammar and practice Student's Book p 140

1 Adverb and prepositional phrases

Check that students understand what adverbs are before getting them to categorize the examples from the article. This is probably best done as a whole class exercise.

ANSWERS

• manner	*quickly*
• place	*in space / on earth / to the top*
• time	*six months later / one afternoon / the next day now / these days*
• frequency	*often / regularly*
• degree	*very / almost / extremely / entirely / absolutely*
• viewpoint	*obviously / amazingly / actually*

Try eliciting a few more examples of each type, especially **manner** and **place** which are not well represented in the text.

Ideas
• manner   *well / badly / angrily / politely / quietly*
• place   *downstairs / somewhere / under the bed / there / left*

2 Position of adverbs

A The correct positioning of adverbs is a very complicated matter and you should not attempt to teach all the rules involved. You may want to avoid giving rules altogether and get students to do this exercise by relying on what sounds or feels right to them. Some phrases which include adverbs can be thought of as set expressions, for example : *to do everything you* **possibly** *can . . .* Alternatively, suggest they refer to the notes in the Grammar reference on page 210 of their books during or immediately after this exercise. Allow students plenty of time for this exercise before eliciting answers.

ANSWERS
Correct word order:
• everything she **possibly** can
• She spends a lot of time **now** talking to schoolchildren. / She **now** spends a lot of time talking to schoolchildren. / She spends a lot of time talking to schoolchildren **now**. / **Now** she spends a lot of time talking to schoolchildren.
• Primary school teachers **often** have no scientific . . . / **Often** primary school teachers have no scientific . . .
• I **definitely** think children should learn about space / I think children should **definitely** learn about space
• scientists themselves aren't always the best people
The other words and phrases are in the correct places.

B If students have not already referred to the Grammar reference on page 210, let them do so now.

3 *Too, enough, very*

These words may not cause your students any serious problems, so allow them to work uninterrupted through A and B. Then check answers.

ANSWERS
A Fill the gaps
1 very
2 too
3 enough

B Meanings
1 very
2 too
3 enough
4 too, very
5 enough
6 enough

Explain any difficulties your students may have or refer them to the Grammar reference notes on page 210 of their books. Then let them continue with C.

POSSIBLE ANSWERS
1 . . . we were too young to get married.
   . . . we were not old enough to get married.
2 . . . is too expensive for us.
   . . . is not cheap enough for us.
3 . . . would be too hot for me.
   . . . would not be cool enough for me.
   . . . would not have a low enough temperature for me.
4 . . . because he realized / found he was too impatient to do the job.
   . . . because he realized / found he wasn't patient enough for the job.
   . . . because he realized / found he didn't have enough patience for the job.

Workbook: Grammar 2, p 64

Vocabulary Student's Book p 141

1 Clothes

A This exercise is designed to elicit some less commonly used clothes vocabulary. Students should write lists individually and then compare with a partner.

POSSIBLE ANSWERS
Winter clothes: boots, gloves, hat, scarf, mac, overcoat, raincoat, parka, anorak
Summer clothes: sandals, shorts, T-shirt, short-sleeved shirt
Sportswear: jogging suit, tracksuit, swimming costume (women), swimming trunks (men), leotard, trainers
Indoor clothes: blouse, cardigan, dress, jeans, pullover, sweater, shirt, skirt, slippers
Nightwear: dressing-gown, nightie, pyjamas

Elicit ideas for other categories, e.g. work clothes, party clothes, formal clothes, footwear, headwear, underwear.

B Before setting this exercise, brainstorm some descriptive vocabulary students might need to use. Write appropriate lists on the board.
Materials and patterns: see page 218 of the Vocabulary reference.
Colours: check main colours and related shades, e.g. green, dark green, etc.
Styles: tight, loose (fitting), baggy, smart, casual, formal, informal, short-sleeved, long-sleeved.
Students write sentences individually and compare ideas in pairs.

Extra activity
Get students to describe the clothes or uniforms worn by the people in the three photographs on this page.

2 Prohibition

ANSWERS _____
1 B banned	4 A forbidden
2 A prohibited	5 C permitted
3 D compulsory	

3 Phrasal verbs

ANSWERS _____
1 carried out	(= did)
2 taking up	(= starting to do)
3 give in	(= agree / surrender)
4 wrote down	(= wrote on paper)
5 sent off	(= wrote a letter)

Workbook: Vocabulary 1, 2, 3 pp 65–66

Exam techniques Student's Book pp 142–143

Use of English: Key word transformations

Note: The main differences between this kind of transformation exercise and ones students may have done before are:
- The word given cannot be changed in any way.
- Students are limited to using a certain number of words.

The intended effect of these two features is that only **one** grammatical structure can be used to provide the correct answer.

1 Guidelines

Work through the guidelines, following the ideas given in the Introduction on pages 13–14 of this book.

2 Recognizing structures

A Get students to read through this introductory description of this exercise type, or read through it with them, making sure they understand everything. It is important that students realize that, above all, these exercises are a test of their grammatical knowledge and accuracy.

B Students could work through sentences 1–10 individually or in pairs, or this could be done as a whole class activity.

ANSWERS _____
1 ✓
2 ✗ He'd **rather stay in. . .** (*rather* + infinitive without 'to')
3 ✗ Is this **the earliest flight**. . . (not **earlier** – superlative adjective)
4 ✗ Six months **ago he started**. . . (not **has started** – simple past, not present perfect with specific time reference)
5 ✗ This is the **first time** I **have eaten** snails. (not **I am eating** – present perfect after superlative expressions)
6 ✓
7 ✓
8 ✗ I was **brought up** . . .(not **me**; this is a normal passive construction.)
9 ✓ (note correct Conditional type 3 tense sequence)
10 ✗ It was **such a boring film**. . . (not **a such** boring film – note correct word order)

3 Guided practice

Let students work individually and independently on the next 10 sentences. Remind them to pay careful attention to the clues.

ANSWERS _____
1 A holiday in Bermuda is **more expensive than one** in Miami.
2 I **haven't seen Jimmy since** Stephen's party.
3 Many people **regret starting to** smoke.
4 My brother never **used to be late** until he got friendly with Mick.
5 You can't come in **unless you are** a member.
6 I **prefer to drive than** (**to**) be driven.
7 By Monday **I will / I'll have finished** this book.
8 He is overweight **because he eats** so much chocolate.
9 My parents **congratulated me on passing** my driving test.
10 He was **banned from driving** for a year after the accident.

Writing Student's Book p 144

Bringing descriptions to life

1 Introduction and models
Check students understand the difference being made here between factual details and descriptive details and then let them work through the two short texts making lists. Elicit answers.

Factual details

Text 1 (left) *The Toros mountains meet the sea at Antalya. Lots of sports are played in this region.*

Text 2 (right) *Four individuals / £2500 from vegetarian author Rebecca Hall / The cage has no toilet / (it) is one metre square by two metres high*

Descriptive details

Text 1 *the pine-covered Toros mountains / irregular coastline / rocky headlands / secluded bays / brilliant sunshine*

Text 2 *brave individuals / human chickens / boiled brown rice / metal tray*

2 Practice

A Work through the first sentence of the text to be expanded with the whole class to make sure students understand what to do, then let them continue individually or in pairs.

Finally elicit a version of the text from the class which is made up of students' own additional words and phrases rather than those listed in their books.

Possible expanded text

Yesterday morning [1] **thousands of** [2] **middle-aged** protesters marched [3] **solemnly** through the [4] **middle of** town. When they arrived at the town hall, they stopped and formed an [5] **angry** crowd. Some of them were carrying [6] **enormous** placards with [7] **anti-war** slogans. Others were shouting and shaking their fists [8] **energetically** at the [9] **faceless** officials working inside the [10] **grey concrete** building.

B Don't spend too long on this exercise at this stage – it is more important to allow students to write their own description. Work quickly through the six phrases with the whole class.

ANSWERS

1 a large old Spanish city
2 a beautiful tall modern building
3 correct
4 wonderful green cotton baseball caps
5 impressive ancient narrow streets
6 small sixteenth-century wood houses

If adjective order is a problem for your students, make a point of revising rules in a future lesson. You may also refer students to the Grammar reference on page 211 of their books.

3 Think, plan, write
Get students to follow the usual preparations for writing, then set the writing itself for homework.

Your students are now ready to take Unit test 10, which is on page 157 of this book. The key is on page 171.

11 Speculation

Follow that

Unit focus   Expressing certainties, possibilities and wishes

Topic 1   Gadgets, appliances and other inventions
Listening
Grammar and practice   The modals *must*, *can't*, *may*, *might* and *could*
Vocabulary   Gadgets and appliances, adjectival suffixes, phrasal verbs
Writing   Connecting ideas

Topic 2   Volcanoes and other environmental disasters
Reading
Grammar and practice   The verb *wish*
Exam techniques   Listening: Selecting from two or three answers
Writing   Describing places – paragraphs, punctuation
Exam training: Compositions 2

Introduction   Student's Book p 145

Aim: To introduce the topic of the first part of the unit – gadgets, appliances and other inventions.

A Students read the dictionary definitions. Explain that 'esp.' is an abbreviation for 'especially'. Students then work in pairs to answer the questions on the photos. Some of their answers will probably be guesses. Do not confirm whether these ideas are correct or not; students will find out when they do B.
Do not name any of the items when checking the answers to A.

ANSWERS
1 appliances: 4, 7
  gadgets: 2, 3, 5, 6
  either appliances or gadgets: 1
2 1 for extracting juice from oranges, lemons, etc. (juice-extractor)
  2 for shining light into awkward spaces (a flexible torch)
  3 for finding out about the weather (a barometer)
  4 for washing dishes (a dishwasher)
  5 for opening bottles and jars (a bottle-opener)
  6 for making fuel from waste paper (a briquette maker)
  7 for cleaning floors by sucking up dirt (a vacuum cleaner)

B ANSWERS
1st text: 6   2nd text: 3   3rd text: 2

C Points for discussion
Pairs or small groups should spend a few minutes noting down all the appliances and gadgets that they have at home (or at work) before discussing the questions. Selected class feedback can follow their discussion.

Listening   Student's Book pp 146–147

1 Think ahead

Even if students can't pick up satellite television where they live, they may know what equipment is needed to receive it. If they don't, tell them.

ANSWER
a satellite dish, a TV monitor and a receiver

Ask students to imagine the sort of things that could go wrong if they installed their own satellite dish.

Background information
Commercial broadcasting direct from satellites began in the USA in the 1980s and in Europe in 1989.

2 Comprehension

A Before students hear the recording, check that they know what a panel game is: a game on radio or television, usually with an audience, in which teams compete against each other. Elicit a few examples of panel games that students are familiar with (or other contests if students are unfamiliar with panel games). Establish the type of things that the competitors have to do, what the rules are, etc. Ask students to read the incomplete sentences carefully and to try to work out the kind of information that might be missing. Elicit a few ideas but don't confirm whether they are correct or not. Finally, remind students that they are required to complete the sentences with a word or short phrase only. They will be expected to write between one and five words.
Play the recording twice and allow students time between and after listenings to decide their answers.

ANSWERS
1 three people
2 what comes next
3 two points

SPECULATION   **UNIT 11**   113

4 (next-door) neighbour
5 before colour TVs
6 tell everyone
7 there was no picture
8 moved the dish about
9 Eric's satellite dish
10 some (net) curtains

Tapescript

P1 = Presenter; P2 = Peter; A1 = Anita; A2 = Angie; S1 = Suzanne; S2 = Sue; N = Nigel; J = Jim

P1 Good evening and welcome to another session of your favourite panel game 'Follow that'. As usual we have two teams in the studio. On Nigel's team this evening we have Suzanne Nightingale and Angie Somerville and on Sue's team we have Peter Burke and Jim Livingstone.

Let me just remind you of the rules. A member of the studio audience will relate a story which may or may not be true. From time to time they will stop and the teams will have to guess what comes next. They can do one of two things: a team member can answer on his or her own without any help from the other members of the team – a correct answer will give the team five points – or the team can confer and in this case they'll get two points for a correct answer. If the answer is wrong, it'll be passed over to the other team who can confer and will also get two points for a correct answer.

Okay? Right. Let's hear our first story which is from Anita Bishop of Llandudno in Wales. Hello, Anita.

A1 Hello. The man who lives next door to us – his name is Eric Robinson – is gadget-mad. You name it, he bought it first. He was the first to get colour TV when that came out, the first to get a microwave, and the first. . . (*Pause*)

P1 Okay. Follow that . . . Suzanne.

S1 Erm. . . Could be anything, couldn't it? Can I confer? (*To Nigel*) It could be a dishwasher. There again it might be a mobile phone. What do you think?

N Mm, the only other thing I can think of is satellite television. What do you think, Angie?

A2 I'd . . . I'd go for the phone.

S1 The first to get a mobile phone?

P1 Sorry. Over to your team Sue.

S2 (*To Jim and Peter*) Any ideas?

J Well, if it wasn't a phone, it must be satellite television.

S2 What about a dishwasher?

P2 No, it can't be a dishwasher. I'm pretty sure they were around before colour television.

S2 Okay. We'll go for satellite television.

P1 Correct. That's two points to your team Sue. Back to you, Anita.

A1 The moment he got his satellite dish, he got his ladder out, put it up against the side of the house, climbed up it, fixed the dish and climbed back down

again. I should tell you that Eric likes to get things done as quickly as he can because he's desperate to tell everyone. So he doesn't always do things properly.

Anyway, when he went into the living room and switched on the telly, he found that there was no picture. So out he went again, and back up the ladder. But this time he left his wife in front of the telly so she could shout up to let him know when he had a decent picture. He moved the dish about and after a while his wife called up to say it wasn't brilliant but it was okay. He thought the dish was pointing a bit low, but it was a hot day and he was a bit fed up by this time so he decided to leave it as it was. A few hours later, a fire-engine drew up outside. The house across the street was on fire. What had happened?

P1 Okay. Peter.

P2 I'll try this one on my own. Well, it must have been something to do with the satellite dish. Anita said something about . . . he thought it was too low and then she told us that he didn't spend a lot of time doing things properly. Erm . . . So I suppose the dish might have reflected the sun onto something in the other house. Am I on the right track?

P1 I'm not really allowed to say. Not if you're going for full marks.

P2 Okay. Erm . . . Do you want more detail?

P1 Yes.

P2 Well, it can't have been anything solid, like a table, because the dish had only been up for a few hours. Erm . . . It must have been something flammable and near the window. Oh, I know! It was curtains!

P1 Is that your answer?

P2 Yes.

P1 Well done. It was net curtains at the window. (*Pause*) So at the halfway stage Nigel's team has no points and Sue's team has seven. Now, let's go on to our next story, from John Hamilton of Glasgow.

B Vocabulary

ANSWERS

1 e 2 f 3 c 4 g 5 b 6 h 7 d 8 a

Extra activity

Writing task: Have you ever tried to set up or repair a machine or appliance? Were you successful or did something go wrong? Write a paragraph explaining what happened.

3 Over to you

A Suggested procedure

1 Students think about the question individually and jot down their ideas.
2 They now form groups of up to four students who share

the same opinion, to brainstorm ideas to support their view.
3 Students reform into mixed groups of three, in which each person argues for a different invention.
4 Ask for selected feedback.
This is a fluency activity so don't interrupt students to correct mistakes. Any help should be given at the earlier stages.

B 'The mysterious hitchhiker' in the Workbook on page 32 is another example of an urban myth.

Grammar and practice Student's Book pp 148–149

1 Certainties and possibilities

Aim: To focus on the use of the modal verbs *may*, *might*, *could*, *must* and *can't* to express certainty and possibility.

Students should spend only a few minutes discussing the answers to the inductive grammar questions in A, B and C. Check their answers to each one before allowing them to go on to the next stage.

A ANSWERS
1 Uncertain: *might*
2 Almost certain: *can't*
3 Almost certain: *must*
4 Absolutely certain: full verb *was*

B ANSWERS
1 b   2 b   3 a   4 c

C ANSWERS
1 *could*: might, may, maybe, possibly, perhaps
2 *might*: as above
3 *must*: probably*
4 *can't*: probably not*
* *Probably* and *probably not* are not as strong as the modal verbs *must* and *can't*.

Check that students know how the sentence structure would change if the alternative forms were used:
It may be a dishwasher.
Maybe it's a dishwasher.
Perhaps it's a dishwasher.
It's possibly a dishwasher.
It's probably satellite television.
It probably isn't a dishwasher.

2 Past, present or future?

A/B Students can work alone, then compare answers with a partner before checking their answers in the Grammar reference on page 211 of their books.

ANSWERS
1 Past: *have* + past participle
2 Present: *be* + present participle
3 Future: infinitive without *to*
4 Present: infinitive without *to*

3 Practice

You may wish to point out that the adverb *maybe* is one word, and should not be confused with *may* + *be*. *Maybe* has the same meaning as *perhaps*.

ANSWERS
2 He may / might / could be in the canteen.
3 He may / might / could have gone home early.
4 It can't have been pork that you had.
5 They may / might not have arrived yet.
6 She must have got them.
7 She must still be very angry.
8 It can't be.
9 Your watch may / might / could be slow.
10 Water must have got into it.

4 Picture discussion

Make sure that students know what they have to do before they start the activity. Encourage them to use the modals they have practised in this unit, but don't insist on it. Don't interrupt them or allow them to ask you questions while they are doing the activity. You can deal with mistakes and questions at the end. Students should spend about five minutes on each photograph.

Workbook: Grammar 1, 2 p 70

Vocabulary Student's Book p 150

1 Gadgets and appliances

Students can work on their own and then compare answers, or in pairs. Before they begin, explain any unknown vocabulary in the definitions but not the names of the actual appliances and gadgets. Ask them which are gadgets and which are appliances and what they are used for.

ANSWERS
1 tin opener (gadget; for opening tins)
2 food processor (appliance; for preparing food)
3 tumble dryer (appliance; for drying clothes)
4 egg timer (gadget; for timing boiled eggs)
Supply any vocabulary students need for writing their own definitions. When they have written their definitions the other students can guess which item they are describing, say whether it is a gadget or appliance and what it is used for.

1 It's made of plastic and has a lot of buttons on it. When you press these you operate the machine. (remote control: a gadget for operating e.g. a TV set from a distance)

2 The part which you hold is made of hard plastic; the blades are usually made of metal. You can make it go faster or more slowly. (electric whisk: a small electrical appliance which is used for whisking and beating liquids)

3 It's a rectangular shape and is made of glass and plastic. You put things inside it and they turn round on a sort of turntable. (microwave oven: an appliance which is used for heating and cooking food)

4 There are many kinds of these. The simplest is made of clay. You can get some made of plastic, which have places inside where you can put refrigerated panels. (wine cooler: a gadget for cooling or keeping wine cold)

2 Word building

Note: *Flammable* and *inflammable* have the same meaning.

ANSWERS

1 uncomfortable	5 reliable
2 reasonable	6 unforgettable
3 available	7 changeable
4 suitable	8 advisable

3 Phrasal verbs

ANSWERS

1 found
2 come to my house / flat
3 regained consciousness
4 unexpected has happened which I have to deal with
5 thought of

Workbook: Vocabulary 1, 2, 3, 4 pp 71–72

Writing   Student's Book p 151

Connecting ideas

Aim: This section focuses on joining ideas together at clause, sentence and text level. It examines the types of words writers use both to make clear the relationship between ideas and to make the text cohesive.
Students work on their own and then compare answers, or in pairs. Check each section before students go on to the next one.

1 In sentences

ANSWERS

1 so that (*in case* someone should steal his idea)
2 in case
3 and
4 unless
5 which
6 despite
7 or

2 Between sentences

ANSWERS

1 In contrast (However)		4 What is more (As a result)
2 On the contrary		5 On the whole
3 As a result		6 However

3 Referring words

ANSWERS

1 *they* refers to *camcorders*
2 *it* refers to her decision to get an answering machine
3 *them* refers to *researchers*
4 *it* refers to *the appliance*
5 *this* refers to the fact that less money is being spent on space exploration.

Playing with fire

Introduction   Student's Book p 152

Aim: To introduce the topic of the second part of the unit – volcanoes and other environmental disasters.

1 Establish the names of the natural phenomena which are illustrated: earthquake, flooding, hurricane, volcanic eruption.

2 Elicit ideas from the whole class. Some possible ideas are:
Earthquake: land disappears, buildings and bridges collapse, roads break up, cracks appear in the earth, people lose their homes, people die from being crushed or buried in falling buildings.
Flooding: areas are submerged in water and mud, trees are uprooted, buildings are destroyed, people and animals are drowned.
Hurricane: trees are uprooted, buildings and vehicles are destroyed, people are killed.
Volcanic eruption: people and animals in the vicinity may be killed, vegetation is destroyed, everything is covered with ash. (Don't mention at this stage that the ash makes the land more fertile or that people and animals are killed by molten lava or hot gases.)

Reading   Student's Book pp 152–153

1 Think ahead

Students should spend a couple of minutes in pairs making a list of countries where there are volcanoes. (See below for answers.)

2 Reading

Ask students to read the article fairly quickly for gist and to tick off the countries which are on their list.

ANSWERS

The countries mentioned in the article which have volcanoes are: Italy, Indonesia, Hawaii, Iceland, the Philippines, Japan, New Zealand, the USA, Columbia. Others which students may know are: Mexico, New Guinea, Ecuador, Peru, Chile, Cameroon, Cape Verde, the Canary Islands, Ethiopia, Kenya, Tanzania, Zaire, Guatemala, Costa Rica, Honduras, Nicaragua.

3 Points of view

Students should spend a few moments exchanging experiences and / or opinions with a partner.

4 Comprehension

A ANSWERS

Where there is more than one answer to a question the answers can be given in any order. Make sure that students can justify their answers by reference to the article.

1 E	2 I	*studies; growing scientific understanding*
3 A	4 C 5 E	*Vesuvius and Krakatoa; Mount Etna; Pinatubo*
6 G	7 H	*the fertility it adds to the soil . . .* (coffee, vines and rice grow well on volcanic soils); *the heat is used to generate electricity.* Also the lava flows concentrate minerals in one place.
8 F	9 G	*If a major eruption were to occur in Japan, New Zealand or California . . . in the near future; There are 15 capital cities in a position to be wiped out by volcanic eruptions.*
10 G		*. . . the soils from volcanic ashes are light, easily worked, drain well and are full of plant nutrients.*
11 B		*The types of eruption vary greatly . . .*
12 A	13 C 14 F	*. . . killing an estimated 16,000 people. More than 36,000 people were killed; killed nine tourists; counting the dead in millions.*
15 E		*disrupting the ozone layer and the planet's climate.*

B Reading between the lines

POSSIBLE ANSWERS

1 Presumably because volcanoes that have been thought extinct have erupted.
2 One that behaves predictably.

C Vocabulary

POSSIBLE ANSWERS

1 killed a lot of people
2 approximately, about
3 the volcanoes don't erupt as often
4 everyone in the world
5 which could be

5 Over to you

You may like to devote a whole lesson to this discussion. Elicit types of man-made environmental disasters, then divide the class into groups of three or four students for the discussion. Each group should discuss one type of disaster and take notes so that they can report their ideas, opinions and recommendations back to the class. Students will find the Vocabulary reference on page 218 useful. Some possible ideas follow.
Note: You may prefer not to do the ones asterisked as they feature in the Writing section on page 156 of this unit.

*Oil spills (e.g. the *Exxon Valdez* supertanker disaster Alaska, 1989)
Causes: bad weather, overcrowded waterways (collisions), old tankers.
Effects: beaches and sea polluted (oil slicks), marine life and birds killed.
Preventative measures: restricted routes, check that tankers are sea-worthy.

Nuclear accidents (e.g. the Chernobyl disaster, Ukraine 1986)
Causes: breakdowns in nuclear reactors, leaks, human error.
Effects: land contaminated by radiation and can't be used for hundreds or thousands of years, people killed or get cancers, radioactivity gets into the food chain, radioactive fall-out thousands of miles away.
Preventative measures: develop alternative sources of energy, stricter safety procedures.

Forest fires
Causes: human carelessness (e.g. cigarettes, matches, picnic fires), arson attacks.
Effects: people and wildlife killed, property and large areas of forest destroyed.
Preventative measures: advertising campaigns, harsher punishment for arsonists.

*River poisoning
Causes: dumping of chemical waste from factories, use of chemical fertilizers on agricultural land.
Effects: plant and animal life killed, rivers unfit for recreational use (e.g. swimming)
Preventative measures: heavy fines.

Environmental disasters could result from:
Global warming / the greenhouse effect
Causes: excess carbon dioxide in the atmosphere caused by pollution from factories, car exhaust fumes, CFCs (chlorofluorocarbons used in aerosols, refrigerators and foam packaging), deforestation.
Effects: disturbed weather patterns, rising temperatures (drought), increased sea levels (flooding).
Preventative measures: reduce number of cars, unleaded petrol, reduce fossil fuel consumption, cut down fewer trees / plant more.

The hole in the ozone layer
Causes: CFCs (see above).
Effects: skin cancer (caused by ultraviolet radiation, which the ozone layer protects against), damage to eyesight.
Preventative measures: use of pump sprays rather than aerosols, correct disposal of fridges, develop new packaging materials.

Acid rain
Causes: factory and car emissions combine with rain to form sulphuric acid and nitric acid.
Effects: rivers, lakes and soil poisoned, trees and dependent wildlife destroyed, buildings and archaeological remains damaged.
Preventative measures: cleaner fuels, stricter controls on factory emissions, lead-free petrol.

Workbook: Reading pp 68–69

Grammar and practice   Student's Book p 154

1 Wishes

A Form and use
Students can work in pairs to study the sentence. Check their answer.

ANSWER

People would wish these things if the volcano erupted.

B/C Students can work in pairs. Refer them to the Grammar reference on pages 211 and 212 to check their answers.

ANSWERS

| 1, 6, c | 2, 4, b | 3, 5, a |

2 Practice

A Use of English

ANSWERS

1 I wish I **could afford to go** away this year.
2 I **wish you would clean** the bath when you've finished!
3 Pete wishes **he had remembered to send** Sally a Valentine card.
4 'I wish I **had gone to bed earlier**,' said Justin, yawning.
5 Jodie wishes **she was / were as tall as** her sister.
6 If only I hadn't told John.

B POSSIBLE ANSWERS

1 I wish I hadn't stolen that money.
2 I wish I could answer this question. / I wish I had worked harder.
3 I wish I'd checked the petrol before we left. / I wish I'd remembered to fill up with petrol.
4 I wish I'd known there was a bull in this field. / I wish I hadn't put on this red shirt. / I wish I hadn't come into this field. / I wish I hadn't taken a short cut.

Workbook: Grammar 3 p 71

Exam techniques   Student's Book p 155

Listening: Selecting from two or three answers

1 Guidelines
Go through the guidelines with students.

2 Practice

Ask them to predict from the questions and information given what the topic might be about and some words and phrases they might hear. If students have no ideas of their own use the following ideas to try to elicit some.

Ideas

The conversation takes place between two people in a village shop. The woman is the owner of the shop and the man is a customer. The new information pleases at least one of them. The news may be about a change, which is probably quite an important change because of the word 'affected'. It might be the reason why one of the people leaves the village. Perhaps the change would affect one of them negatively. The 'work schedule' may or may not refer to the news / change. We have no real way of knowing what the change is. Students may have some ideas of the types of changes that would affect people in a village. Don't tell them if their ideas are right or wrong.

ANSWERS

1 M 2 M 3 B 4 W 5 M 6 M 7 W

Tapescript

M = Man (Graham); W = Woman (Vera)
M   And I'll take an Evening News, please, Vera. (*Pause*) Hey, have you seen this?
W   What?
M   It says here they're going to start building the new ring road next year. Plans to build a new road, which will bypass the villages of Marsden and Brantham, have finally been approved. Work will start next October.
W   I'm surprised you didn't know that, Graham.
M   No, first I've heard of it. I didn't even know it'd got to the discussion stage, never mind been accepted. Well, that's good news.
W   It might be to you, but my trade's certainly going to suffer. At least half of my customers are people who are just passing through. Once the new road's built, I'll notice a big drop in profits. And I won't be the only one. But I imagine it'll mean a change for the better for you.
M   Yes, it'll make a big difference to us. We'll be able to get a decent night's sleep for a change instead of being woken up by lorries going down the main street at 3 o'clock in the morning.
W   I thought you were moving anyway.
M   Well, we certainly thought about it. I obviously didn't want to but Sally's just been so worried about the kids with all this heavy traffic going through the village. Anyway, now we won't have to move, will we?
W   Well, if things start going downhill for me, I'll probably sell up. I've always fancied running a café somewhere on the coast anyway.
M   It'd be quite a change for you, though.
W   Oh, yes, there's no doubt about that. It seems like I've lived here all my life.

M	Yeah, you seem more like a native than me and I come from here.
W	That's because you've spent as much time away from Marsden as you have in it.
M	That's true enough. I can't understand why they're starting in the autumn though.
W	I suppose it is a bit unusual.
M	With all the snow we get round here, they'll just have started all the digging when they'll have to stop.
W	I suppose they'll have their reasons.
M	Well, it seems a bit silly to me. Still, I mustn't go on. After all, who cares when they build it, just so long as they do.
W	Mm. It'll mean a big improvement for you.
M	Yes. It always was a worry for us. What with the school being so near the main road, you always felt there was bound to be an accident sometime. I'm sorry it'll affect your business though.
W	Oh, don't worry about me. I'm just pleased for you and Sally and everyone else. I'll get by.
M	Right, well, better be off. Can't stand here talking all day. See you, Vera.
W	Bye, Graham.

Writing

Exam training: Compositions 2

Student's Book pp 156

Aim: In this section students are prepared for writing an opinion composition. The opinion composition is contrasted with the advantages and disadvantages composition in Unit 8, where a model is given (see page 116). Words which preface opinions are revised in this section.

1 Preparation

Check that students remember typical words and phrases which indicate that a writer is giving his or her opinion.

2 Think, plan, write

It will be useful if students study the Vocabulary reference on page 218 in their books before starting this section. Students can work in pairs or groups or, if vocabulary is going to be a major problem, this can be a whole class activity.

If your students are interested in ecological issues work through all three questions with them. You may find the background information on page 118 of this book useful for questions 1 and 2. If your students are not very interested in ecology or animal rights choose one question only.

Some ideas

1 What other kinds of pollution are there? What effect do they have? What measures can be taken?
2 As above
3 In what other ways are animals threatened?
• For their skins (e.g. shoes, handbags)
• For their tusks (elephants) or horns (rhinos), because ivory is very valuable and because rhino horn is considered to be an aphrodisiac in the East
• They are captured to be sold as pets. (e.g. parrots, monkeys)
• They are hunted for sport. (e.g. fox-hunting; safaris)
• They are hunted for food.
In what other ways are they treated cruelly?
• They are experimented on.
• They are hurt or killed in sports like bull-fighting or cock-fighting.
• They are made to perform tricks. (e.g. in circuses)
• They are kept in captivity. (e.g. zoos)
What other solutions are there?
• Stop experiments on animals.
• Make people aware through advertising campaigns. (e.g. *Greenpeace* protection of dolphins, whales)
• Enforce harsh punishments for the killing of endangered species.

C/D The planning and writing can be set as homework.

MODEL

Experiments are carried out on animals to test everything from new drugs for asthma sufferers to new beauty products. In my opinion, scientific research on animals, for whatever purpose, should be stopped immediately.

In the first place it is not right that animals should be used in this way. Animals feel pain just as much as humans do and the torture and killing of hundreds of thousands of monkeys, guinea pigs, rabbits and rats every year in the name of scientific research is both cruel and morally wrong.

Scientists argue that cures would not be found if they were unable to experiment with new techniques and drugs. This is probably true, but human volunteers could be used instead. No matter how like humans some animals are, they are not humans and drugs will not necessarily have the same effect on them as on us.

In conclusion, there are alternatives to using animals in scientific research. There are no good reasons why these alternatives should not be used.

Workbook: Writing p 73

Your students are now ready to take Unit test 11, which is on page 158 of this book. The key is on pages 171–172.

12Information

Sleep tight

Unit focus   The passive

Topic 1   Sleep
Reading
Grammar and practice   Passives
Exam techniques   Speaking: Parts 3 and 4

Topic 2   Festivals
Listening
Grammar and practice   Passive constructions with the infinitive
Writing   Reporting an opinion
Vocabulary   Celebrations and festivals, confusing verbs, phrasal verbs
Writing   Exam training: Reports 2

Introduction   Student's Book p 157

Aim: Several short prediction, interpretation and information-exchange activities introduce students to the topic of the first part of the unit – sleep.

Note: The topic heading is taken from an English expression, 'Night, night, sleep tight!', which means 'Goodnight. Sleep well.' It is typically said to young children at bedtime.

Students discuss the questions in pairs or as a whole class.

A The woman in the photo is participating in a scientific research programme into human sleep patterns. Her eye-movements and the electrical activity of her brain are being measured through the electrodes attached to her scalp and face. The tube running from a vein in her arm allows blood samples to be taken to assess the variation in hormone levels during sleep.

ANSWER ———————————————————
We dream when we are in *deeper sleep*.

B In Britain most children under seven go to bed before eight o'clock and most children up to the age of three-and-a-half also have an afternoon nap.

C Students respond personally. You may like to find out the class average.

Possible effects of lack of sleep: It makes you bad-tempered, irritable, forgetful, indecisive, clumsy, liable to make mistakes, etc.

Reading   Student's Book pp 158–159

1 Think ahead

Elicit words from the whole class and write them on the board. Some possible prompts are: *a word of three letters which means a short sleep* (nap); *a word borrowed from Spanish which means a short sleep in the afternoon* (siesta); *to start sleeping* (to fall asleep, or more informal, to drop off); *to have a short, light sleep* (to snooze – Unit 5, page 64).

Note: It is not necessary to pre-teach this vocabulary, as it is covered later in the vocabulary section.

Extra activity
In groups, or as a whole class, students brainstorm and write down any words or ideas related to the word sleep, e.g. *bed, dreams*. If working in groups, students could be awarded one point either for each answer accepted or for each answer that the other groups haven't got. This activity could be used to recycle sleep vocabulary at a later date.

2 Reading

Students read the text for gist and guess the source.

ANSWER ———————————————————
The text comes from a magazine. It is not factual enough and the language is too informal to be any of the other options.
Students can be asked to find examples of informal language e.g. *nod off, the telly* and to give their more formal equivalents.

3 Comprehension

Students work on their own, then compare answers. Make sure they are able to justify their choices.

A ANSWERS ———————————————————
1 H *it* links with *it* (repeated twice) in the previous sentence and refers to sleeping.
2 E *injured, wounds healing* link with *damage, illnesses* and *curing* in the same paragraph.
3 A *These* refers to *chemicals* in the previous sentence.
4 G *They* refers to *scientists* in the previous sentence. *Slows down* links with *more slowly* in the next sentence.
5 B *dream* links with *dreams* in the previous sentence. *One*, in the next sentence, refers to one of the theories mentioned in B.
6 C *it* refers to *sleep* in the previous sentence. The strange effects of going without sleep are outlined in the following sentences.

7 F *They* refers to *airline pilots* in the previous sentence. *Landing* a plane is one of the jobs an airline pilot has to do.

B Paragraphs

This exercise focuses on the role of topic sentences in text. The topic sentence (usually the first or second sentence in the paragraph) tells us what the paragraph is going to be about. The remainder of the paragraph contains further details and examples.

SUGGESTED ANSWERS

Paragraph 3: What controls sleep? / What makes us sleep?

Paragraph 4: What have scientists discovered about sleep? / What goes on in people's heads while they sleep?

Paragraph 5: Why do we dream?

Paragraph 6: What can happen if we don't get enough sleep?

Paragraph 7: How are people's and animals' sleeping habits different? / How could we improve our sleeping habits?

4 Points of view

Students discuss the questions in pairs. Ask for selected feedback.

5 Vocabulary

ANSWERS

1 B 2 B 3 A 4 C 5 C

6 Reading between the lines

Ideas

1 Coffee, tea, cola as they all contain caffeine, which helps keep you awake.

2 Young people might feel embarrassed as it's behaviour which is typical of the old.

7 Over to you

Students will need a few minutes thinking time before they begin this activity. They may also need to ask for or look up vocabulary. Most students should be able to take part, but those who insist that they never dream could be made responsible for giving some general feedback on their group's dreams to the class.

Extra activity

Writing: Write down the description of your dream, including as many details as you can.

See suggestions for using model texts on page 15 of this book.

MODEL

I don't remember most of my dreams but there are two that I remember very clearly. I had one of them a long time ago when I was seven years old and in hospital for an operation to have my tonsils out. I remember that I was very worried because it was my first time in hospital.

I had the dream when I was under the general anaesthetic. It was in colour and like a cartoon. It could only have lasted a few seconds. This is what happened. A brown cartoon dog walked on from the right of the 'screen', was sick and then walked off again. I suppose that was what had happened to me in hospital but I didn't dare ask.

I had the second more recently. It was more like a nightmare than a dream. Again, it was a cartoon and very short. A baby was suspended in a bright blue sky. It got bigger and bigger, as if it was a balloon which someone was blowing up. Finally, it burst with a bang and I woke up with a jolt.

Workbook: Reading pp 74–75

Grammar and practice

Student's Book pp 160–161

1 Passives

A Form and use

Students work in pairs.

ANSWERS

1 a *is*: active (present simple)
can be repaired: passive (present modal verb)
isn't being used up: passive (present continuous)
doing: active (gerund)

b *is controlled*: passive (present simple)

c *can control*: active (present modal verb)

2 The passive is formed with a form of the verb *be* + the past participle.

3 b *Certain chemicals control sleep*.
If we use the passive form beginning with the word *sleep*, we maintain the topic of sleep in the text. If we use the active form, as here, we introduce a new topic and lose the cohesive link with the preceding paragraph.

c *The effects of these chemicals can be controlled to some extent*. By using the active form, we focus on the performer of the action, i.e. we. If we use the passive form, as here, the focus is on the recipient of the action, i.e. *the effects of these chemicals*. This is the main difference between the active and the passive.
The agent in sentence (b), by certain chemicals, is included because it is important for us to know what controls sleep. No agents are mentioned in sentence (a) because the agents 'by us' or 'by our bodies' are obvious.

B Refer students to the Grammar reference on page 212 of their books.

2 The agent

ANSWERS

1 c/d	4 b/c
2 c (by everyone here)	5 a
3 a/b	6 c (by the judge)

3 Practice

A Advertising
Students match the correct photos with the five sentences, saying which words helped them to choose.

ANSWERS

1 c Abbey Hotel – *welcome, guests*
2 e washing machine – *electrical, install, appliance, electrician*
3 Carlsberg lager is extra.
4 d coffee – *pack, airtight container*
5 a Opal Fruits – *wrapper*
6 b shoes – *shoes*

Now students complete the sentences, using passive forms of the verbs in the box.

ANSWERS

1 was bought	4 be stored
2 are fitted	5 is required, be carried out
3 is made	

B Students should be asked to explain why they have or haven't included an agent in each case.

ANSWERS

1 Smith was arrested at Newtown Hospital last night. He was being taken to the operating theatre when the police arrived. He had been accidentally shot in the knee * during the get-away by one of his accomplices. Smith is being interrogated at Sunhill Police Station. **He will be charged with armed robbery. He has been charged twice for similar offences in the last five years.
* The agent can also come here.
** The text sounds more natural if the relative pronoun *where* is used to link the two sentences.

Note: The only agent which needs to be included is the one which tells us who shot Smith. The other agents are obvious (the police are the only people who can arrest, interrogate and charge in these circumstances) or unimportant (the doctors).

2 Three more coal mines will be closed (by the government)* over the next two years. A total of six have already been closed since they / the government** came into office. Miners are being asked to consider voluntary redundancy.
* The agent is probably not necessary since the government is usually the only body with the authority to close a coal mine.
** Depending on whether the government was mentioned in the previous sentence.

In the last sentence the agent (the government) is obvious, so it would not be included.

C Services
1 **Background information**
British hotel guests usually expect to be able to make tea and coffee in their rooms, and facilities and ingredients are therefore provided. (It is less common for British hotel rooms to have a mini-bar.)
An *English breakfast* is cereal or fruit juice followed by a hot meal, usually consisting of fried bacon, eggs, sausages and tomatoes, and toast and marmalade.
en suite facilities are a private bathroom adjoining the bedroom.

ANSWERS

1 is guaranteed	4 are equipped	7 is served
2 is situated	5 are reserved	8 be booked
3 are furnished	6 is included	9 is charged

2 **MODEL**
Guests at the Miramar are guaranteed an enjoyable stay. This modern three-star hotel is situated only five minutes' walk from the sandy beach, and also has its own swimming pool and tennis courts. All 150 bedrooms are comfortably furnished and equipped with colour televisions; the en-suite facilities include showers and hairdryers. Our popular breakfast buffet, which is included in the price, is served in the Coffee Shop from 7.30 to 10.30 a.m. Lunch and dinner are also available in the Cocteau Restaurant, and all our food is prepared with fresh local ingredients wherever possible. There are two luxurious bars, and 24-hour room service is provided. During the high season, we offer a full programme of evening entertainment.

4 Use of English

Students work on their own, then check their answers in pairs or small groups. Remind students to read through the whole text first to get a general idea of what it is about, and to look for clues which will help them fill the gaps. (Or refer them to the guidelines for grammar cloze completion on page 40 of their books.)

When checking the answers, you may wish to point out or elicit some of the clues, particularly where students have left blanks.

ANSWERS

1 in	6 nor	11 because / since / as
2 have	7 been	12 but
3 the	8 in / into	13 more
4 was	9 by	14 it
5 and	10 of	15 be

Extra activity
Speaking: questions for discussion
1 Are you superstitious?
2 What popular superstitions are there in your country?
3 Is Friday the 13th a superstitious date in your country? Are any other dates or numbers superstitious?

Workbook: Grammar 1, 2, 3, 4 pp 76–77

Exam techniques Student's Book pp 162–163

Speaking: Paper 5 Part 3 and Part 4

1 Guidelines for Part 3

Read through the guidelines with the students. It is worthwhile looking at them again once students have heard the first recording.

2 Model

A Students in pairs carry out the first speaking task. Make sure that they understand what they have to do before they begin. Don't interrupt them as they do the task, unless they have misunderstood the instructions. Don't give any help with vocabulary, as in the exam they will have to manage with the language that they have. Allow between three and four minutes for the discussion and then get selected feedback.

B As students listen to the recording of the candidates' discussion they should make a note of the candidates' ideas. Check students' answers. It is not important whether their answers are the same as the candidates' or different. There are no right or wrong answers. What is important is that students discuss their ideas and reach a decision. The recording can be played a second time and students asked to note down the language used by the candidates when giving an opinion, giving a reason and interacting with each other generally.

Giving an opinion: *I suppose they should; I don't think (it would be a good idea to . . .)*
Giving a reason: *because; so*
General interaction: *What do you think?*
Asking for information: *How many bedrooms are there? What about Mrs Black?* (The candidate who asks has this information but asks the question as a way of including the other candidate).
Asking the other person what their opinion is: *I don't think . . . Do you?; Shall we . . .?; What about . . .?*
Showing agreement or disagreement: *Yes; No; Okay; Mm*

Tapescript

I = Interviewer; C = Chantal; M = Monique	
I	I'd like you both to look at this plan of the upstairs and downstairs of a house. Can you also read the information which is given alongside about the White family, who are going to move into the house. (*Pause*) What I'd like you to do is to talk together and decide which you think would be the best bedroom for each member of the family. Alright?
C	Yes.
M	Yes.
C	Right. There are one, two, three, four, five people.

	How many bedrooms are there?
M	Four. But Mr and Mrs White are married so they would probably share a bedroom.
C	Yes. I suppose they should have the biggest bedroom because there are two of them. What do you think?
M	Yes. It's probably their house too.
C	So shall we say bedroom 1 for Mr and Mrs White?
M	Yes.
C	Now what about Mrs Black?
M	It says that she's old and she can't walk very well so I don't think it would be a good idea to put her upstairs. Do you?
C	No. Bedroom 4 would be a good one for her. And there's a toilet downstairs too.
M	Yes – and it looks onto the garden so it would probably be a bit quieter. It says she's a light sleeper.
C	Okay, bedroom 4 for Mrs Black.
M	What about James and Angela? It says she's quiet and studious so she probably needs a quiet room to work in.
C	Bedroom 3's quieter than 2. 2 looks onto the road and it's a main road so there's probably quite a lot of traffic. It would probably be quite noisy.
M	Mm. So we'd suggest 2 for Angela and 3 for James?
C	The only problem is if he plays loud music it would disturb his sister.
M	He can wear headphones! (*Pause*)
I	Have you finished?
B	Yes.
I	That's fine. Thank you.

3 Practice

Students work in pairs. They must first decide which two people they are going to choose and then discuss how they think these people would decorate and furnish their bedrooms. Tell students that there are no right or wrong answers and that they can either agree or disagree with each other's ideas. Remind them that they should include each other in the discussion as much as possible. Allow about four minutes for this and then hear a selection of ideas.

4 Guidelines for Part 4

Follow the same procedure as for Part 3.

5 Model

A Students discuss their ideas in pairs. Elicit a selection.

B Follow the same procedure as for 2B.

Tapescript

I = Interviewer; C = Chantal; M = Monique	
I	Now, I'm going to ask you one or two questions and I'd like you to answer as fully as you can. We'll start with you Chantal. How important do you think it is

for young people to have their own bedroom?

C I think it's very important. Your bedroom isn't only where you sleep. It's where you study too. You need somewhere quiet to study and if there is someone else there, maybe they want to do something else and it's difficult.

M Yes, I agree. I have to share my bedroom with my younger sister – she's only 12 – and it's difficult.

C But also you need somewhere private. Sometimes you want to be alone. Sometimes you need to be alone. You need your own room.

I Monique, You said it was difficult to share with your sister. Can you explain why?

M Yes. She has to go to bed earlier then me, at 9 o'clock, so I can't make a noise after that because she's asleep. So I have to do my homework in the kitchen and it's not so good.

I Why not?

M Because it's next to the living room and I can hear the television and I can't concentrate. And if I ask my father to turn it down, he gets angry . . .

6 Practice

This is an opportunity for further pair oral practice. Allow students three or four minutes to discuss their ideas and then hear a selection.

Remember, remember

Introduction   Student's Book p 164

Aim: To introduce the second topic of the unit – festivals. The topic heading comes from an old English rhyme about Bonfire Night:

Remember, remember, the fifth of November
Gunpowder, treason and plot;
There seems no reason
Why gunpowder treason
Should ever be forgot.

Students discuss the questions in pairs and give feedback to the class. If possible, pairs should be from different countries or, if that is not possible, from different regions. After describing the photos, students may be given the following information on the festivals illustrated. Don't give them any information on Bonfire Night until Think ahead.

Listening   Student's Book pp 164–165

1 Think ahead

Elicit any information students know about Bonfire Night.

Background information
Bonfire Night is celebrated in Britain on the evening of November 5th. Many people light bonfires (large fires built outdoors either to burn rubbish or as part of celebrations) and let off fireworks. This is to celebrate the failure of the Gunpowder Plot to blow up the parliament in 1605. The plot was to kill the Protestant King James 1, to put his young son on the throne and turn England back into a Catholic country. The effigy of Guy Fawkes, who was one of the conspirators, is put on top of the bonfire and burnt. In actual fact, Guy Fawkes was hanged.

2 Comprehension

A Ask students to read the information sheet carefully so that they know what information they will be listening out for. Play the recording twice allowing time between listenings and at the end for students to write their answers.

> **ANSWERS** _____
> **Venue**
> 1 The Green Man
> 2 *St Mary's Hospital*
> 3 *The Castle Park*
> **Date**
> 1 4 Nov
> 2 5 Nov
> 3 *5 Nov*
> **Time of firework display**
> 1 *9 p.m.*
> 2 *7.30 p.m.*
> 3 6 p.m. and 9.30 p.m.

Entrance fee

	Adult	Child
1	*free*	free
2	*£3.50*	£1.00
	and includes a baked potato and *a soft drink*	
3	*£3.75*	£1.25
		and includes *a hot dog or hamburger*

Tapescript

> ### Radio broadcast
>
> Well, and here we are again and have those pencils and paper ready to jot down the details of Bonfire Night celebrations in your area.
>
> And we start off with one at the Green Man pub in Stanway and that's on tonight. It starts at nine p.m. and there's no charge to its customers so get along there tonight and start the celebrations early.
>
> And tomorrow night we have those traditional Fifth of November celebrations at St Mary's Hospital and the Castle Park. The St Mary's do starts at seven-thirty and the gates open half an hour earlier at seven o'clock. Tickets are three fifty for adults and a pound for children and pensioners and that includes a soft drink of your choice and a baked potato. Can't be bad! And finally we have the Charity Firework Display in the Castle Park. This proved so popular last year that they've decided to have two displays this year. This first one will be at six o'clock for the kiddies and there'll be another one later on for those who just can't get along to the first one. And that'll be at nine thirty. Tickets can be bought in advance and the price is three seventy-five for adults and one twenty-five for children and that includes a hot dog or hamburger. And remember all proceeds go to charity so you can really enjoy yourself and help someone in need at the same time.
>
> Now over to Bob Wilson to bring you up to date on the latest traffic news.

B Allow the students two minutes to read the questions. They should spend this time checking that they understand what they have to do and predicting the type of language or vocabulary they might expect to hear. Elicit a few examples before you play the recording. For example, for question 1:

- You will hear more than one festival mentioned.
- The information may be more general, e.g. how people lived, dressed, etc.
- One event only will be mentioned and possibly a date.

Remind students that they should be able to justify their choice of answer.

ANSWERS

1 C The title of the book is *Guy Fawkes and the Gunpowder Plot*.
2 B *I don't want you wandering off; you'll get left behind; if we do get separated; head for the white tent, give them your* name and I'll come and get you.
3 A *Anyway, do you want me to write it up? ...it's not really worth a long article . . .*
4 C *. . . what gets me is the wrappers and stuff that get blown into the garden; clear up the mess.*
5 A *I'll leave you in charge of that.* (sandwiches; fish and chips)

Tapescript

> **1 W = Woman   P = Professor Ellett**
> **W** . . . Professor Ellett is considered to be one of the leading authorities on 17th century British history. Professor, tomorrow, November 5th, children all over the country will be putting their guys on top of their bonfires and yet in your book *Guy Fawkes and the Gunpowder Plot*, you say that it was not Guy Fawkes who masterminded the plot to blow up the parliament in 1605. So, why do we give him so much importance?
> **P** Well, although Guy Fawkes is believed by the man in the street to have been the brains behind the plot, historians know that the plot was in fact hatched by Thomas Winter and Robert Catesby.
>
> **2 W = Woman**
> **W** Now there are going to be a lot of people there so I want you to stick together. Charlotte, you can hold Jamie's hand. Alex, I don't want you wandering off. If you meet any of your friends, for goodness sake don't start talking to them, you'll only get left behind. But, look, if we do get separated then just head for that big white tent over there. Do you see it? There's an ambulance outside. Yes? Give them your name and they'll put it out over the Tannoy and I'll come and get you. Okay? Is that clear?
>
> **3 M = Man** (Reporter)
> **M** There's not really all that much to report. More near misses then actual accidents. Someone threw petrol on the bonfire because it wouldn't light but he was unhurt. They had to send for the fire brigade because the wind got up a bit and some sparks set fire to the grass, but they managed to put that out before the fire engines arrived. Apart from that, not a lot. One or two minor injuries, but nothing serious. A good turnout too. The organizers say they've made over a thousand pounds. Anyway, do you want me to write it up or will you do it? It's not really worth a long article unless you can think of a good angle. (*Pause*) Alright, I'll see to it when I get back then.
>
> **4 W = Woman; F = Friend**
> **W** I don't know why they can't have it somewhere else? This is the third year in a row that they've had it there. Honestly, you'd think they'd have some consideration.
> **F** Yes, it must be a bit noisy.

W Oh, it's not really the noise that I mind. The smoke's more of a nuisance, well it can be, though as long as you keep your windows shut it's not really a problem. No, what really gets me is all the wrappers and stuff that get blown into the garden because they never send anyone round afterwards to clear up the mess. It really makes me cross.

5 M = Man

M I don't think there's much point in changing the venue, do you? We didn't have too many complaints last year and it's a nice clear area, lots of space. But I think we need to do something about the food. Some people said there wasn't much choice. It might be nice to have a fish and chip van there as well as the burger vans. What do you think? Maybe some people would be interested in doing sandwiches or something vegetarian as well. Anyway I'll leave you in charge of that. Frank Forsyth says his brother-in-law might be able to get a discount on the fireworks. If that's the case we'll buy direct from him.

Extra activity
Use of English: grammar cloze

Bonfire Night is celebrated all (1)_____ Britain on November 5th. The festival dates from 1605 (2)_____ a man called Guy Fawkes tried to blow (3)_____ the Houses of Parliament. He was caught and hanged, along (4)_____ the other conspirators.
Preparations for Bonfire Night usually start weeks (5)_____ the event itself. Children go from house (6)_____ house collecting old furniture, newspapers and anything else (7)_____ will burn for their bonfires. They make (8)_____ 'guy', a figure that represents Guy Fawkes, from an old sack and wheel (9)_____ round the streets asking (10)_____ money which they use to buy fireworks.
   On the day itself, as (11)_____ as it is dark, the guy is put on top (12)_____ the bonfire, which is then lit. Fireworks (13)_____ set off (14)_____ everyone enjoys the display as they stand round (15)_____ bonfire keeping warm, eating baked potatoes and hot dogs.

ANSWERS _____

1 over	6 to	11 soon
2 when	7 which / that	12 of
3 up	8 a / their	13 are
4 with	9 it	14 and
5 before	10 for	15 the

3 Over to you

1 If students come from different countries, the information exchange can be done in pairs or groups. Otherwise the activity is best done with the whole class. The type of special day that may be celebrated is a Saint's Day, Valentine's Day, Father's Day, National No-Smoking Day.

2 This could be a particular event. It could be something serious like a day to commemorate someone famous who has died. Or it could be something silly like National Left-handers Day, when only left-handed people have a holiday.

Grammar and practice Student's Book p 165

More passives

Aim: To introduce the use of the passive + infinitive forms of verbs like *think, believe* when (a) we do not want to say where our information came from or (b) we do not know if our information is true.

A Students work in pairs or as a whole class to study the example sentences.

ANSWERS _____

The speaker presents the information as being factual in sentences 1a and 2a.
The passive constructions *is considered / is believed* + infinitive distance the speaker from the information. We do not know if the speaker agrees with the information, which is presented as a generally accepted opinion.
Consider in 1b could be replaced by *think*.
Believe in 2b could be replaced by *think* or *report*.

B Refer students to the Grammar reference on page 213 of their books.

C Practice
Go through the instructions and example carefully with the students. Before they start the exercise, make sure they are also able to form an example with a perfect infinitive. If necessary, give some extra practice. Ask students to convert these statements of fact:

Several passengers survived the crash.
Several passengers are thought to have survived the crash.
One of them is a baby.
One of them is believed to be a baby.
The survivors were sitting at the rear of the plane.
The survivors are thought to have been sitting at the rear of the plane.

SUGGESTED ANSWERS _____

1 Several of the passengers are believed to be British. It is thought to have run into problems as it was coming in to land.
2 The coins are thought to be Roman. They are believed to date from the first century BC.
3 One of the men is reported to have a scar on his left cheek. The other is said to speak with a northern accent.

Writing Student's Book p 166

Reporting an opinion

Aim: This section prepares students for the Writing section Exam training: Reports 2 on pages 169–170. It contrasts the giving of personal opinions with the reporting of other people's opinions, which students may be required to do in a report.

All the activities can be done in pairs, groups or with the whole class except for the actual interview in 3 Practice.

1 Extracts

Ask students to justify their ideas when checking their answers.

SUGGESTED ANSWERS

1 In a report possibly made for *Burger Express* or the City Hall on whether people think *Burger Express* have done enough to satisfy complaints made about litter.
2 In a food and drink guide / magazine. It is recommending a white wine.
3 In a report or article on people's eating habits.
4 In a restaurant guide. It describes / recommends a restaurant.
5 In an article on the advantages and disadvantages of the microwave.
6 In an article on diets / slimming products.

2 Analysis

A The writers give their own opinion in extracts 2 and 4. The writers report other people's opinions in extracts 1, 3, 5 and 6.

B The verbs which are used to introduce other people's opinions are: *said; felt; thought; consider; argue; believe*. Other verbs are: agree; disagree; claim.

C The words and phrases which indicate the writer's attitude to the opinions they are reporting are: *Surprisingly. It is interesting that . . .*. Some other similar words and phrases that students might be expected to know at this level are: strangely; as might be expected; not surprisingly.

D The opinion words and phrases in extracts 2 and 4 are:
a light, crisp aroma; excellent value for money (2)
simple but pleasing; could be better; rather over-priced (4)

The writers do not use opinion words like *I think* to introduce the opinions because they are trying to present the opinions as being widely held and from different sources.

3 Practice

Students prepare their questionnaires in pairs or groups. Check that the questions are correctly formed before students interview others. With very large classes it may not be possible or advisable for students to interview everyone. The results of the survey could be written up at home as a short report.

Vocabulary Student's Book pp 167–168

1 Celebrations

A Title 2 is the most suitable.

B Use of English

ANSWERS

1 D	6 A	11 D
2 B	7 C	12 B
3 A	8 B	13 C
4 D	9 D	14 D
5 C	10 A	15 A

2 Confusing verbs

Quickly revise the meanings of *raise / rise* and *lay / lie*. Then check that students know the past tense and present and past participles of the verbs.

Infinitive	Past	Past participle	Present participle
lie	lay	lain	lying (intransitive)
lie	lied	lied	lying
lay	laid	laid	laying (transitive)
rise	rose	risen	rising (intransitive)
raise	raised	raised	raising (transitive)

ANSWERS

1 raise (meaning 2e)	4 have risen (2c)
2 lying (1a)	5 lying (1c)
3 laying (1f)	6 was raised (2h)

Note: The meanings in brackets refer to those given in the extra activity below.

Extra activity
The following sentences could be made into a gap-fill exercise for extra practice, before students do the exercise in their book, or they could be given the sentences and the meanings (mixed up) and asked to match them.

1 a She *lay* on the sofa with her eyes closed. (be in a horizontal position)
   b United are *lying* second in the League. (be in a position in a competition)
   c He *lied* to me when he told me he was single. (not tell the truth)
   d He *laid* his cards face down on the table. (carefully put something in a particular position)
   e All birds *lay* eggs. (produce)
   f Can you *lay* the table, please? (put plates, knives, forks, etc on the table for a meal)
2 a They *rose* at dawn. (get up (formal))
   b The sun *rises* in the east and sets in the west. (appear above the horizon)

c Unemployment is *rising* steadily. (increase)
d The smoke from the bonfire *rose* into the air. (move or travel upwards)
e He *raised* the glass to his lips and drank. (lift)
f The government are going to *raise* taxes again. (increase)
g The concert *raised* £2,000 for the homeless. (get / collect money)
h He *raised* the question of his promotion with his boss. (bring up a subject for discussion)

3 Phrasal verbs with *up*

Before students do the matching exercise, point out that the verbs in the example sentence and in column A are separable.

Elicit an alternative word order for the example: *I was so angry that I tore up the letter into small pieces.*

Then ask students to substitute a pronoun for the noun *letter*: *I was so furious that I tore it up*, to remind them that there is no choice of word order with a pronoun object – it must come between a separable phrasal verb and its particle.

ANSWERS

1 desk / mess	4 dinner	6 mess
3 milk	5 car	7 present

Possible sentences:
These could be used as a gap-fill exercise to recycle vocabulary at a later date.
1 I'll have to *tidy* up my desk. I can't find anything.
3 *Drink* up your milk! It's good for you.
4 You can't leave the table until you *'ve eaten* up all your dinner.
5 He *filled* the car up with unleaded petrol.
6 It took them the whole morning to *clean* up the mess after the party.
7 She *wrapped* the present up in tissue paper and tied it with a blue ribbon.

4 Phrasal verbs with *get*

A ANSWERS

. . . so our body can *get on* with curing us = start or continue doing an activity
We can't *get by* without sleep = survive, manage

B ANSWERS

1 to get away	5 get (me) down
2 was getting on	6 got by
3 didn't get on	7 get over
4 to get away	8 got out

> Workbook: Vocabulary 1, 2, 3 pp 77–78

Writing   Student's Book pp 169–170

Exam training: Reports 2

Aim: This writing section revises the main features of reports, introduced in Unit 6 (see Student's Book page 82). It focuses on the formal language of reports and reporting opinions objectively.

Most of the activities can be done in pairs, groups or with the whole class. Check answers and ideas after each section.

1 Model

ANSWERS

Report 2 would get a better mark. It answers the question. It sounds factual and objective. It has a suitable top heading and each paragraph has a suitable sub-heading. The personal opinion comes at the end.

Report 1 doesn't really answer the question, as it doesn't consider two sites. The layout is not appropriate to a report and there are no sub-headings; the language is often too informal and subjective and the information, although mainly relevant, is not very well organized.

2 Analysis

A ANSWERS

1 assess the suitability of the sites
2 It is assumed that . . .
3 attend the event
4 easily accessible
5 provide parking facilities
6 minimizes the risk of fire
7 The Community Hall will allow the use of their toilets
8 Food and drink stalls could be set up here
9 The school will allow free use of their toilets
10 It is recommended . . .

B Some examples:
I think the best site The best site would seem / appear to be
In my opinion, it has It is felt that it has
lots of many
big large
won't be will not be
so there won't be any parking problems so parking will not be a problem
You could have a bonfire It would be possible to have a bonfire
you built it it was built
the landlord of Green's has said that we can use their toilets We will be allowed to use the toilets in Green's
we could put a big tent up a large tent could be put up
and (we could) serve the food and drink there and the food and drink could be served there

3 Think, plan, write

Brainstorm ideas in pairs, small groups or with the whole class. The previous listening extracts should give students some ideas. Students can write up the report for homework.

Ideas

Complaints about: noise; rubbish; cars parked outside houses blocking exits.

Causes: loud music and cars and motorbikes; food wrappers left behind after the concert; insufficient parking space provided.

Effects: dogs barked, people got angry and phoned the police to complain; mess (litter blown into gardens); people couldn't use their own cars (couldn't get them out of garages).

Minimizing problems in future: have the event on a Saturday (most people don't work on Sunday); finish the event by 11p.m.; provide better car parking facilities; provide more litter bins and clear up litter immediately or next day.

MODEL

To: Mr Wilson
From: Joanna Morgan

Introduction

The aim of this report is to summarize the results of a survey into the reactions of people living in the area where the outdoor music festival was held, and to make suggestions for improvement. The survey was carried out on 100 families living in Stirling Road.

People's reactions

Surprisingly, only 15% of the people interviewed had complaints to make. The most common complaint was about the level of noise. Some people felt that playing loud music after 11p.m. on a weekday was quite unacceptable. There were also several complaints about litter. Three people complained about cars parked on pavements and in front of exits.

Conclusion

It is recommended that the residents of Stirling Road are invited to any future events and that these finish before 11p.m. People attending the concert should be reminded to take their litter home with them and to park in the school car park or use public transport.

> Workbook: Writing p 79

Your students are now ready to take Unit test 12, which is on page 159 of this book. The key is on page 172.

After they have taken the Unit test, students can do Revision 3, on pages 80–81 of the Workbook. Encourage them to look up anything they have difficulties with. This will help to consolidate their learning, and will prepare them for Progress test 3. Revision 3 could be set for homework.

Your students are now ready to take Progress test 3, which can be found on pages 166–167 of this book. The key is on page 173.

13 Skills and abilities

Memory

Unit focus   Expressing abilities

Topic 1   Memory
Reading
Grammar and practice   *Can, be able to, manage, succeed*
Writing   Exam training: Set book

Topic 2   The cinema
Listening
Grammar and practice   Question tags
Vocabulary   The mind and the senses, money, *remind / remember*, phrasal verbs
Writing   Exam training: Applications 2

Introduction   Student's Book p 171

Aim: To introduce the topic of the first part of the unit – memory.
Students do A on their own. B can be done with the whole class or students can discuss in pairs or small groups with selected feedback.

A ANSWERS

From left to right: Princess Diana, Jack Nicholson, Madonna.

C Points for discussion
Some ideas
1 Tie a knot in a handkerchief; draw a ring round a calendar date; write a note in a diary; ask someone to remind you; change over a watch to the other wrist / a ring to another finger; write a note in pen on the hand.
   Note: The discussion can be extended to how students memorize people's names (e.g. use the person's name immediately; repeat the name over and over to yourself) and how they memorize information for exams (e.g. write down the information and repeat it to yourself; ask someone to test you).
2 Forgetting a birthday or anniversary; forgetting that you've left something cooking; forgetting to post a letter.

Reading   Student's Book pp 172–173

1 Think ahead

Students answer the pre-reading questions on their own and then discuss their answers in pairs. Don't confirm whether their answers are right or wrong until after they have completed 2 Reading.

2 Reading

Check students' answers to 1 Think ahead. Ask them to justify their answers.

ANSWERS

1 False *Memory, it seems, is almost limitless.*
2 True *. . . you are unusual if you can remember much from before the age of three.*
3 True *Our capacity for memory is determined by our genes.*
4 True *. . . events associated with pain and anxiety are repressed and forgotten more readily than pleasant incidents.*
5 True (According to some theorists) *Some theorists say that once something is learnt it is never forgotten.*

3 Comprehension

Students work on their own then compare answers in pairs. Ask them to note down or underline any words or phrases in the text which helped them to decide their answers. Remind them that there is one extra heading.

ANSWERS

1 G The whole paragraph, excluding the first line
2 E *Memory is **defined** as the ability to store and receive information.*
3 H *. . . people have no memory before they can speak; memory may actually begin before birth.*
4 B *We recall . . . more vividly because chemicals like adrenalin boost memory.*
5 F *The reason we cannot remember something is a problem of access. There are two traditional theories of forgetting.*
6 A The whole paragraph
7 D *. . . the probability of remembering something depends on how often it has been called to mind and reinforced.*

4 Points of view

Short pair, group or whole class discussion.

Suggested ideas
Advantages:
It would eliminate embarrassment / annoyance caused by forgetting names, birthdays, anniversaries. It would make swotting for exams easier and would probably result in better exam results.
Disadvantages:
It might harm personal relationships, e.g. you wouldn't be able to forget any negative things people said or did.

5 Vocabulary

ANSWERS
a amazing; incredible
b infinite; without limit
c in any case
d not equal to others
e remember
f clearly
g easily
h getting at information
i becomes fainter
j keeping hold of something

6 Over to you

Pair, group or whole class discussion. Students may remember their first day at school; their first holiday or something unpleasant like falling off a bike or having a tooth out. Encourage students to describe how they felt at the time.

7 I remember . . .

This short writing activity could be set for homework.

Workbook: Reading pp 82–83

Grammar and practice Student's Book pp 174–175

Aim: To revise the forms and uses of verbs used to talk about ability: *can, be able to, manage, succeed.*

1 *Can, be able to*

A Ask students to substitute *can* and *be able to* in sentences 1 and 2 to show how they are interchangeable in these examples.

ANSWERS
1 We can learn complex skills like driving a car.
2 The reason we are not able to remember something is a problem of access.

Students should then spend one minute in pairs discussing the inductive grammar question for 3 and 4. Check their ideas.

ANSWERS
3 Because there is no present perfect form of *can.*
4 Because there is no infinitive form of *can.*

B Practice

ANSWERS
1 He can
2 I could . . .
3 . . . they couldn't . . .
4 There is no future form of *can*
5 . . . I couldn't have spent . . .
Note: As a general rule, where *can* is possible, it is the more usual alternative.

C/D Allow students no more than two minutes to discuss the inductive grammar question in pairs. Ask them for their ideas, then refer them to the Grammar reference on page 213 to check their own answers.

ANSWERS
1 When we are talking about a general ability in the past, both forms are possible.
2 When we are talking about an unsuccessful event in the past, both forms are possible.
3 When we are talking about a successful event in the past, only the *be able to* form is possible. *He could swim across the Channel* means he has the ability to do it (now) if he wants, or that he had the ability in the past, but not that he actually did it. *He was able to swim across the Channel* means he swam across the Channel.

2 Other ability structures

Allow students a maximum of two minutes to think of a reason, then check their ideas.

ANSWER
Because *manage* and *succeed* can only be used to talk about a specific attempt to do something. Sentence 1 talks about a general ability.
Draw students' attention to the form of the verbs after *manage* (to do) and *succeed* (in doing) before they do the practice exercise.

3 Practice

A POSSIBLE ANSWERS
2 didn't succeed in finding
3 wasn't able to finish
4 succeeded in passing
5 managed to break in
6 was / wasn't able to swim
7 managed to get
8 wasn't able to (get to) sleep

9 were able to identify
10 succeeded in opening

Sentences 2, 3, 6 and 8 can all be rewritten with *could* or *couldn't*:
2 couldn't find
3 couldn't finish
6 could / couldn't swim
8 couldn't (get to) sleep

B POSSIBLE ANSWERS
1 managed to persuade / succeeded in persuading
2 was good at
3 learnt how to
4 managed to win / succeeded in winning

C Quiz
Students do the quiz in small groups. Give a demonstration first, eliciting other possible question forms, e.g. Do you enjoy doing it? Can you do it anywhere? Can you only do it in a particular place? Could you do it with your hands tied? Could you teach me how to do it?

4 Use of English
ANSWERS

1	is	6	neither	11	although
2	for	7	not	12	and
3	which	8	able	13	by
4	in	9	his	14	has
5	when	10	than	15	more

Workbook: Grammar 1, 2 p 84

Writing   Student's Book pp 176–177

Exam training: Set book

Aim: The aim of this section is to introduce students to the types of writing task they may be required to do for Question 5 of Paper 2 (Part 2), and to revise the function of paragraphs.
Note: The list of set books for FCE is changed each year.

Students work on their own (then compare answers), or in pairs or small groups for 1–4, and in small groups of three or four students for 5A.

1 Introduction
Point out to students that although there is a choice of two tasks, one may be more suitable to the particular set book they have studied. See also 5 Think, plan, write in the next column.

2 Sample questions
ANSWERS

a	1, 2, 3	c 6, 7
b	4, 5, 6, 7	d 3, 5, 6

3 Model
Question 4 is being answered.

4 Analysis
SUGGESTED ANSWERS
1 The purpose of the first paragraph is to make clear which question the writer is answering; to say how the writer feels about the character; to say which story the character appears in, and to name the character.
2 The purpose of the first sentence in paragraph 2 is to give the reason why the writer feels as he or she does about the character.
3 Its function is to give selected examples of the character's kind-heartedness. The writer divides this information into two paragraphs because otherwise the paragraph would be too long, and because the writer gives two different examples.
4 The purpose of the last paragraph is to give some concluding remarks on why the writer feels as s/he does about the character. The words which indicate the writer's purpose are *In short*.

5 Think, plan, write
Begin by deciding with the class which question or questions are inappropriate to the set book the class is studying. Then elicit a few ideas from the class for each of the remaining questions before students decide which one they are going to answer. It is important that students brainstorm ideas before looking at their books as they will not have their books to refer to in the exam. Remind students to only select the parts of the plot which illustrate or support their ideas and arguments. The selection of best ideas, planning and writing can be set for homework.

13

The silver screen

Introduction   Student's Book p 178

Aim: To introduce the topic of the second part of the unit – the cinema.

A Divide the class into pairs or small groups. Give them five minutes to name the actors and to think of the films that each of the actors in the list is famous for. Award one point for each correct answer. It doesn't matter if the film titles are not in English, but you may like to award an extra point for a reasonable guess at the English title.

ANSWERS

From left to right: Andie McDowell, Tom Cruise, Michelle Pfeiffer, Sylvester Stallone.

Possible films:
Andie McDowell – *Four Weddings and a Funeral*, *Green Card*
Tom Cruise – *Top Gun*, *The Firm*, *Rain Man*, *Cocktail*
Michelle Pfeiffer – *Batman 2*, *Wolf*
Sylvester Stallone – *Rocky*, *Rambo*, *Demolition Man*

B Personal response.

C Discussion questions and ideas

Ask students whether more or fewer people go to the cinema in their countries than five or ten years ago. Have cinemas been closed down in their home towns or have new ones been built? How many of the students watch home videos? How many do they watch a week? Do they prefer watching a video at home or going to the cinema? Why? What are the advantages of each form of entertainment?
Advantages of home videos:
You can watch a film in the comfort of your own home. They are useful for couples with children, who may not be able to get out very often. They are a cheaper alternative for families.
Advantages of the cinema:
It's a 'night out'.
Most films look and sound better on the big screen.

Listening   Student's Book pp 178–179

1 Think ahead

Aim: To give students the opportunity to revise some of the vocabulary in the Vocabulary reference (Unit 3: Entertainment and the Arts) and to anticipate some of the vocabulary they may hear in the listening.
Divide the class into small groups. Give students a few minutes to write down as many words connected with the cinema as they can. Then check their answers. Either award one point for each correct answer or award one point for each answer none of the other groups has. The group with the most points is the winner.

2 Comprehension

Give students a few minutes to read through the questions and possible answers before they listen, explaining vocabulary if necessary. The tape includes exam-length pauses and each extract is repeated. After students have listened, try to elicit any words and phrases which helped them to identify the answers.

ANSWERS

1 C *It's more to do with the image he puts across than anything else. He always plays the part of a tough, macho man . . . and I suppose he appeals to young people for that reason.*
2 A *I'm tall and blonde. You said that was what they were looking for . . . to be an extra.*
3 C *the bit where he arranges to meet the girl was well-done. And the scene with his father at the end.*
4 A *. . . come another day instead . . . sell these tickets and give me some others.*
5 B *. . . dividing it up into four or five smaller cinemas . . . lower the original ceiling . . . replace the seats.*
6 C *I said not the back row. I'm not paying for those seats.*
7 C *We'll have to do without that scene.*
8 A *It was an all-girls' secondary school. We were all quite envious of her.*

Tapescript

1   You are going to hear part of an interview. Why does the speaker think the actor is so popular?
A Because he is very attractive.
B Because he is a very good actor.
C Because of the parts he plays.

W = Woman
W   Yes, he is one of the big box-office draws. They make millions of dollars out of his films so he's obviously popular. I think it's more to do with the image he puts across than anything else. He always plays the part of a hard, tough, macho man and I suppose he appeals to young people, particularly boys, for that reason. I mean, well, he's quite nice to look at if you like men with muscles – which not everyone does of course, but you wouldn't exactly call him a brilliant actor, would you? So I suppose it must be that.

2   Listen to this woman speaking to a friend. What does she want him to do?
A get her a part in a film
B arrange a meeting with the director
C introduce her to an actor

W = Woman; M = Man
W   I don't see what the problem is. Can't you just say you're a friend of the director's. I mean you are anyway.
M   That won't make any difference. It doesn't really have anything to do with him.
W   Well don't you know thingy? . . . What's'isname? . . . The main actor?

M Steve Andrew? Yes, but I can hardly bother him with this, can I?

W Well, can't you do something? I'd be ideal! After all I'm tall and blonde. You said that was what they were looking for. It's not as if I need loads of experience to be an extra, is it?

3 You will hear someone talking about a new film. What was his opinion of it?
A He thought it was too long.
B He thought it was excellent.
C He thought parts of it were good.

M = Man

M I wouldn't say it was his best film but it was a lot better than his last one, that's for sure. That was far too long; they could have cut it by at least thirty minutes. But the bit where he arranges to meet the girl and there's that incredible mix-up was well-done. And the scene with his father at the end. Yeah, it was a pleasant way to spend an afternoon.

4 Listen to this man phoning a box-office. What does he want the woman in the box-office to do?
A change his tickets
B change his seats
C refund his money

M = Man

M No, I know you can't give me my money back... That's not why I'm ringing. I just want to know if it's possible to come another day instead... Yes, I understand that, but surely you can sell these tickets and give me some others... No, that doesn't matter... That would be fine, actually. The seats aren't too near the front, are they?... Row M. No, that'll be fine. Well, thanks a lot. That's great. I'll pick them up tomorrow.

5 Some people are discussing plans for an old cinema. What does the speaker want to do?
A knock it down and build a new one
B make alterations and modernize it
C turn it into a conference hall

W = Woman

W Well personally, I think making it into a conference hall would be too expensive. I agree with John's idea of dividing it up into four or five smaller cinemas. And I also think we should seriously consider lowering the original ceiling. We'd save a lot on heating costs and it should improve the sound quality as well. Obviously we'll have to replace the seats too.

6 You are going to hear part of a telephone conversation. What has the man's son done?
A forgotten to buy some tickets
B lost some tickets
C bought the wrong tickets

M = Man

M What?... Oh, for goodness sake. I don't believe it! You can't do anything right, can you? I distinctly said not the back row. You know your mother can't see a thing unless she's practically sitting on top of the screen. Well, you'll just have to phone up the box-office and get it sorted out, won't you? Cos' I'm not. And I'm not paying for those seats either.

7 Listen to this conversation. What are the film director and his producer talking about?
A changing an actor
B refilming a scene
C cutting a scene

M1 = Man 1; M2 = Man 2

M1 Who chose Branson for the part anyway?

M2 Me, I'm afraid. The agency didn't have anyone else even remotely suitable. I knew he wouldn't be brilliant but I didn't think he'd be this bad, I have to admit.

M1 Well, it's too late to do anything about it now. We're already behind schedule. We'll just have to do without that scene. Let the scriptwriter know, will you? In case he needs to make any changes.

8 Listen to the woman on TV talking about someone famous. How does the woman know her?
A They went to the same secondary school.
B They went to the same university.
C They went to the same drama school.

W = Woman

W It was an all-girls' secondary school and it was very much geared towards preparing pupils for university. So when Mary said she wanted to go to drama school to study acting instead of taking up her university place, the headmistress wasn't at all pleased. It didn't really fit in with the image of the school. We were all quite envious of her. It sounded much more glamorous than what we were going to do.

3 Points of view

Short pair, group or whole class discussion.

Ideas

Go to university: A university education gives better career prospects. There is a high rate of unemployment among actors.

Go to drama school: If you have a talent you should make the most of it. You may become a big star and if you don't you can always go to university later.

4 Over to you

Students discuss the questions in groups of three or four.

Ideas

1 Acting seems to be a natural talent, though it can be improved by training and practice (most actors go to Drama School). Since many actors have parents who are actors, it might appear to be an inherited skill. However, it is difficult to get into acting, and having a father or mother who is well-known must open doors.

2 They would probably find ordinary life boring. They are used to being in the limelight and would want the money and success their parents have. Many children of ordinary people follow in their parents' footsteps too. This could be because they inherit the sort of characteristics suited to the job because they know something about the job or because their parents pass on their enthusiasm for the job.

Grammar and practice   Student's Book p 179

Question tags

A Play the recorded examples as many times as necessary, then check students' answers.

ANSWERS

The speaker is asking a real question in 1, but simply expecting agreement in 2. Rising intonation on the question tag indicates a real question; falling intonation on the question tag indicates that the speaker expects agreement.

B Listening

1 Play sentences a–f, pausing between each one to give students time to write down their answers. Let them compare answers with a partner, then play again for a final check.

ANSWERS

a Q b Q c A d A e Q f A

2 Play again for choral and individual repetition.

C Forming question tags

Allow students a few minutes to discuss the rules in pairs, then check their ideas. You may wish to refer them to the Grammar reference on page 213 of their books.

D Students now have practice in forming question tags themselves.

• Play each incomplete sentence, pausing the tape after each one.

• Ask all the students to decide what the missing question tag is, then name one student to repeat the question and add the tag with falling intonation.

• If necessary, prompt by repeating the incomplete sentence. It is important that students do not simply say the question tag.

• If the tag is not correct, ask another student. If the form is correct but not the intonation, indicate this with a downward movement of the hand.

• Finally, let students check their version with the model on the tape.

• When you have repeated this process with all the sentences, play them again straight through from beginning to end for choral repetition.

Tapescript

Note: Each sentence is recorded twice – first without and then with the question tag. For reasons of space, only the full versions are given here.

1	You won't forget, *will you*?
2	You never know if he's angry or not, *do you*?
3	They've just bought a new house, *haven't they*?
4	Bill used to work for the government, *didn't he*?
5	She doesn't understand, *does she*?
6	The film was absolutely brilliant, *wasn't it*?
7	It finishes after 11, *doesn't it*?
8	You can't swim, *can you*?
9	You're coming on Friday, *aren't you*?
10	You really should try harder, *shouldn't you*?
11	You have to be a member to get in, *don't you*?
12	I've seen you before, *haven't I*?
13	You didn't enjoy that, *did you*?
14	You'd rather not go, *wouldn't you*?
15	He'd better not do it again, *had he*?
16	You will be careful, *won't you*?
17	She hasn't been here before, *has she*?
18	He never said a word, *did he*?
19	I'm buying the wine to take to Mandy's, *aren't I*?
20	They wouldn't answer, *would they*?

Workbook: Grammar 3 p 85

Vocabulary   Student's Book pp 180–181

• Give students ten minutes to study the relevant Vocabulary reference sections on page 219. They can use dictionaries to look up any words they don't know.

• Then divide them into groups of three or four and allow them ten minutes to complete exercises 1 and 2A together. Don't allow them to use dictionaries or refer back to the Vocabulary reference at this point.

• When time is up, give them three more minutes to refer to dictionaries or the Vocabulary reference.

• Check through answers with them, or collect in one set of answers from each group and mark this while students are doing exercise 2B.

• Hand back students' answers, indicating which are incorrect. Then give groups five minutes to try to correct their work. Allow them to use dictionaries and to refer to the vocabulary reference.

• Check through their answers.

1 The mind and the senses

ANSWERS

1 hearing	5 glimpse	8 memory
2 (eye)sight	6 smells	9 listening
3 touch	7 staring	10 memorizing
4 taste		

2 Money

A Quiz

ANSWERS

1 This varies from country to country. In Britain, women over 60 and men over 65 are entitled to a state pension.
2 Parents
3 Students
4 In Britain, taxi-drivers, waiters, hairdressers
5 For speeding, parking illegally, dropping litter, if your library book is overdue
6 If an article you have bought is faulty
7 With cash, by cheque or credit card, or on hire purchase (a credit agreement)
8 A net salary is after tax and any other deductions have been taken off.
9 Someone who is buying a house
10 A tenant

B Phrasal verbs

ANSWERS

1 pays, into	5 to pay it back
2 have been saving up	6 ran out / had run out
3 put down	7 would put, towards
4 took out	8 to pay off

C Use of English

ANSWERS

1 C 2 B 3 D 4 A 5 C

3 Memory verbs

ANSWERS

A

1 remind	4 reminds	6 don't remind
2 don't remember	5 don't remember	7 remind
3 remember		

B

- To remind someone to do something: to help someone to remember to do something
- To remind someone of someone: to cause someone to think of a particular person because of similarities of appearance or character
- To remember to do something: to do an action you had intended to do
- To remember doing something: to have a memory of a past action

Workbook: Vocabulary 1, 2, 3, 4, 5 pp 85–86

Writing Student's Book p 182

Exam training: Applications 2

Aim: This writing section prepares students for writing a letter of application for a grant.

Students do 1 on their own (then compare answers), or in pairs or small groups. Before they begin, check what they remember about writing applications. Applications 1 in Unit 7 (page 96) covered letters of application for a job, focusing on the presentation of relevant personal information in an appropriate formal style.

1 Grant application

A SUGGESTED ANSWERS

Dear **Sir or Madam**,
I saw your **advertisement** in **the (name of newspaper) on Friday** and I **would like** to **apply** for a grant to study in Britain for one month this summer. **I am sixteen years old** and have been studying English **for five years. I am** taking the **First Certificate examination**. In June and, if I **pass**, I **would like** to study for a higher exam next year. I have never had the **opportunity** to go abroad before and **it would be wonderful** to be able to improve my English and learn about the British way of life at the same time.
I hope you will **consider my application. I look forward to hearing from you soon.**
Yours faithfully,
Federico Accinni

B The applicant could say that he has a good level of written English but finds speaking in English difficult. This would be an opportunity to improve his fluency. The applicant could also say that his parents could not afford to send him to Britain (e.g. because of a large family; father unemployed, etc.).

2 Think, plan, write

Students should use their improved versions of Federico Accinni's letter of application as a model and add their own personal details and ideas. Remind them that the information need not be true and that they should use their imaginations. The writing can be done in class or set for homework.

Workbook: Writing p 87

Your students are now ready to take Unit test 13, which is on page 160 of this book. The key is on page 172.

14 Cause and effect

That'll teach you

Unit focus   Causative structures

Topic 1   Education
Reading
Grammar and practice   Expressing cause and effect
                        Expressions of purpose
Vocabulary   Education, word building
Writing   Checking and editing

Topic 2   Music
Listening
Grammar and practice   Causative verbs: *have / get*
                        something done
Vocabulary   Health, phrasal verbs
Writing   Exam training: Stories 2
Exam techniques   Taking FCE

Introduction   Student's Book p 183

Aim: To introduce the topic of the first part of the unit – education. Since this is the final unit of the book, the focus is on taking exams in general and on the First Certificate exam in particular. The final section on pages 195–196 gives advice on taking the exam.

A Get students to look at the four photographs and discuss them in pairs. They could choose two of the photos and talk about them as they will have to in Paper 5 Part 2, and as they did on page 62 of the Student's Book. They could then go on to discuss the five questions.

Round this off with a brief class discussion. Elicit class reactions to questions 2, 3, and 4.

The photos show, clockwise from bottom left, the following learning situations:
Secondary school: normal classroom situation in which some children are well-occupied and interested, while others are bored and inattentive.
Vocational training session: this kind of learning is usually related to training for a particular job, often skilled manual work requiring practical skills. Students learn by doing.
University lecture: typical method of teaching and learning at universities, where groups are large. Lecturers talk, students take notes and there is little contact between them.
Class on a field trip: students studying geography or biology often go on field trips. This type of learning is very practical and related to real life.

B Education

1 Students read the five statements and discuss them in pairs or as a class. They could then reformulate the sentences to say what they believe, for example, 'Continuous assessment is the best way to find out how good students are'.
2 Class discussion.
   Some possible purposes of education are:
   • training for a particular job
   • training for the world of work in general
   • personal development

   • acquisition of life skills
   • intellectual training and development
   • moral and political conformity

Reading   Student's Book pp 184–185

1 Think ahead

This task focuses attention specifically on examinations in preparation for reading the article. Students may discuss the two questions in pairs or groups.

2 Reading

These two questions check students' general understanding of the article. Allow students a maximum of five minutes for this first reading.

Background information
In the British education system there are two important exams. GCSE (General Certificate of Secondary Education) is taken at the age of about 16. The best students take eight or nine subjects at this level. A (Advanced) Level is taken at the age of 18. Most students take three subjects at this level. Their results determine whether or not they succeed in getting a place at a university.

ANSWERS
1 C From the tone of the introduction the text is clearly aimed at students waiting for their exam results. The examples of well-known (in Britain) people who have succeeded in life without examination passes are intended to make students feel better about the possibility of failing.
2 B

3 Comprehension

A Multiple matching

Remind students of the need to scan the article for the information required to answer these questions. They do not need to read the text from beginning to end. Set a limit of five minutes to encourage students to scan, but extend this if necessary.

ANSWERS

1	B	
2/3	A / E	*a journalist; presenter of the Channel 4 TV programme . . . / TV presenter*
4/5	B / D	*I don't see any problem with competitive exams. / I still feel education has to be taken seriously.*
6/7	A / C	
8	A	*My higher education was pubs and music.*
9	B	*. . . left university after just 2 years.*
10	E	*. . . the kids with degrees are usually too self-centred.*
11	E	*Kids from the middle and upper classes just don't have the same hunger.*
12	B	*There are contests for everything . . .*

B Vocabulary

ANSWERS

1 to succeed in the area / job you have chosen
2 to be born lucky, usually into a rich or advantaged family
3 from the very beginning
4 to leave the family home, become independent, earn your own living
5 to know something instinctively / to know deep down, even if you are not prepared to admit it publicly
6 when everything has been considered and taken into account
7 the education, knowledge and wisdom that come from the experience of life

C Reading between the lines

SUGGESTED ANSWERS

1 She found out about the lives, interests, problems and difficulties of ordinary people.
2 Competitive exams are thought by some people
   • to cause unhealthy levels of stress in students
   • to emphasize passing and failing at the expense of genuine learning
   • to be elitist / unfairly selective
   • to favour certain kinds of students.
3 Having passed exams proves only that people can pass exams. It doesn't mean that people are better or even more intelligent than others.
Note: Only discuss this last statement if students have not previously had much opportunity to talk about the subject of exams.

4 Over to you

These questions are probably best discussed as a whole class.

5 My last exam

Students could prepare for this writing activity by asking each other questions about the last exam they took.

MODEL PARAGRAPHS

On the morning of the exam I was incredibly nervous. I'd spent the whole of the week before revising and I felt quite confident, but I hadn't slept very well, so I was rather tired. I remember I couldn't stop yawning on the way to the exam centre.

The exam lasted three hours. When it was all over I felt absolutely exhausted but I was also very relieved, because it meant I could stop working and look forward to the holidays. I went out with my friends that evening. We forgot all about the exam and just enjoyed ourselves.

> Workbook: Reading pp 88–89

Grammar and practice   Student's Book p 186

1 Cause and effect

A This exercise introduces a number of ways of expressing causes and effects. Elicit answers from the class.

ANSWERS

2 will cause
3 will make
4 made me

B Students could work in pairs to produce a note-form chart.

ANSWERS

Cause	*Effect*
2 particular results	more problems than they solve
3 news reports	people who are not happy
4 growing up in Caribbean	confidence in child

C *Make*
1 Sentence 3: *make* + object + infinitive without *to* ; sentence 4: *make* + object + adjective
2 Refer students to the Grammar reference on page 214 of their books.

D Students ask each other questions in pairs. This is mainly for accuracy practice, but if they are interested in the questions, it may develop into a fluency activity. Monitor, correcting their use of *make* if necessary.

POSSIBLE ANSWERS

1 Cartoons like *Tom and Jerry* make me laugh.
2 I can move my ears up and down – that makes people laugh.
3 Putting off replying to friends' letters makes me feel guilty.
4 Politicians who tell lies make me angry.
5 The fact that I'm often late makes other people angry.

You could round off this activity with a survey of students' answers to one of the questions.

2 Purpose

A ANSWER
in order to + infinitive

B ANSWERS
1 *to* + infinitive (*to keep themselves fit*)
2 *so* + clause (*so I can have Friday off*)
3 *in order to* + infinitive (*in order to improve his spoken French*)
4 *so that* + clause (*so that he could study in peace*)

C Refer students to the Grammar reference on page 214 of their books.

3 Practice

This is mainly for accuracy practice of purpose expressions, but if students are interested in the questions, it may develop into a fluency activity. Monitor the activity, discouraging students from answering too many questions with *because* clauses.

POSSIBLE ANSWERS
1 to impress their friends, to get to places quickly, because they're impatient
2 to lose weight, to feel healthier, to improve their appearance
3 to relax after a hard day, to dance, to drink, to meet people
4 to get better jobs, to become qualified, to prove how good they are

4 Fluency

This activity continues the theme of cause and effect and may involve some of the language previously practised, but it is primarily a fluency activity. Students read about the three situations, decide how they would react in each case and then compare ideas in pairs or small groups. Alternatively they could think about and discuss the situations one at a time.

When groups have had sufficient time to discuss the three problems, ask one member from each group to report back any ideas and suggestions agreed upon.

Background information
Situation 2: According to experts, the best position to take up if you find yourself in a lift that is in 'freefall' is to stand with your legs slightly bent. Jumping upwards doesn't work for three reasons. Firstly, it is very difficult to time. Secondly, by the time you have thought about this tactic you will already have hit the bottom. Thirdly, if you have enough time to think you have already fallen too far to survive.

Workbook: Grammar 1, 2 p 90

Vocabulary   Student's Book p 187

1 Education

A Quiz
1 Make sure students have unjumbled all the words correctly before they attempt to match them to the symbols.

ANSWERS
a geography	symbol 6
b history	symbol 4
c maths	symbol 2
d foreign language	symbol 1
e science	symbol 3
f economics	symbol 7
g physical education	symbol 5

2 biology, chemistry, physics
Here are some more: anthropology, astrology, entomology (insects), philology (development of language), physiology.

3 ANSWERS
1 psychology	4 sociology
2 technology	5 archaeology
3 geology	

B Elicit ideas before students start writing. Stress that their reasons for liking or disliking subjects are also important.

MODEL
My favourite subject at school was definitely French. I've always been good with words and I'm interested in speaking to people from other countries. When I was 15, I spent a week with a French family in Paris. Because I always got high marks, I was popular with the French teachers.

My least favourite subject was maths. I was good at numbers until I was about 12 and then suddenly the subject got harder, and I understood almost nothing. The problem was that we had a very impatient teacher. He had no sympathy with children who were no good at maths.

2 Word building

A ANSWERS
Noun	Person	Verb	Adjective
1 examination	examiner	examine	X
2 education	educator	educate	a educated
			b educational
3 competition	competitor	compete	competitive
4 qualification	X	qualify	qualified
5 intelligence	X	X	intelligent
6 revision	X	revise	X
7 failure	failure	fail	failing

B ANSWERS
1 taking	3 revised	5 re-sitting
2 pass	4 fail	

Workbook: Vocabulary 1 p 92

Writing

Student's Book pp 188–189

Checking your work

1 Introduction

This writing section summarizes what many teachers urge their students to do every time they write. Get students to read the introductory notes. Follow this up with a short discussion, perhaps by asking students to decide which piece of advice they think is the most useful or important. Try to impress upon them the need to use all the time available in the exam to check what they have written.

2 Answering the question

This first practice section considers what is the most fundamental point of all in regard to the tasks in Paper 2 – the absolute need for students to answer the question given (as opposed to one small part of it, or a different but related question of their own.)

In the first instance students should ignore the grammatical errors and simply read the model to check whether it does,

in fact answer the question. Allow about ten minutes for this and encourage students to discuss their ideas.

SUGGESTED ANSWER

On the whole this model does answer the question. The writer does actually express the opinion, in the last paragraph, that boys and girls should **not** be taught separately. Paragraph 1 provides the reasons for boys and girls being educated separately; Paragraph 2 gives some reasons against (and Paragraph 3 gives the writer's personal opinion). From a structural point of view, however, this model lacks an introductory paragraph, outlining the purpose and scope of the composition.

3 Editing

Students could work through the model looking for and correcting mistakes, and then work through the checklist of questions. Alternatively, they could work through the questions one at a time, looking for errors in the text. Allow plenty of time for students to do this individually or in pairs.

Text – see below.
Note: The errors are underlined and corrections are suggested alongside.

The fact that girls and boys are separated can be good	Boys and girls being separated
because they have different interest. The communication is	interests / **the** not needed
easier if there are only girls or boys. For example, boys and	
girls seldom play together because the first ones prefer	boys / the former
fighting or playing cars, whereas the others like puppets.	girls / the latter / dolls
Also that permit to organize the subjects in different ways.	this system allows schools to organize
So, the boys could have more sport, and the girls could do	
cooking or drawning.	drawing
However, we can notice some disadvantages as having a	there are / such as / there being
bad atmosphere. I explain: if girls are all the time together, it	I will explain (Let me explain) / together all the time
can makes problems. Otherwise, because girls are more	cause (no **-s**) / What is more is better than otherwise
mature, they can help the boys to grow up. At last, if boys	Finally
and girls are mixed, that contribute to a rivalry between	this contributes / a sense of rivalry
each other and the results **can** be better___	the two groups / may / add **full stop**.
In my opinion to separate boys and girls is not a good idea	
because they have to live together and they should learn it	this
the youngest as possible. Apart from that I don't see the	as young as possible / any
reason to separate them. They can bring something each	**to** missing
other.	

ANSWERS TO QUESTIONS

1–3 Grammar, Vocabulary, Spelling and punctuation
These are dealt with in the corrected model above.

4 Organization
- The main ideas are clear.
- The introductory paragraph is missing.
  Paragraph 1 is rather long in comparison with paragraph 2.
- Linking expressions used:
  Para 1   *For example*   ✓
  Also   This is rather weak; *In addition to this* would be better.
  So   This is weak; *In this way* would be better.
  Para 2   *However*   A stronger word is needed at the beginning of a paragraph to introduce the other side of the picture, e.g. *There are arguments against separate schools*.
  I explain   This phrase is wrong, but the correct version, *Let me explain*, is too colloquial here. A better alternative might be *In my opinion / experience*.
  Otherwise is used incorrectly here – *What is more* is more appropriate.
  At last is incorrect here – see above.
  Para 3   *In my opinion*   ✓

5 Style
- On the whole, the style is appropriate – it is reasonably formal, but not too stiff or unnatural.
- Only one short verb form is used, in the last paragraph. This is reasonable as it is part of the writer's expression of his / her own opinion.

4 Correct your own writing

A Students could write the two opening paragraphs in class or for homework. Stress the importance of answering the question and of checking accuracy. Refer students back to the list of questions in the previous section.

Notice that the two suggested questions require different types of writing: the first is an article, the second a report.

B/C Students check their own accuracy and then pass their writing on to a partner for further corrections. They should then write a final version, which should be corrected by you, the teacher.

MODEL ANSWERS

1 'I can't wait to leave!' 'The best time of your life!' These are just two common opinions about school. In my experience, young people may have strong views about schools, but they all agree that they need a good education.

2 Introduction
We asked 100 people what they thought the new English exam should contain. Although more than half said they were happy with the current exam, 90 per cent wanted a higher proportion of the marks given to spoken language.

Extra activity

Here are two more model answers to the same questions. Both are in need of substantial correction and improvement.

1 Lot of my friends want to leave the school getting jobs. I'm not so sure – there are things about school that I loves, like science experiments and the drama, however everyone have their own opinions, don't they. In my country we can leave when we're 16.

2 I ask students in my class what they thought should be in new English exam. Most them didn't really have some ideas, but a few do. Everyone want to get rid of the writing paper because is more difficult.

14 Cause and effect

Face the music

Introduction
Student's Book p 190

Aim: To introduce the topic of the second part of the unit – music.

In groups, students brainstorm answers to these questions. Draw attention to the time limit suggestion, and if you wish to introduce an element of competition, let groups try to get longer lists than each other.

POSSIBLE ANSWERS

1 baroque, blues, rhythm and blues, choral, classical, country and western, dance music, early music, film music, folk, gospel, heavy metal, jazz, military, opera, pop, punk, rap, reggae, religious, rock, soul, traditional, World
2 ballets, car radio, concerts, films, home, lifts, opera, in planes, shops, waiting to be connected on the phone, on a walkman, while jogging
3 for relaxation, to dance to, to do exercise to

Listening
Student's Book pp 190–191

1 Listening

The first time students hear the recording they should listen for the kinds of music mentioned by the speakers. This may be a style of music (e.g. jazz) or the reason for which music is played (e.g. to help patients in hospital). In this task, students are listening for specific information and you should play the recording once only. When eliciting answers, don't go into too much detail about the types of music or you will give away the answers to some of the comprehension exercise which follows.

ANSWERS

1 Indian music
   Note: do not mention the connection with dentists yet.
2 disco music
   Note: do not mention that this is music from other people's personal stereos.
3 music played on a radio request programme
4 pop or rock music (bass and drums / words)
   Note: do not mention the idea of a live concert yet.
5 Madonna's first hit
6 an unusual French instrument (perhaps an old one, like an accordion, or a hurdy-gurdy)
7 jazz (traditional or modern)
8 music played to patients recovering in hospital

Tapescript

1   It's something I've always been terrified of – but it was absolutely killing me. In the end it got so bad that I just had to get it seen to. Actually, I only had it

filled – which wasn't so bad as having it taken out. Anyway, I was sitting there in the chair, feeling very nervous, waiting for the drill, when this wonderful Indian music started playing. It was incredible – in just a few seconds my anxiety disappeared, I unclenched my hands and relaxed my body. Believe it or not, I actually felt myself smiling.

2   It's everywhere you go these days – I was on the train on the way to work last week, a girl came and sat next to me. I was trying to read a report and all I could hear was this repetitive mechanical drumming noise – sort of disco music, I suppose. I just couldn't concentrate. I've got a friend who listens when he goes jogging – he wears those special headphones that fit into your ear so they won't fall out. Well, that's okay, because he's not disturbing anyone. But in public places they're a real nuisance – a blatant case of noise pollution, I'd call it.

3   I've got a letter here from Mrs Johnson. She'd like to have *Love Hurts* played for her son Michael. Mum sends you her love Michael, wherever you are. She's asked me to tell you that she loves you very much and says please, please, please contact her before your birthday – she doesn't want to lose touch with you. Just a phone call would do. You don't have to tell her where you are if you don't want to. So, for Michael Johnson here's *Love Hurts* – from your Mum. And don't forget, she's looking forward to hearing from you.

4   It was incredible – my friend and me were right at the front – we were in the most expensive seats. But even there it was almost impossible to hear anything. As soon as they came on and started playing everyone went mad – you could just about hear the bass and the drums from time to time, but the words were completely inaudible. We could see their mouths opening and closing, but nothing seemed to come out. Even so, it was one of the most exciting nights of my life.

5   It's just incredible, you just have to hear a certain sound or catch whiff of a particular smell and everything comes flooding back – I mean I can remember exactly where I was when I heard Madonna's first hit – it was a winter evening – I was in my mother's kitchen making myself a cheese sandwich. I only have to hear that first guitar chord and I'm back in my Mum's kitchen. It's like the smell of sun-tan lotion – it always takes me straight back to a holiday I spent in Spain when I was four years old.

6   I remember seeing someone in a French group playing one and I thought 'I'd like to do that'. It took me a few months to save enough money for a decent one – after that I became completely obsessed – I practised several hours a day every day. I can't even read music, but I listened to records and tried things out for myself. No-one told me how to play properly – I never had any formal lessons – I

just picked it up. People seem to enjoy what I do – in the end that's all that matters.

7 It has to be jazz – all kinds – traditional, modern. I don't know exactly what it is about it – it's not only the music itself, it's the atmosphere of the clubs, the people you meet at concerts – everything about it. I like other kinds as well – blues, folk, classical even – though I have to say I'm not that keen on pop or rock. But if I had to pick just one, it'd have to be jazz.

8 We now use music to help them recover – especially if they're long stay. Experimenting with different kinds of music, we've found that certain sounds have the power to change moods and emotional states for the better. Many of them come to us shattered, angry and full of pain, both physical and emotional. They have had their lives reduced to a bed and a locker. We work to bring peace of mind to both their body and mind.

2 Comprehension

This is a multiple choice listening exercise of the kind students will have to answer in Part 1 of Paper 4. The questions and possible answers are included on the tape, as in the actual exam. For space reasons, they are not reproduced here.

A Allow students time to read through the questions and the choice of answers, and then play the recording. Elicit answers with reasons – these can sometimes be in the form of clue words and phrases from the recording.

ANSWERS
1 B *filled / chair / drill*
2 A *repetitive mechanical drumming noise / headphones*
3 A (Not B – it is not her son's birthday yet.)
4 C *As soon as they came on* shows that this is a live performance.
5 B The speaker mentions the way smells as well as music can bring back memories.
6 A *I can't read music / No-one taught me how to play.*
7 B This is the only question that can be answered by It. . .
8 C *recover / long stay / pain / a bed and a locker*

B Listening between the lines
Allow students about five minutes to discuss the questions in pairs or small groups, then elicit answers.

POSSIBLE ANSWERS
1 to stop himself becoming bored / to have a rhythmic sound to run to / just for enjoyment
2 This suggests that Michael may not want his mother to know where he is. It is a way of trying to persuade the son to contact his mother without worrying about being found.
3 The audience was very excited by the sight and sound of their favourite group that they made a lot of noise.

4 Patients may be so ill or disabled that they have to spend a long time in hospital. Their freedom is taken away from them and the bed and locker (cupboard to put a few personal belongings) is all they have.

Extra activity
Here is an extra vocabulary exercise students could be asked to do.

Choose the best meaning for the words or phrases in italics in these extracts from the recordings.
1 It was absolutely *killing me*
   A making me cry
   B hurting me
   C poisoning me   (Answer B)
2 I just had to get it (the tooth) *seen to*.
   A examined
   B treated
   C taken out   (Answer B)
3 I *unclenched* my hands
   A opened
   B wiped
   C closed   (Answer A)
4 . . . a *blatant* case of noise pollution . . .
   A definite
   B probable
   C public   (Answer A)
5 *I became completely obsessed.*
   A I took an interest
   B I became quite keen
   C I couldn't stop thinking about it   (Answer C)
6 I never had any formal lessons – I just *picked it up*.
   A learnt without any conscious effort
   B taught myself
   C learnt from a book   (Answer A)

Grammar and practice   Student's Book p 191

Have / get something done

Aim: A brief revision of causative verbs.
The Grammar reference on page 214 points out to students that *to have / get something done* can be used in preference to a passive verb when we want to indicate that, although someone does not do something themselves, they are nevertheless instrumental in bringing about the action.

By extension, these verbs are often used to refer to actions that people cannot or will not do for themselves:
That tree is getting too tall. We ought to get it cut down.
The President does absolutely nothing for himself – he even has his feet washed by one of his servants.

A Elicit answers to the questions following each example sentence.

ANSWERS
1 the dentist
2 because this is not something it is possible to do for yourself
3 the disc jockey / DJ

B The main difference between the passive and *have / get done* is related to the attitude of the speaker. By saying *I had my tooth filled* the speaker shows that he was responsible for the action although he didn't do it himself. The passive seems to emphasize that the speaker had nothing to do with the action, but was simply the passive recipient of dental treatment which he didn't necessarily want.

We might use the passive to emphasize that we have no responsibility for an action, for example:
I went to the doctor's to have my blood pressure checked, but by the time I came out half an hour later, I'd been given three injections, I'd been examined by the doctor and a couple of nurses, and I'd been told to stay in bed for three weeks.

C This question draws attention to two different meanings of *have something done*. Elicit students ideas.

ANSWER _____

In the first example the verb is used **causatively** – the speaker brings about the action even though he does not do it himself.
In the second example, people have been the victim of something outside their control, so the verb is not being used causatively.

D Students should read the Grammar reference on page 214.

E ANSWERS _____

2 I had my hair cut in a completely different style.
3 We have had the front of our house repainted.
4 I'm going to get my video repaired next week (by a friend of mine who's an electrician).
5 I'm having my jacket cleaned at a specialist cleaner's.
6 The council has just had the town hall rebuilt.

F Students could work through these questions orally in pairs or groups, or in writing for homework. It is quite likely that students will not know all the vocabulary necessary for this exercise.

POSSIBLE ANSWERS _____

1 You can have your teeth cleaned, filled, taken out
  You can have false teeth fitted
2 They go to have their hair cut, coloured, waved, washed, trimmed.
3 They go to have them serviced, repaired. They have the oil changed.
4 I'd have my hair dyed; my nose made smaller; I'd have the shape of my face changed.

G Ideas
I have my windows cleaned, rubbish collected, milk delivered, post and newspapers delivered, car repaired, serviced, and cleaned. I have my hair cut, clothes washed and ironed and my shoes polished. Occasionally, I have a pizza delivered to my flat.

When students compare and discuss their lists in pairs, they may want to use expressions like I don't have my clothes ironed for me: I iron them myself.

Workbook: Grammar 3, 4, 5 pp 90–91

Vocabulary   Student's Book p 192

1 Health

A Work through the definitions of words 1–10 before students start. Elicit possible answers, but do not confirm or reject suggestions until they have done the wordsearch.

ANSWERS _____

1 midwife	3 patient	5 bandage	7 plaster	9 cure
2 nurse	4 surgeon	6 pill	8 catch	10 treat

P	A	T	R	E	A	T	O	S
U	B	A	N	D	A	G	E	U
S	L	L	I	P	A	P	E	R
H	M	I	D	W	I	F	E	G
P	L	A	S	T	E	R	A	E
B	C	O	F	F	I	N	G	O
L	U	H	C	A	T	C	H	N
U	R	T	N	E	I	T	A	P
D	E	E	S	R	U	N	F	U

2 Use of English

Students will meet this type of exercise in Paper 3 Use of English. Remind them of the importance or working out what type of word is needed to fill the gaps (noun, adjective, etc).

ANSWERS _____

1 infection	4 injection
2 specialist	5 painful
3 examination	6 recovery

3 Phrasal verbs

Work through the instructions and explanations with the class. Point out that students must work out the correct form of the verbs – this may include using negative forms. Stress that three-part verbs are never separable.

ANSWERS _____

1 come up against (= encountered)
2 to cut down on (= to reduce)
3 kept up with (= made sure I was informed about)
4 don't go along with (= don't agree with)
5 catch up with (= reach) keep up with (= go as fast as)
6 had gone / come down with (= had caught / become ill with)
7 came up with (= invented / thought of). Note the use of past simple after 'It's time . . .'

Note: There are two more combinations of the verbs and particles from the table.
• catch up on (= do something which has been neglected)
  I'm going to bed early tonight. I really need to catch up on my sleep.

- come down on (= to criticize someone for something)
  If our handwriting isn't neat, our teacher comes down on us very hard.

Extra activity

Students could be given this 'confusing words' exercise. Most of the word are related in some way to health.

Choose the correct word to fill the gaps in these sentences.

1 The tablets I took had absolutely no _____ on my headache.
   A power
   B effect
   C influence
   D affect   (Answer B)
2 The doctor examined me and then wrote out a _____ for me to take to the chemist.
   A paper
   B recipe
   C prescription
   D ticket   (Answer C)
3 I don't mind when you go on holiday. It doesn't really _____ me.
   A effect
   B affect
   C matter
   D suit   (Answer B)
4 I've had two teeth taken out – it was OK at the time, but now my mouth really _____
   A pains
   B harms
   C hurts
   D injures   (Answer C)
5 After I'd run for the bus my heart was _____ very hard.
   A beating
   B hitting
   C striking
   D blowing   (Answer A)

Workbook: Vocabulary 2, 3, 4 p 92

Writing   Student's Book pp 193–194

Exam training: Stories 2

1 Introduction

Remind students of the main features of stories introduced in Unit 5, and, if necessary, allow them to read through the summary box on page 69 of their books.

2 Model

A Make sure students understand the reading task, then let them read the model answer underlining those parts which say what happened.

I was travelling through northern Italy, listening to a Paul McCartney cassette on my personal stereo. Although it was sunny, it was cool for April. The coach was comfortable, light and airy – occasionally, the smartly-dressed attendants brought cold drinks and delicious snacks.

Just after midday, the road started to climb and the temperature fell rapidly. When we reached the highest point of the hills, it was snowing hard. Suddenly, there was a bang, and the coach drove off the road and stopped. For a moment everything was quiet and nobody moved. In my headphones, Paul McCartney went on singing sweetly. Fortunately nobody was hurt and soon we were all chattering excitedly. The driver had lost control after a puncture. He said he couldn't change the wheel in such terrible weather conditions.

Twenty hours later the breakdown truck arrived and soon we were able to continue our journey. By the time we arrived in Milan, I was tired and hungry – I must have listened to my cassette over twenty times. Every time I hear that music now, it reminds me of that amazing day.

B Students now have a chance to analyse the descriptive language which fills out the story and makes it interesting.

Allow them to work in pairs on this exercise.

ANSWERS

1 Appearance, character, behaviour
   smartly-dressed attendants / I was tired and hungry
2 Place or thing
   northern Italy / the coach was comfortable light and airy / delicious snacks
3 Situation or atmosphere
   it was sunny / cool for April / everything was quiet / excitedly / terrible weather conditions
4 Explanation
   The driver had lost control after a puncture.

Approximately 40% of the story is narrative and 60% is descriptive.

3 Think, plan, write

Students are now going to write their own stories ending with this same sentence.

Students should work individually through the A–E sequence, writing their story for homework.

Workbook: Writing p 93

Exam techniques   Student's Book pp 195–196

Taking the First Certificate exam

This final section of the book consists of advice to students about taking exams in general, and about each of the five paper of the First Certificate exam.

It would not be advisable to work through this section in class, but make sure students know it is there and read through it for themselves some time before the exam. It should be read in conjunction with the Exam Factfile at the beginning of the book. Suggest students read the information about the papers again the day or night before they take those papers. If there are any specific exercise types students are worried about, suggest they look back at the relevant Exam techniques sections.

It is worth drawing particular attention to the last section *The answer sheet*, and checking that students understand the need to transfer their answers to a separate answer sheet in Papers 1, 3 and 4. There is a sample answer sheet on page 196.

Your students are now ready to take Unit test 14, which is on page 161 of this book. The key is on page 172.

After they have taken the Unit test, students can do Revision 4, on pages 94–96 of their Workbooks. Encourage them to look up anything they have difficulties with. This will help to consolidate their learning, and will prepare them for Progress test 4. Revision 4 could be set for homework.

Your students are now ready to take Progress test 4, which can be found on pages 168–169 of this book. The key is on

Tests

Unit tests and Progress tests

The tests appear in numerical order, the Unit tests first, followed by the Progress tests. Unit tests should be taken on finishing the relevant unit. Progress tests should be taken after Revision at the end of Units 4, 8, 12 and 14.

The keys to all the Unit tests are on pages 170–172. Those to the Progress tests are on pages 173–74.

There is further information about the tests in the Introduction on pages 8–9 of this book.

The following section contains pages marked 'photocopiable'. The publisher grants permission for those pages to be photocopied in accordance with the following conditions. Individual purchasers may make copies for their own use or for use by the classes they teach. School purchasers may make copies for use by their staff and students, but this permission does not extend to additional schools or branches.

In no circumstances may any part of this book be photocopied for resale.

Unit 1 test

Vocabulary

A Put the correct form of one of these key verbs in the gaps.

have   get   give   set   take

1 They _____ John the sack for stealing money from the company.

2 Yesterday it _____ me nearly an hour to get to college.

3 Usually I just _____ a sandwich and a cup of coffee for my lunch.

4 My sister and her boyfriend have decided to _____ married next April.

5 Dave accidentally _____ light to his ne[...] when he dropped his cigarette.

B Match a beginning 6–10 with an ending a–[...] careful attention to the meaning of the phra[...]
6 I've been feeling ill for nearly a week.
7 Although I live in England now,
8 We thought we had enough money to [...] whole holiday
9 My mother often asks me when I'm go[...] down
10 We saw a crowd of people at the end [...]

a but actually we got through most of it in the first week.
b and get a steady job.
c I think it's something I picked up while I was on holiday.
d so we went to see what was going on.
e I grew up in Australia.

C Which shop would you buy these items from?
11 sugar, biscuits, butter   _____
12 medicine, tablets, bandages   _____
13 a flight to London, a rail ticket to Edinburgh, a holiday in Crete   _____
14 steak, chops, sausages   _____
15 apples, carrots, lettuce   _____
16 tools, knives, keys   _____
17 envelopes, paper, pencils   _____
18 chocolate, chewing gum   _____
19 rolls, cakes, bread   _____
20 cod, prawns, crabs   _____

Grammar

D Fill the gaps in these sentences with the correct form of one of the verbs below. Use each of these verb tenses or forms at least once.

past simple / present continuous / present simple / tend to / used to / would

complain   do   eat   go   have   leave   start think   wash   work

21 A hundred years ago many people _____ for 15 hours a day.

22 My grandfather _____ home at 6 o'clock in the morning and not return until 10 at night.

23/24/25 When he got home he always _____ something, _____ and _____ straight to bed.

26 Today very few people _____ more than about ten hours' work a day.

27 Most of us _____ work at 9 am and [...] between 5 and 6 pm.

[...]en _____ at least an hour's break [...]htime.

[...]e such a short day we _____ about [...]g too much to do.

[...]ardly ever _____ about what things [...]like for our grandparents.

[...]se the correct verb in these sentences.
[...]ed in Africa for nearly five years but I *never got [...] to / was never used to* the heat.
[...]t used to smoking / I used to smoke*, but I gave up nearly three years ago.

33 Even though my parents are in their eighties *they are used to looking after themselves / they used to look after themselves.*

34 Foreigners *get / are* used to driving on the left quite quickly when they come to England.

35 Where *did you use to live / were you used to living* before you moved to New York?

F Fill the gaps in the following sentences with a suitable preposition.

36 My parents live _____ the tenth floor of an apartment block in the centre of Manchester.

37 When I retire I'd like to live in a bungalow _____ the sea.

38 Harwich is a small port _____ the east coast of England.

39 These days more and more people live _____ the suburbs of large cities.

40 When I was a child I spent every holiday _____ the seaside.

© Oxford University Press

Unit 2 test

Vocabulary

A Put the correct form of one of these verbs in the gaps. You do not need to use one of the verbs.

blow freeze pour rain shine snow

1 We had to postpone the barbecue because it _____ with rain.

2 It was so cold that the water in the river _____.

3 We're going to the beach tomorrow. Let's hope the sun _____ for us.

4 When we looked out of the window, everything was white – obviously, it _____ for several hours.

5 During the storm the wind _____ over nearly all the trees on the island.

B Choose the correct adjective in these sentences.

6 Just before lunch there was a very *strong* / *heavy* shower of rain.

7 It's dangerous to drive fast in *heavy* / *thick* fog.

8 We had to wear sunglasses because of the *bright* / *light* sunshine.

9 They closed the bridge over the river because of *fast* / *strong* winds.

10 Even though it was only a *light* / *thin* drizzle, we got surprisingly wet.

C Put the correct form of one of these key verbs in the gaps.

go have make run take

11 It took me six months to _____ a complete recovery after the accident.

12 When I was in France everyone _____ to a lot of trouble to make me feel at home.

13 If you drink and drive, you _____ the risk of losing your licence.

14 My parents always _____ hundreds of photographs when they go on holiday.

15 _____ a good time at the party, but don't be too late home.

Grammar

D Fill the gaps in the following sentences with a suitable preposition.

16 My grandfather left school _____ the age of 12.

17 You've been _____ the phone for ages. Please hurry up.

18 I don't like driving _____ my own at night.

19 The headteacher is _____ charge of everything that goes on in the school.

20 The electricity went off right _____ the middle of the film.

E Fill the gaps with the correct future form of the verb in brackets.

21 My father _____ (be) 80 years old on his next birthday.

22 I feel terrible – I think I _____ (faint).

23 I won't be at work tomorrow – I _____ (go) for an interview for a new job.

24 We'd better hurry up – the train _____ (leave) in ten minutes.

25 This time tomorrow you _____ (work) in this office for ten years.

26 A 'The music's terribly loud.'

B 'Sorry, I _____ (turn) it down straightaway.'

27 Next year I _____ (learn) to drive – and that's definite.

28 I hope the exam goes well. We _____ (think) of you all the time.

29 I've eaten so much I think I _____ (burst).

30 I _____ (carry) your shopping for you, shall I?

F Fill the gaps in these sentences with the correct article. If no article is needed, write ✗.

31 I was ill all last week so I stayed at ___ home.

32 Monica Seles is probably ___ best woman tennis player in the world.

33 Would you like ___ cup of tea?

34 Have you still got ___ books I lent you?

35 I've always wanted to visit ___ United States.

36 ___ politicians often have to work long, unsociable hours.

37 Before he retired my father was ___ engineer.

38 My grandparents still go to ___ church every Sunday.

39 Nearly ___ million people were made homeless by last week's floods.

40 John's sight quickly got worse and at the age of seven he was sent to a special school for ___ blind.

Unit 3 test

Vocabulary

A Fill the gaps in these sentences with one of the words below. There are six extra words.

aisle audience conductor encores exhibited lines magician perform plot row scenery script set spectators stalls subtitles

1 The group played two _____ at the end of the concert.

2 The _____ repeated the word 'Abracadabra' and pulled a rabbit from his hat.

3 I've never seen such a bad play. One of the actors kept forgetting his _____.

4 A lot of people don't like watching foreign language films because they hate having to read _____ .

5 The _____ applauded loudly at the end of the concert.

6 When I go the cinema I don't like to sit on the front _____ because you're too near the screen.

7 The Beatles always used to _____ in front of hundreds of screaming teenage girls.

8 When the _____ raised his baton, the orchestra started to play.

9 I didn't like the film much. The _____ was far too difficult to follow.

10 The _____ was very simple. It consisted of a table, four chairs, a bottle of wine and two glasses.

B Write the nouns which correspond to these adjectives in the gaps.

Example intelligent *intelligence*

11 secure   _____

12 dark   _____

13 lonely   _____

14 admired   _____

15 fit   _____

16 popular   _____

17 shy   _____

18 sincere   _____

Grammar

C Fill the gaps in these sentences with a verb below in the gerund or infinitive form.

be change get have lay lose meet pay see steal take work

19 David considered _____ his job when they increased the hours.

20 I don't think we can afford _____ a holiday this year, do you?

21 You risk _____ your driving licence if you drink and drive.

22 Being a nurse means _____ long hours, nights and weekends.

23 When you've finished _____ the table, could you make the beds?

24 I've arranged _____ John outside the cinema at 8 o'clock.

25 We didn't want to speak to Mike so we pretended not _____ him.

26 The man admitted _____ a bottle of whisky from the shop.

27 I don't expect _____ late but you never know.

28 No one can prevent you _____ married when you're 18.

29 I can't resist _____ another piece of apple pie.

30 I always put off _____ my bills until the last moment.

D Choose the correct form: gerund or infinitive.

31 Jason tried *to open / opening* the window but it was stuck.

32 Marie stopped *to go / going out* with her friends when she started dating Richard.

33 I regret *to go / going* straight to university after I left school. I wish I'd travelled a bit first.

34 The alarm clock went off but Chris just went on *to sleep / sleeping*.

35 Sorry! I meant *to tell / telling* you but I forgot.

36 If you want to make new friends, try *to join / joining* a sports club.

37 Being famous means *to be / being* recognized wherever you go.

38 Sorry we're late! We had to stop *to ask / asking* the way several times.

39 British Airways regrets *to announce / announcing* the late arrival of flight BA 467 from Athens. This flight is now expected to arrive at 23.00 hours.

40 The teacher first of all explained to the students what they had to do then went on *to demonstrate / demonstrating*.

© Oxford University Press

Unit 4 test

Vocabulary

A Write the family word for these people.
1 your father's or mother's brother _____
2 one of two children born at the same time to the same mother _____
3 man whose wife is dead _____
4 daughter of your brother or sister _____
5 your father's father _____
6 your wife's or husband's mother _____
7 son or daughter of your mother's sister _____
8 woman whose husband is dead _____
9 son of your brother or sister _____
10 all the people who are part of your family (two answers are possible) _____

B Write the name of the person who does these jobs. You are given the first letter of each job and you will need to use each of these five job endings twice.

-ant   -er   -ian   -ist   -or

11 someone who looks after a large building, like a school or a block of flats   c_____
12 someone who answers the telephone in a large organization like a company, a college, etc.   t_____
13 someone who installs and repairs electrical equipment   e_____
14 someone who serves customers in a shop   s_____ a_____(two words)
15 someone who keeps or checks business accounts   a_____
16 someone who writes a book, play, poem, etc.   a_____
17 someone who gives legal advice, writes legal documents and speaks in law courts   s_____
18 someone who repairs water pipes, baths, etc.   p_____
19 someone who works in a hotel or office, dealing with guests, visitors, etc.   r_____
20 someone who tests eyes and sells glasses   o_____

Grammar

C Fill the gaps in these sentences with the comparative or superlative forms of one of these adjectives.

busy   comfortable   common   depressing   difficult

far   frightening   good   popular   wet

21 Easy? You must be joking. That was by far _____ exam I've ever taken.
22 We seem to have been travelling for ages. London is much _____ than I thought.
23 Daniel used to be quite an unusual name. It seems to have become much _____ in the last ten years.
24 Most countries in the world play football – in fact it's probably _____ sport in the world.
25 I didn't think I was going to enjoy the journey, but actually it was much _____ than I expected.
26 I've never felt so miserable after going to the cinema – that was definitely _____ film I've ever seen.
27 I'm used to the traffic and the crowds in Paris, but I found London even _____.
28 Why don't you sit on the sofa? It's far _____ than the chair you're sitting on.
29 It rained every day last week, but then April is well-known for being _____ month of the year.
30 I had a terrible dream last night. In fact it was _____ nightmare I've had for a long time.

D Match a beginning 31–35 with an ending a–f. You do not need to use one of the endings.
31 The harder you work
32 It was raining so hard
33 I hope I see you again –
34 They're such intelligent students
35 Ireland's a wonderful place. I've never met

a that the children were sent home early from school.
b such warm, friendly people.
c that they're certain to get into university.
d the more chance you have of passing your exam.
e so generous people.
f the sooner the better.

E Fill the gaps in these sentences with a suitable preposition.

36 When I was twelve years old I fell in love _____ my French teacher.

37 The President should resign. He never seems to be _____ control of the political situation.

38 When I was a child, my brother and I were always competing _____ our parents' attention.

39 I liked a few lessons, but _____ the whole I didn't enjoy going to school.

40 I intend to get married _____ my mid-twenties.

Unit 5 test

Vocabulary

A Put the correct form of one of these verbs in the gaps.

beat   dive   draw   miss   ride   serve   train   win

1 Cindy _____ into the pool and swam to the other side.

2 Last Saturday Everton _____ Manchester United 2–1.

3 Arsenal _____ 1–1 with Leeds.

4 During the match Sampras _____ 15 aces.

5 Johnson _____ all his races last year.

6 The winner 'Shakatan' _____ by the jockey Willie Carson.

7 If Peters _____ the penalty, we would have won.

8 The team _____ twice a week and plays on Saturday afternoons.

B Put the correct form of one of these verbs in the gaps.

come   go   see   spend   take   cost

9 Ten thousand competitors _____ part in last year's marathon.

10 Jenny felt such a fool when she realized her

mistake but eventually _____ the funny side of it.

11 We were pleased with the results as we _____ a lot of time and energy on the project.

12 Go to drama school. Don't let your talent _____ to waste.

13 Drink driving _____ the lives of many innocent victims each year.

14 If you throw a coin into the fountain and make a

wish it's supposed _____ true.

Grammar

C Write the missing past tenses and past participles of the following verbs.

Example

see   *saw*   *seen*

15 shrink   _____   _____

16 rise   _____   _____

17 bring   _____   _____

18 freeze   _____   _____

19 choose   _____   _____

20 hold   _____   _____

21 lay   _____   _____

22 bleed   _____   _____

23 sting   _____   _____

24 catch   _____   _____

D Fill the gaps in these sentences with one of these time expressions. Use each one once only.

after   as   as soon as   before   then   whenever

25 _____ I feel depressed, I go for a long walk.

26 _____ we start the meeting, I'd like to thank you all for coming at such short notice.

27 I promise I'll let you know _____ I find out myself.

28 Can you do the washing-up _____ you've finished your homework?

29 _____ I was waiting for the bus, I realized I'd left my money on the kitchen table.

30 Cut the chicken into quarters and fry in a little oil.

_____ add the mushrooms.

E Some of these sentences are correct and some contain mistakes in the verb form or tense. Tick (✓) the correct sentences and correct the sentences which are wrong.

31 Mandy picked up Spanish when she was living in Spain.

32 Josie took off her coat and hanged it up in the cupboard.

33 I never saw anything like it before.

34 John found it strange that David had never eaten octopus before.

35 Having two large slices of chocolate cake, I was full.

36 My hands are dirty because I've worked in the garden.

37 Receiving no answer, I knocked more loudly.

38 Matthew has looked for a job for ages before he finally found this one.

39 Leaving his car parked outside, he went into the station.

40 I have gone on holiday twice already this year.

Unit 6 test

Vocabulary

A Put the correct form of one of these key verbs in the gaps.

do   make   play   run   take

1 Most parents _____ an important part in their children's education.

2 You shouldn't _____ exams too seriously. There are more important things to worry about.

3 The police are _____ enquiries into the theft of my car.

4 Falling into the river made me feel very cold and wet, but it didn't _____ me any real harm.

5 You need a certain sort of personality to _____ a business successfully.

B Put the correct form of one of these key verbs in the gaps.

say   speak   talk   tell

6 I asked my father if I could borrow his car and he _____ Yes.

7 Did I ever _____ you the story of how I broke my leg?

8 I'd love to be able _____ Italian. It's such a romantic language.

9 Apparently George Washington never _____ a lie.

10 There's no point in being shy. You've just got to _____ your mind.

C Write the words for these definitions about the body.

11 one of the two passages in your nose that you breathe through _____

12 you kiss with these _____

13 the back of the lower part of your leg _____

14 the red liquid that runs through veins round your body _____

15 you bite and chew things with these _____

16 a closed hand which boxers use to hit each other _____

17 to open and close both eyes at the same time _____

18 the front of the lower part of your leg _____

19 you do this to make food go out of your mouth into your stomach _____

20 the narrow part around the middle of your body _____

Grammar

D Fill the gaps in these conditional sentences with the correct form of the verb in brackets.

21 If it _____ (stop) raining, we'll go out for the afternoon.

22 I _____ (not tell) you if I'd known you were going to get so upset.

23 If I won the lottery, I _____ (give) most of the money away.

24 If you hadn't broken my arm, I _____ (be able) to play tennis with you tomorrow afternoon.

25 Her eyes get tired if she _____ (wear) her glasses for too long.

26 I'd go and see the doctor, if I _____ (be) in your position.

27 If I _____ (meet) your parents, I won't tell them I've seen you.

28 We wouldn't be in this terrible position now if we _____ (be) more careful with our money.

29 John _____ (get) toothache if he eats ice cream.

30 If we _____ (check) the car before we left, we probably wouldn't have had the accident.

E Choose the correct word or phrase in these sentences.

31 You'll be late *unless / provided that* you leave now.

32 I'll give you a lift in my car *as long as / unless* you don't smoke.

33 *If / Unless* you don't stop drinking you're going to make yourself ill.

34 I'm sure we'll have a good holiday, *provided that / unless* the weather's good.

35 *If / Unless* you tell me what's wrong, I can't help you.

F Fill the gaps in the following sentences with a suitable preposition.

36 Every time I drink milk I get a headache – I think I must be allergic _____ it.

37 Hi! How are you? I haven't seen you _____ ages.

38 Can't we watch something else? I'm not very keen _____ sports programmes.

39 I don't know about you, but _____ my point of view this is the best thing that could have happened.

40 _____ general I prefer French food to English.

Unit 7 test

Vocabulary

A Fill the gaps in these sentences with one of the words below.

average   medium   mid   middle

1 Some _____-aged people, to the embarrassment of their children, never grow up.

2 Graham is in his _____ -twenties and studying to be an engineer.

3 Julie has dark-brown, _____-length hair, which she sometimes wears up.

4 At 1.50 metres William is below _____ height.

B Put the following adjectives in order from the fattest (5) to the thinnest (8).

plump   skinny   slim   thin

5 _____   7 _____

6 _____   8 _____

C Add a prefix to these adjectives to give their opposites.

Example   loyal   *disloyal*

9 enthusiastic   _____

10 logical   _____

11 patient   _____

12 responsible   _____

13 organized   _____

14 convenient   _____

15 reliable   _____

16 secure   _____

D Match the phrasal verbs with their definitions. You will need to use two of them twice.

turn down   turn into   turn over   turn up

17 arrive; appear   _____

18 decrease the volume   _____

19 become   _____

20 refuse an invitation _____

21 increase the volume   _____

22 change sides   _____

Grammar

E Fill the gaps in these sentences with one of the prepositions below.

at   by   in   on   over

23 The boy has been _____ trouble with the police on several occasions.

23 People all _____ the world will be celebrating the event.

25 Don't worry. I'll have repaired it _____ the time your father gets back.

26 Please let me finish this _____ my own time.

F Two relative pronouns are given in brackets (Ø means no relative pronoun). Cross out the pronouns which are not correct or tick (✓) the sentence if both are correct.

Examples
I'd never seen the man (Ø) (that) she was talking to before. ✓
The woman (who) (̶Ø̶) is speaking to Joe is his Aunt Mary.

27 Can you return the book (that) (which) I lent you as soon as possible please?

28 The house, (which) (that) was situated on the edge of a lake, had an incredible view.

29 Those (who) (which) arrive late will not be allowed to enter until the end of the act.

30 That nice boy (who) (which) I told you about will be there.

31 Margaret Thatcher, (who) (that) was Britain's first lady prime minister, is still actively involved in politics.

32 The woman (which) (whose) house was almost destroyed in the explosion is going to sue the gas company.

33 Bradford, (that) (which) is situated about ten miles from Leeds, used to be an important manufacturing town.

34 George's dad lent him £200 so that he could come on holiday with us, (which) (that) I thought was very generous.

35 The person to (who) (whom) I spoke told me there were still some tickets left.

36 That restaurant (Ø) (that) closed down last month has re-opened under new management.

37 Stephen really likes the C.D. (Ø) (which) you gave him.

38 Please don't look at the answers, (that) (which) are at the back of your book.

39 The last book (which) (Ø) he wrote was a best-seller.

40 It was Maria's brother (which) (that) you met, not her cousin.

Unit 8 test

Vocabulary

A Fill the gaps with a noun made from one of these verbs.

argue   forgive   occur   populate   punish   secure

1 As a _____ for being rude to his father, Paul wasn't allowed to go to the party.
2 He begged _____ for what he had done.
3 Most young people have _____ with their parents about the time they have to be home.
4 Children who lack the _____ of a good home are more likely to break the law.
5 The _____ continues to increase alarmingly despite birth control programmes.
6 Nowadays muggings are an everyday _____.

B Fill the gaps with an appropriate word. The first letter is given.

Example Someone who commits a crime is a *criminal*.

7 Someone who sees a crime take place is a w_____.
8 The crime of demanding money from somebody in exchange for keeping information about them secret is called b_____.
9 The decision made by a jury about whether a person is innocent or guilty of a crime is called a v_____.
10 Someone who brings goods into or out of a country illegally is called a s_____.
11 The person with the authority to decide cases in a court of law is the j_____.

C Put the correct form of one of these verbs in the gaps.

arrest   ban   charge   fine   investigate   steal

12 O'Sullivan _____ from driving for a year.
13 Simpson _____ by police officers last night.
14 Scotland Yard detectives _____ the case.
15 _____ is wrong.

D Put the correct form of one of these verbs in the gaps. There is one verb you will not need.

get   keep   set   take

16 I've decided _____ Monday off and go away for a long weekend.
17 Some parents _____ a bad example by smoking in front of their children.
18 Demonstrators demanded that Hughes be _____ free after serving four years of her sentence.
19 Always make sure you _____ hold of your handbag when travelling on public transport.

E Replace the part of the sentence in italics with the verb *go* in the correct tense and an appropriate particle.
20 The custom's officer *searched* the contents of our suitcase. _____
21 The teacher told the class *to check* their work carefully before handing it in. _____
22 The fire *had stopped burning* because no one had put more coal on it. _____
23 Her clothes *don't match* her image. _____
24 Fortunately the bomb *didn't explode*. _____

Grammar

F Choose the correct option in these sentences.
25 She advised *that I go / me to go / that I should go*.
26 He told me *don't be late / to not be late / not to be late*.
27 My boss asked *to me to work late / me can you work late / me if I could work late*.
28 James warned me *not to start smoking / not start to smoke / to don't start smoking*.
29 Melanie suggested *us to leave early / that we left early / us leaving early*.
30 Sandra told me *to give it to her / give that to her / give it to her*.
31 She said she *saw me the next day / would see me the following day / sees me tomorrow*.
32 The tourist asked me *where is the post office / where was the post office / where the post office was*.

G Fill the gaps in these sentences with one of the following discourse markers. Use each one twice.

besides   in fact   on the other hand   on the whole

33 John is very clever. _____ he's the most intelligent person I've ever met.
34 Smoking is expensive, _____ being unhealthy.
35 _____ nowadays most crimes are drug-related.
36 Flying is the most expensive way to travel. _____ it's the fastest.
37 I'm not going to Emma's wedding. I don't like her and _____, I've got nothing to wear.
38 Camping's cheaper. _____ it's less comfortable.
39 The weather could have been better, but _____, we enjoyed our holiday.
40 The film was excellent. _____, it's the best film I've seen for ages.

Unit 9 test

Vocabulary

A Put the correct form of one of these verbs in the gaps.

do   have   lose   make   reach

1 I know he can be very irritating, but try not to _____ your temper with him.
2 It's too late now. Nothing you can do will _____ any difference.
3 Last week's storm _____ at least £100,000 worth of damage to our school.
4 I work hard all week. I think I deserve to _____ fun at the weekends.
5 We talked for over three hours without _____ a conclusion.

B Put the correct form of one of these words in the gaps below.

addict   amuse   envy   luck   observe

6 Some people say that coffee is _____, but I can stop drinking it any time I like.
7 My brother has just won £1000 on the lottery, but then he's always been a _____ person.
8 My sister has always been _____ of my success.
9 It was one of the worst comedy programmes I've ever seen. Hardly anyone in the audience found it _____.
10 If you want to make a good detective, you need to develop your powers of _____.

C Write the travel word for which these are the definitions.

11 cars and other vehicles using the road   _____
12 a long journey by sea or space   _____
13 part of a wide road for one line of cars   _____
14 travel by getting free rides in other people's cars   _____
15 place at an airport where you show your ticket and hand in your bags   _____
16 a holiday in which you travel on a ship and visit different places   _____
17 another word for underground (train system)   _____
18 come down from the air to the ground (a plane does this)   _____
19 place to stay overnight for people who are travelling by car (usually on or near main roads and motorways)   _____
20 bags, suitcases, etc. you take with you on a journey   _____

Grammar

D Choose the correct word or phrase in these sentences.

21 *You'd better / Let's* eat less fried food. You know what the doctor said.
22 *If I were you / Whatever you do,* don't forget to turn off the oven.
23 *How about / Why don't we* going to Crete for our next holiday?
24 *I suggest we / What about* start saving up straightaway.
25 *We could / How about* visit the temple of Knossos.

E Fill the gaps with one of these verbs. Sometimes more than one answer is possible.

could   ought to   should

26 I haven't got any money. _____ you lend me £10 until the weekend, please?
27 I ordered my new guitar over a month ago. It _____ be here by now.
28 You really _____ stop smoking. You've got a terrible cough.
29 My sister _____ read by the time she was two.
30 If my watch is right, we _____ be landing any time now.

F Match a beginning 31–35 with an appropriate ending a–e and fill the gaps with one of these linking words or phrases.

although   but   despite   however   in spite

31 _____ I've been driving for nearly five years.
32 We had intended to arrive by lunchtime.
33 _____ the bad weather
34 _____ of being scared of flying,
35 I had to take my driving test three times

a _____ my sister passed at the first attempt.
b I'm still not confident about going on motorways.
c _____ the roads were icy and we had to drive slowly.
d Sue decided to travel by air.
e we had a fantastic holiday in Ireland.

G Fill the gaps in these sentences with a suitable preposition.

36 Thanks _____ my brilliant teacher, I managed to pass the maths exam.
37 I like Indian and Chinese food, but I'm not familiar _____ Thai cookery.
38 _____ average we go to the cinema five or six times a year.
39 Stop shouting _____ me – I'm not deaf.
40 Over the past 10 years there has been a great improvement _____ the standard of driving in Britain.

Unit 10 test

Vocabulary

A Put the correct form of one of these verbs in the gaps.

change   find   have   make   take

1 On the first day all students have to _____ an English test.

2 After I lost my job it took me nearly six months to _____ work again.

3 Before you go away on holiday _____ sure you've closed the windows and locked the doors.

4 The neighbours didn't _____ any objections to our party even though they knew the music would be very loud.

5 Once you've made a decision, don't _____ your mind.

B Complete these sentences with an item of clothing. All these words are plural, e.g. *shoes* or *tights*.

6 I wish I'd brought my _____. My hands are really cold.

7/8 In summer many men wear _____ instead of long _____.

9 I can't see a thing. I wish I'd remembered my _____.

10 When my brother goes in the sea, he usually wears bright red swimming _____.

11 These days people of all ages wear blue denim _____.

12 In winter I wear striped _____ to keep me warm in bed.

13/14 In games like football and hockey the players wear _____ and thick woollen _____ on their feet.

15 _____ are shoes that are open and are worn when the weather's hot and dry.

C Write the natural material that is being described.

16 It is strong, is made from the skin of animals and is used to make shoes, coats and bags. _____

17 It is a delicate soft material which is produced by a special kind of worm. _____

18 It is a strong elastic material used for making waterproof boots. It is made from the juice of trees. _____

19 It is the soft hair of sheep and goats. _____

20 It is cloth made from the white hairs of a plant of the same name. _____

Grammar

D Choose the correct verb in these sentences.

21 You *mustn't / needn't* wear uniform for school if you don't want to.

22 I'm sorry, I'd love to come to your party, but I *should / have to* finish writing a report for my boss.

23 You *have to / must* go and see that film! You'll love it.

24 Be careful. And remember, you *mustn't / don't have to* cross the road without looking right and left.

25 It hasn't rained for six weeks, so the garden really *needs to be / could be* watered every day.

26 If your tooth aches you *have to / should* make an appointment to see the dentist.

27 It hasn't rained once, so *I needn't have brought / I didn't need to bring* my umbrella after all.

28 It's great – I *don't have to / mustn't* start work until midday tomorrow.

29 I was about to make myself something to eat when Paul came round and we decided to go out for lunch. That meant I *needn't have cooked / didn't need to cook.*

30 You *should / must* drive on the left in Britain.

E Choose the correct adverb in these sentences.

31 I didn't realize the path was so icy until I fell *flat / flatly* on my back.

32 Sorry, but I'm *too / very* tired to come out tonight.

33 I can't talk *free / freely* at the moment. Let's meet somewhere tomorrow.

34 I love drinking *too / very* hot coffee.

35 Every night several thousand people sleep *rough / roughly* in London.

F Fill the gaps in these sentences with a suitable preposition.

36 The attic room is quiet – it's perfect _____ studying in.

37 You should only phone for an ambulance _____ an emergency.

38 I opened the door and _____ my surprise two dogs ran into the house.

39 The students of the school co-operated _____ the staff to prepare for the annual inspection.

40 I feel very _____ of place in expensive restaurants and hotels.

Unit 11 test

Vocabulary

A Fill the gaps with an adjective made from these verbs. You may need to add a negative prefix.

advise   avail   change   comfort   reason   rely

1 The bill came to just over £10, which was very
_____ for a three-course meal.

2 The shoes were _____ as they were a size too small.

3 _____ people frequently let you down.

4 The sweater is _____ in three sizes; small, medium and large.

5 When you're abroad it is _____ to carry large amounts of cash on you in case you're robbed.

6 The weather in April is very _____ ; sunshine and showers.

B Fill the gaps with an appropriate word. The first letter is given.

7 Most gadgets are both b _____ – or mains-operated.

8 You don't have to get out of your chair to operate the television. Everything can be done by
r _____ c _____ .

9 The obvious advantage of a p _____ phone is that you can be contacted wherever you are.

10 Oliver is doing r _____ into the causes of cancer.

11 Ronnie didn't feel he was driving fast but the
s _____ showed he was going at well over 80 mph.

12 It is more convenient to f _____ information than to send it by post.

13 E _____ are carried out in a laboratory.

14 Scientists worldwide are competing to
d _____ a cure for AIDS.

15 Live events can be transmitted all over the world
via s _____ .

16 The m _____ magnified the specimen 100 times.

Grammar

C Choose the correct answer in these sentences.

17 Joe and Liz can't have *gone / been* on holiday. Dave says he saw them yesterday.

18 Andrew *mustn't / can't be* tired. He wants to play another set.

19 Diana *may / can* be coming later.

20 She *can't / mustn't* have meant to upset you.

21 You *can / could* be right I suppose.

D You would like to change the following situations. Fill the gaps with an appropriate verb in the correct form.

22 You're thirteen. I wish I _____ older.

23 You haven't got a car. I wish I _____ a car.

24 You can't swim. I wish I _____ .

25 You've argued with your father. I wish I _____ with my father.

26 You didn't go to university. I wish I _____ to university.

E Choose the correct answer in these sentences.

27 I wish you *didn't promise / hadn't promised* to go.

28 I wish you *would stop / stopped* whistling.

29 I wish I *would / could* be sure he was telling the truth.

30 I *wish / hope* I see you on Friday.

31 He wishes his exams *were / would be* over.

F Fill the gaps in these sentences with one of these linking words or phrases. Use each one once only.

despite   in case   so that   unless

32 Take your empty bottles to the bottle bank
_____ they can be recycled.

33 _____ something is done soon, many endangered species will soon be extinct.

34 People were evacuated from the area _____ the volcano erupted.

35 The oil slick is still advancing towards the coast
_____ efforts to break it up.

G Underline the word, clause or sentence which the word in italics refers to.

36 Although *he* was actually younger than my mother, my father seemed much older.

37 School dinners are much better than they used to be. Despite *this* many pupils still prefer to eat snacks.

38 *It* was a good idea to buy the tickets in advance.

39 I disagree with his views on nuclear power. In my opinion, *it* is an extremely risky source of energy.

40 The climbers have been missing since Wednesday evening and *this* is giving cause for concern.

Unit 12 test

Vocabulary

A Write the different ways of cooking.
1 Cook in oil or fat _____
2 Cook in very hot water _____
3 'Cook' bread, cakes and biscuits in the oven _____
4 Cook by heating gently in a small amount of liquid _____
5 Cook slowly in liquid in a closed saucepan _____

B Match the adjectives with the food products. Use each one once only and give their opposites.

cooked   fresh   ripe   tender

6 steak _____ _____
7 apples _____ _____
8 bread _____ _____
9 carrots _____ _____

C Fill the gaps in these sentences with a suitable preposition.

10 The man _____ the street is not in favour of arming the police.

11 The answers are written _____ the foot of the page.

12 What are you arguing with me for? I'm _____ your side!

13 'Quicksave' products represent good value _____ money.

14 I'm afraid we can't come for dinner on the 18th. We're already going something _____ that date.

D Fill the gaps with an appropriate particle.

15 I'm really fed up with this weather. This heat is really getting me _____.

16 How are you getting _____ in your new job, Vicky?

17 Jackie's beginning to get _____ her operation but she won't be back at work until she's completely recovered.

18 Let's try and get _____ this weekend. We could do with a break.

19 Sorry I can't lend you any money. I've only just got enough to get _____ myself.

20 You should get _____ more and meet people.

E Put the correct form of one of these verbs in the gaps.

lay   lie   raise   rise

21 The government always cuts taxes before elections and then _____ them again when they get back in.

22 Alan _____ on the bed fully clothed.

23 The sun _____ over the rooftops.

24 I don't think she's telling the truth. I'm almost sure she _____.

25 You can watch TV after you _____ the table.

26 Ricky _____ his hand to show that he knew the answer.

Grammar

F Put the verb in brackets in the correct form of the passive.

27 Your essays should _____ (hand in) on Friday at the latest.

28 *Jurassic Park* _____ (direct) by Steven Spielberg.

29 The winner of our competition _____ (announce) on tomorrow's show.

30/31 We can't cancel the wedding now. The church _____ (book). Apart from that, all the invitations _____ (send out).

32 Food must _____ (not bring) into the classroom.

33 The dog _____ (feed) once a day, in the evening.

34 Angie thought the woman _____ (follow) her for a moment.

35/36 In Britain the post _____ (deliver) twice a day but the dustbins _____ (empty) only once a week.

37 The film's special effects must _____ (see) to be believed.

38 This room looks much nicer now that it _____ (paint).

39 Wine _____ (make) from grapes.

40 Picasso's masterpiece _____ (sell) to a private art collection.

Unit 13 test

Vocabulary

A Fill the gaps with an appropriate word. The first letter is given.

1 look for a long time with the eyes open
s_____

2 a less formal word for *intelligent* b_____

3 the five senses are touch, taste, smell, hearing and
s_____

4 someone who can't hear is d_____

5 someone who has a lot of natural skill or ability is
very t_____

6 a person of exceptional mental or creative ability is
a g_____

7 another word for *feelings* is e_____

8 someone who can express their ideas clearly in
words is a_____

9 a person who can't distinguish red from green is
c_____-b_____

10 people who can't see things close up are
s_____-s_____

B Fill the gaps with the verb *remember* or *remind* in an appropriate tense. You will need to make some sentences negative.

11 Can you _____ Charlie about the meeting tomorrow?

12 I bet you _____ to buy some bread on your way home, did you?

13 The teacher told us to write about our first day at school but I can't _____ anything.

14 Angie _____ me of her mother when she was that age.

15 'Aren't you going to the dentist's tomorrow?' Lisa asked. 'Oh, _____ me,' replied Tracy. 'I'm trying not to think about it.'

C Fill the gaps by adding an appropriate particle.

16 I always run _____ of money halfway through the month and have to borrow from my parents.

17 It took Graham six months to save _____ the airfare.

18 Could you pay me _____ the money I lent you? I'm broke.

19 Did you know Danny's put _____ a deposit on a new motorbike?

20 'I'd like to take _____ £100, please,' Amanda said to the bank clerk.

Grammar

D Some of these sentences are correct and some contain mistakes. Tick (✓) the correct sentences and correct the sentences which are wrong.

21 Does Nicola know to play poker?

22 She could have danced a lot better at the audition than she did.

23 I never been able to run very fast.

24 The whole class succeeded to pass the exam.

25 I was able to see better if I wore glasses.

26 I did my best. I couldn't have swum any faster.

27 Jeremy's never been good in languages.

28 Ryan is certainly capable in running 100 metres in under 11 seconds.

29 Fortunately the doctor could remove the object the woman had accidently swallowed.

30 Did the pilot manage landing the plane safely?

E Add the missing question tags to these sentences.

31 You have told James about the change of plan, _____?

32 Ian usually has lunch at home, _____?

33 You won't forget to write, _____?

34 Let's take a five-minute break, _____?

35 Nobody knows where Daniel lives, _____?

36 I am on time, _____?

37 Remember to give your mother my best wishes, _____?

38 Someone is looking after the children, _____?

39 We used to have great fun together, _____?

40 You didn't walk all the way, _____?

Unit 14 test

Vocabulary

A Put the correct form of one of these verbs in the gaps.

do   go   lose   make   pass

1   When my Dad saw the damage I'd done to his car he _____ mad.
2   Good luck with the exam this afternoon. I hope you _____.
3   Thousands of rock bands make records, but only a few _____ it to the top.
4   I always enjoyed school and I _____ quite well in most subjects.
5   You must promise to write regularly. I don't want to _____ touch with you.

B Fill the gaps with one of the words below.

day   degree   graduate   infant   secondary

6   A schoolchild below the age of seven is called a(n) _____.
7   After primary school children go to a(n) _____ school.
8   Someone who has successfully completed a university degree course is a(n) _____.
9   A non-boarding school (at which children do not live) is called a(n) _____ school.
10 BA, MSc, PhD are different kinds of _____.

C Fill the gaps in this table with an appropriate word.

Noun	Verb	Adjective
11 intelligence	X	_____
12 science	X	_____
13 _____	revise	X
14 _____	qualify	X
15 examination	_____	X

D Fill the gaps with a noun (singular or plural) made from one of these verbs.

inject   injure   recover   prescribe   treat

16 His _____ after the operation was amazingly quick. He was back at work in less than two weeks.
17 The doctor wrote me a _____ for some strong painkillers.
18 One of the victims of the accident had serious leg _____.
19 My father is currently having _____ for a hearing problem.
20 Dentists usually give their patients a(n) _____ before they take a tooth out.

E Fill the gaps with the correct form of one of these three-part phrasal verbs.

catch up with   come up with   go along with
go down with   run out of

21 We've _____ milk again. We'll have to borrow some from the people next door.
22 I agree with most of my father's ideas, but I don't _____ his views on education.
23 Michael's only just left. If you walk quickly, you should _____ him.
24 Everyone at work seems to have _____ a mystery illness. It only lasts two days, but it makes you feel terrible.
25 When the teacher asked me a really difficult question, I couldn't _____ the right answer.

Grammar

F Complete beginnings 26–30 with the correct form of the verbs *make* or *cause* and an ending a–e.
26 Worrying too much can
27 If I sit too near the screen in the cinema, it
28 Cigarette smoke
29 Eating too quickly sometimes
30 No-one has ever proved that a vegetarian diet

a   indigestion or stomach ache.   d   stress.
b   you live any longer.   e   my eyes hurt.
c   me feel dizzy.

G Fill the gaps with the correct form of have something done and one of these verbs.

clean   cut down   deliver   redecorate   repair

Example   My hair's getting very long, so *I'm going to have it cut* this afternoon.

31 The new television is too heavy for him to carry, so he _____ it _____ this afternoon.
32 Next week my parents _____ their bedroom _____.
33 My camera broke while we were on holiday, so as soon as we got back I took it back _____ it _____.
34 I spilt coffee all over my best suit, so I _____ it _____ tomorrow.
35 A tall tree in the garden was making our house very dark, so we _____ it _____ last week.

H Fill the gaps in these sentences with a suitable preposition.
36 When she heard she had been accepted by Oxford University, she jumped _____ joy.
37 My car broke down _____ the way to work.
38 Even though we were right _____ the front of the queue, we had to wait two hours before we got in.
39 My father and I are _____ business together.
40 I've always been terrified _____ snakes.

Progress test 1 (Units 1–4)

A Reading

Choose from sentences A–H the one which fits each gap in the article. There is one sentence that does not fit anywhere. An example is given.

TV Heaven or TV Hell?

There's good news if you're a real TV addict: sit down and prepare for the revolution that's coming to your TV screen very soon. Your idea of TV heaven might, at the moment, be your favourite soap opera or quiz show, followed by a big sporting event and a late night movie, but that's nothing compared with what's to come.

Forget television as you know it today. [**0** | *H*] Within the next few years, thanks to the new digital technology – the television equivalent of changing from black vinyl records to CDs – you can expect seven or eight more terrestrial channels, over a hundred new satellite channels and possibly dozens of cable channels.

[**1**] The real revolution of the future is in 'interactive' TV, which will put viewers in control of what they see in ways that have only been dreamt of. Suppose, from the comfort of your own sitting room, you could watch a sports event from any of the seats in a stadium, change the actions of characters in soap operas or TV dramas, or talk to distant friends as though they were sitting next to you.

Instead of going to the local school, for example, children will be able to 'attend' lessons on TV. [**2**] You'll also be able to buy whatever you want from TV, where every kind of shop from department stores to specialist shops will offer a full range of goods and services. Most of the technology needed for these developments already exists.

At the centre of this TV revolution is the so-called 'information superhighway' – a worldwide computer network. It's the ultimate in electronic communication. [**3**] Eventually the superhighway will replace conventional telephone networks and deliver entertainment to your home as well.

Another major change to expect is in the traditional cube shape of the television itself. [**4**] And instead of several remote controls for the TV, the video recorder and the CD player, you will have a single unit which will control every part of a home entertainment system. Eventually you will be able to control all these systems simply by using your voice – in other words by speaking. [**5**]

So, with all this technology, will you ever want to leave the house again? [**6**] Probably not. Tomorrow's TV will be interactive, so you will have to work hard at it, whether you're learning something new or taking part in the entertainment. Whatever happens it is certain that people will continue to need contact with other human beings. So TV Heaven or TV Hell? It's your choice.

A This could make learning just as enjoyable as playing video games.

B Soon there will be flat screens as big as your living-room wall.

C Could high-tech TV create an unemployable generation content to lie around in front of the 'box'?

D However, more choice is only the beginning of the transformation.

E Everyone will be able to get in touch with everyone else, instantly.

F Within the next ten years, for example, Britain is expected to have at least 6.5 million homes with cable TV.

G If you talk to the TV as you would talk to an intelligent child, it will obey you.

H First, get ready for an explosion in the number of television channels.

B Grammar cloze

Fill each gap in the following text with one suitable word. An example is given.

A nation of telly addicts

In Britain, television causes more arguments between parents and children than anything else. British parents constantly complain that their children spend too much time watching television (0) *and* not enough time doing other activities (1)_____ sports and reading. A survey recently carried out on people's viewing habits (2)_____ not disprove this. It shows young people in Britain spend (3)_____ average 23 hours a week in front of the television, (4)_____ works out at over three hours every day.

What is surprising, (5)_____, is the fact that the average adult watches even (6)_____: an incredible 28 hours a week. It seems we (7)_____ become a nation of telly addicts. Almost (8)_____ household in the country has a television and over half have two or more. According (9)_____ the survey, people nowadays don't only watch television sitting in their living rooms, they watch it in the kitchen and in bed (10)_____ well.

The Education Minister said a (11)_____ weeks ago that Britain's pupils should spend more time reading. Unfortunately, parents (12)_____ not setting a good example: adults read less than young people. In fact, reading is near (13)_____ bottom of their list of favourite pastimes. They would (14)_____ go to the cinema or hire a video to watch on television (15)_____ home. Perhaps parents should change their own habits.

C Key word transformations

Complete the second sentence so that it has a similar meaning to the first sentence. Use up to five words including the word you are given. Do not change this word.

1 Predicting the weather is sometimes difficult. **difficult**

It can _____ the weather.

2 Joe was on the point of going home when Julie finally arrived. **about**

Joe was _____ when Julie finally arrived.

3 Mandy is excited about going to Greece on holiday. **looking**

Mandy _____ to Greece on holiday.

4 We had to wait so long that we got fed up and left. **time**

We had to wait _____ that we got fed up and left.

5 The hotel was cheaper than we'd expected. **expensive**

The hotel was _____ we'd expected.

6 I haven't got enough money to buy a new car. **afford**

I _____ a new car.

7 It wasn't my intention to embarrass you. **mean**

I _____ you.

8 Do you want us to postpone the meeting? **put**

Shall _____ the meeting?

D Vocabulary cloze

Read the text and decide which word A, B, C or D best fits each space. An example is given.

Example:
0 A bank   C seaside
  B coast   D shore

Oban is a small town on the north-west (0) *coast* of

Scotland. It is (1)_____ in the Highlands, an area of lakes

and mountains of outstanding (2)_____ beauty. Oban used to have an important fishing industry but nowadays the population of about 8,000 (3)_____ depends mainly on tourism for its livelihood. Tourists (4)_____ Oban as a base from which to explore the surrounding countryside and the islands of Mull and Iona, which are only a (5)_____ trip away by boat. Oban is just three hours from Glasgow and can be (6)_____ by road and rail.

1 A set   C placed
  B positioned   D situated
2 A natural   C environmental
  B rural   D agricultural
3 A natives   C visitors
  B inhabitants   D neighbours
4 A live   C visit
  B stay   D use
5 A small   C short
  B little   D brief
6 A visited   C arrived
  B reached   D travelled

E Writing

Choose one of these these titles and write an answer in 120–180 words.

1 An international student magazine is running a series of articles on leisure and entertainment for young people. Write an article for the magazine in answer to the following question:

   How adequate are the leisure and entertainment facilities for young people in your town?

   Write your **article**.

2 You have recently gone to live in another town or country. Write a **letter** to a pen friend, telling him or her about your new life.

Progress test 2 (Units 1–8)

A Reading

Read the text and the missing paragraphs. Then choose from paragraphs A–G the one which fits each gap in the text. There is one extra paragraph which you do not need to use.

A stupid mistake

Julie and Simon Kennedy made careful arrangements for their son when they decided to go on a four-day break to Paris. It was the first time they'd left him for so long, but they knew four-year-old James would love staying with Simon's parents.

1 [_____]

Julie had contacted the headmaster at James's school, and the coach company which ran the school bus, to tell them James would be staying with his grandparents for four days. 'When I kissed James goodbye, I never thought anything could go wrong,' said Julie.

2 [_____]

As James watched the bus disappear down the busy road, tears began to stream down his face. He tried the doors of his semi-detached home and the house next door, but nobody was in. James was alone and afraid.

3 [_____]

He knew he wasn't allowed to go out of the front gate, so he climbed over the back garden fence into the field behind, cutting his hand on the barbed wire. He stumbled on across two fields and climbed another fence and a gate. Then he had to face the busy A68 before he reached the farm and safety.

4 [_____]

Meanwhile, James's grandmother, Edna Kennedy was waiting outside her house as the bus pulled up – without James.
'I panicked when the driver said he'd dropped James off,' said Edna. 'James had been left on the main road. The traffic goes very fast and he could easily have been knocked down.'

5 [_____]

By this time James had reached the neighbouring farm, where the woman took him in and tried to calm him down. 'He was in a terrible state, screaming and crying. It was half an hour before he could even say what had happened,' said Julie.

6 [_____]

Although the Kennedys reported it to the education authorities immediately and asked the bus company for an assurance that it wouldn't happen again, they still haven't received either an apology or an explanation.
'It's as if they don't care,' says Simon. 'I still feel angry when I think we could have lost James because of a stupid mistake.

A Edna's husband, Frank, drove straight to Julie and Simon's house but, since there was no sign of James, he drove on to the school, where the headmaster assured him that James had got on the bus. Then, while the headmaster rang the bus company, Frank raced back to Julie and Simon's.

B Even though he was only four, James knew he couldn't stay where he was so he decided to walk to the lady who lived at the next farm. He didn't know the woman's name but she'd always been nice to him. She'd even given him some sweets the last time he'd been there.

C It was term time, so James would still have to go to school. But his grandparents lived only two kilometres further up the road and it would be quite simple for the little boy to get on and off the school bus outside their house.

D In fact, Simon even put James on the bus before he and Julie set off on the Monday morning. 'I kissed him goodbye and told him we would see him soon,' said Simon. 'I promised to bring him back a model of the Eiffel Tower.'

E For weeks afterwards, James had nightmares. 'He seems to have got over that now, but he's still very clingy. Even if we go into the garden, he's got to come with us,' said Julie. 'I wish we'd never gone away. Anything could have happened to him.

F 'He's not used to crossing roads on his own,' said Julie, 'and even though he knows to look left and right, he still can't judge how fast a car's coming. 'It's only a third of a mile to the farm, but to a four-year-old it must have seemed endless.'

G The Kennedy's home is about two kilometres from the school and James is usually dropped off first. But that afternoon he knew he had to stay on the bus. So, when the driver pulled up as usual outside his home, he said, 'Mummy and Daddy aren't here.' However, as Julie's car was parked outside, the driver assumed someone was home, and put him off the bus as usual.

B Grammar cloze

Fill each gap in the following text with one suitable word. An example is given.

Near misses

The skies around the world's airports are becoming more and more crowded. One result of this is that 'near misses', incidents (0) _*where*_ two aircraft almost crash into each other, seem to (1)_____ increasing. Ministry of Transport officials are currently studying a report of one near-miss at Heathrow Airport, (2)_____ a jumbo jet flew so low over houses (3)_____ eye-witnesses could see the terrified expressions on the passengers' faces!

The pilot of the plane (4)_____ so nearly crashed remained calm and so managed to avoid what could (5)_____ been a disaster. One (6)_____ the plane's four engines stopped just after the jumbo jet (7)_____

taken off. Air traffic controllers received (8)_____

emergency call and then saw the jumbo disappear.

Everyone thought a crash (9)_____ inevitable.

Actually, the pilot had put the three working engines on

full speed in order to get high (10)_____ to drop most of

the plane's heavy load of fuel. This enabled him

(11)_____ reach the safer height of 350 metres. Due to

other incoming flights, (12)_____ , it was a further 30

minutes (13)_____ the pilot received permission to

land.

Although this sort of incident is becoming more and

(14)_____ common, it is a fact that it is still safer to fly

(15)_____ to cross the road. But for how much longer

will this remain true?

C Error correction

Most of the lines in this text contain an unnecessary word. A few of the lines are correct. Read the text carefully, find the extra words and mark them. Tick any lines that are correct. Two examples are given.

0	An Irish teenager was resting yesterday after a flight <u>in</u> which had
00	taken her more than 1000 miles off course. Anne Keane, aged 18, ✓
1	left her at home, near Shannon in Ireland, for a day trip to
2	Manchester, but was discovered after two hours in the air that she
3	was travelling to Minsk in Bielarus. Cabin crew on the plane it
4	realized while they were being flying over Northern Europe
5	that they had an extra passenger. Meanwhile, as the flight from
6	Shannon to Manchester was held up by an unsuccessful search for
7	Miss Keane, whose cases they had been loaded on to the correct plane.
8	In Minsk, Miss Keane has had to spend a night in a police cell
9	because of customs officials were suspicious about her lack of visa.
10	An inquiry which is now taking place at Shannon, but staff think
11	that documents for the Manchester flight and for the Minsk journey
12	may have got mixed up. Both flights depart at the similar times,
13	from gates which are right next to each other. Miss Keane's
14	imprisonment was finally ended up by the great generosity of two
15	airlines which had returned her free of charge to Manchester.

D Key word transformations

Complete the second sentence so that it has a similar

meaning to the first sentence. Use up to five words including the word you are given. Do not change this word.

1 I didn't invite you to my party because I didn't know you were back from your holiday. **if**

I would have invited you to my party

_____ you were back from your holiday.

2 The President is opening the new bridge tomorrow morning. **opened**

The new bridge _____ the President tomorrow morning.

3 I'm afraid I can't cook very well. **good**

I'm not _____, I'm afraid.

4 Driving on the left is strange to me. **used**

I am _____ on the left.

5 My brother can't run as fast as he used to. **than**

My brother used to _____ now.

6 I haven't seen dancing like that since I was on holiday in Spain. **last**

The _____ dancing like that I was on holiday in Spain.

7 Your car will probably break down if it isn't repaired soon. **unless**

Your car will probably break down _____ soon.

8 If you worry, you'll find it difficult to sleep. **more**

The _____ difficult you'll find it to sleep.

E Writing

Choose one of these these titles and write an answer in 120–180 words.

1 You have decided to enter a short-story competition. The story must begin like this:

The day started normally. I had got up at the usual time. . .

Write your **story**.

2 There is a lot of discussion in your town about the rights and wrongs of smoking in public places. You have agreed to carry out a survey to find out people's views on this subject.

Write a **report** on the results of your survey.

Progress test 3 (Units 1–12)

A Reading

You are going to read a text which gives information about some British zoos. For questions 1–12 below, choose from the zoos (A–F). Some zoos will need to be chosen more than once. When more than one answer is required, these may be given in any order. An example is given.

A EDINBURGH ZOO
Still a daily event (usually at about 1.30 p.m.) is the penguin parade, started in the 1940s when a keeper accidentally left a gate open. Penguins take a pre-lunch stroll past ranks of visitors. The penguin pool is the world's largest. It is the only zoo in Britain to breed blue poison-arrow frogs. There are 53 species in the zoo's captive breeding programmes. New this summer is a family of tamarins.

B PORT LYMPNE ZOO PARK
The centrepiece of this 300-acre wildlife park, the second of John Aspinall's 'animal banks' of endangered species, is a 2.5 mile zoo walk past many spacious enclosures for rare animals. These include the largest breeding herd of black rhinos in the UK. A new gorilla pavilion houses part of Aspinall's collection of lowland gorillas – the world's largest. Other highlights include snow leopards, Asian elephants, Malayan tapirs and Barbary lions, now extinct in the wild.

C WHIPSNADE ZOO
New this summer is a cheetah enclosure, complete with false rocks on which the animals perch to view the visitors. The only zoo with free-flying macaws and other unusual birds, including red-legged seriema. The dwarf crocodiles, which were bred successfully last year, are in a new enclosure while their fast-growing babies are in the Discovery Centre. Three of the five species of rhino are also here: black, white and Indian.

D CHESTER ZOO
A famous feature is Chimp Island, surrounded by a water-filled moat and home to a group of 24 chimps. Pursuing its plan to eventually hold only animals from endangered species, Chester has acquired a pair of rare Asiatic lions from which to breed. The zoo currently breeds scimitar-horned oryx for reintroduction into the wild. Recent births include a chimp, a camel and some sea lions. The zoo's black rhino is about to give birth any time now.

E JERSEY ZOO
New this summer at Gerald Durrell's famous zoo is an island orang-utan enclosure. Recent arrivals include 10-year-old gorilla Ya-Kwanza and a family of lemurs. Among the primates free in the trees are golden lion tamarins. Jersey-bred animals of this kind have been successfully reintroduced into the Brazilian forest. A baby bear is expected soon.

F BELFAST ZOO
The zoo is celebrating its 60th anniversary with a £12 million redevelopment – imaginative landscaping gives more privacy to animals and birds. One of the zoo's

principles is to keep a small number of species – only 50 mammals – but in larger numbers than is usual. Star features include an award-winning primate enclosure, elephant house, new bird house and underwater viewing facilities for penguins and sea lions. New this year is baby gorilla Djamba.

- Where can visitors see creatures swimming under the water? **0** | F |
- Where are there three types of a particular animal? **1** | |
- Which zoo sent animals back to a natural environment? **2** | |
- Where is there a regular show for visitors? **3** | |
- Which zoo has types of animal that no longer exist in their natural environment? **4** | |
- Where can animals be seen living on land surrounded by water? **5** | | **6** | |
- Which zoo prefers not to have too many different kinds of animal? **7** | |
- In which zoos are baby animals about to be born? **8** | | **9** | |
- Which zoos specialize in species of animals whose existence in the wild is at risk? **10** | | **11** | |
- Which zoo has won a prize? **12** | |

B Grammar cloze

Fill each gap in the following text with one suitable word. An example is given.

Practice makes perfect
Most people believe that musicians are born with special talents. Professor John Sloboda of the Department (0)___*of*___ Psychology at Keele University argues, however, that (1)_____ is no strong scientific evidence to support this view. Professor Sloboda (2)_____ just completed a study of 120 young people who are learning (3)_____ play musical instruments. He concludes that most young people could become competent musicians (4)_____, on the one hand, they had supportive parents and kind and enthusiastic teachers, and on the other they (5)_____ sufficiently motivated. 'Of the thousands of young people (6)_____ take up a musical instrument each year, most give up (7)_____ only a few years,' he commented. 'This (8)_____ partly because they do not get the right parental support. It is absolutely essential (9)_____ parents to remember that no one becomes

© Oxford University Press

Photocopiable

(10)_____ musician overnight. (11)_____ requires hours and hours of practice. Parents need to praise their children even when what (12)_____ produce sounds more (13)_____ noise than music. Children need a huge amount of encouragement.' Professor Sloboda admitted that (14)_____ everyone would turn out to be another Mozart, but pointed out that (15)_____ Mozart had had to put in the practice. Genius in itself was not enough.

C Key word transformations

Complete the second sentence so that it has a similar meaning to the first sentence. Use up to five words including the word you are given. Do not change this word.

1 It is impossible to sit on the grass because it is too wet. **dry**

The grass is _____ on.

2 He wasn't able to convince the jury of his innocence. **succeed**

He _____ the jury of his innocence.

3 It's a pity you didn't tell me earlier! **wish**

I _____ me earlier!

4 They believe the burglar entered the house through an open window. **got**

The burglar is _____ the house through an open window.

5 Mandy's parents won't let her go out with boys. **allowed**

Mandy _____ out with boys.

6 I could play better if I had a decent tennis racket. **able**

I _____ better if I had a decent tennis racket.

7 I'm not sorry I chose teaching as a career. **regret**

I _____ teaching as a career.

8 You won't improve unless you practise. **better**

You won't _____ not practise.

D Word formation

Read through this text and then use the word in capital letters to form a word which fits in the gap. An example is given.

The job situation

One of the biggest problems faced by the youth of today is (0) _unemployment_. For those who have never worked at all, finding a job is (1)_____ difficult. And although the government has introduced a (2)_____ of schemes, none have been particularly (3)_____.

Despite (4)_____ incentives, employers have continued to show a (5)_____ for workers who have work experience.

A (6)_____ solution to the problem has yet to be found.

(0) EMPLOY   (4) FINANCE
(1) SPECIAL   (5) PREFER
(2) VARY   (6) SATISFY
(3) SUCCEED

E Writing

Choose one of these these titles and write an answer in 120–180 words.

1 You see this advertisement in your local paper.

> **Wanted:** We are looking for people aged 17 and over to act as city tour guides to groups of visiting British and American students. If you have some free time, know your town well and can speak English, apply in writing to: *Student Visits, Box 145, Leeds*.

Write your **letter of application**.

2 Your teacher has asked you to write a composition expressing your opinion on the following statement:

Cars should be banned from city centres.

Write your **composition**.

Progress test 4 (Units 1–14)

A Reading

Read the article. Then choose the most suitable heading from the list A–I for each part (1–7) of the article. There is one extra heading which you do not need to use. An example is given.

Anti-freeze diet

| 0 | *H* |

The polar regions are where you learn most quickly that survival is a question of physics. If you want to keep the body warm, you burn fuel in it. If you want to keep moving as well, you have to burn even more fuel. While slimmers talk a lot about the calories they don't want to consume, polar travellers talk about the calories they have to consume just to stay alive. For them the body is a machine, and like any other machine it has to be looked after if it is to function properly.

| 1 | |

Next month The Transpolar Expedition Group will travel from Siberia to Canada via the Pole, a journey which will take 100 days. Each man will have to pull a sledge weighing around 162 kilos. They cannot pull or carry any more than that. They need to take tents, sleeping bags, equipment, and paraffin, so 100 kilos of food per person is the absolute maximum. That works out at only one kilogram per day.

| 2 | |

The food has to be super-fattening and high in calories as arctic explorers have to keep their body temperature at 37°C when the temperature around them could be –40°C. In Arctic conditions calories are burned up much faster than they can be replaced so, if not enough calories are consumed, the body's fat reserves can disappear very quickly.

| 3 | |

Dr Michael Stroud, who travelled with Sir Ranulph Fiennes across the Antarctic, calculated that on average they had used up 6,500 calories a day, although on some days they had got through as many as 10,000 calories. So far, the Transpolar Expedition leaders haven't been able to get more than 6,000 calories into each of their one kilo rations but they're still trying.

| 4 | |

The daily ration will consist of peanut butter, dried meat, milk, chocolate and nuts. The explorers will have to get used to it before they set off otherwise it will come as a huge shock to their bodies, which are not accustomed to such a high-fat, low-carbohydrate diet.

| 5 | |

Although there is really no room for luxuries, most expeditions still manage a celebratory change of diet now and then. The Transpolar Expedition Group plans to make space for some Christmas cake and brandy to have when the moment seems right.

| 6 | |

They hope that they will be able to save some of their food over the first few days when they will only be travelling three or four hours a day. If they can, they'll use the food they have saved on 'laydays'. A layday is a rest day – quite often a day when the weather is so bad that the most sensible thing to do is to crawl inside your sleeping bag and stay there until the storm blows itself out. If they manage to keep warm, they won't need to eat so much.

| 7 | |

There will be plenty of difficult moments at the end of the trip. They will have to climb ridges of ice each up to 20 metres in height. Getting over those will take all the energy they have. The only good thing is that it will be at the end of the trip. They will no doubt be exhausted but they won't be pulling 100 kilos of food each – they'll have eaten most of it by then.

A Improving the daily intake
B They'll have one advantage
C A high-fat diet can be depressing
D What they can take is limited
E Making the food last
F You won't get fat in the Arctic!
G Treats for a special occasion
H The human engine
I It's a major change

B Grammar cloze

Read the text and fill each gap with one suitable word. An example is given.

Little green monsters

Biologists in the south of France have reported that hundreds of tiny turtles bought as children's pets are turning into monsters. Flushed down toilets (0) _*or*_ thrown into lakes, the little green terrapins only a few centimetres long (1)_____ growing into creatures weighing up to five kilos and over 30 cm (2)_____ length.

They are appearing in waters all over (3)_____ South of France, eating fish and threatening swimmers. One holidaymaker has already (4)_____ bitten while bathing in a lake near Cannes.

The situation is (5)_____ bad that the lake, which supplies the Riviera with its drinking water, may have to (6)_____ emptied and cleared of the turtles. According (7)_____ experts, the hot climate and lack of natural enemies explain (8)_____ the turtles are mutating.

A biologist at *Marineland,* a tourist attraction at Antibes, said: "They are ferocious, very aggressive (9)_____ dangerous. An adult turtle (10)_____ cut off a child's foot with one bite. Now the real problem is that (11)_____ are beginning to breed."

Sales of turtles in France are estimated to be (12)_____ 200,000 and 300,000 (13)_____ year. Most are miniature green terrapins imported from Florida, but some shops (14)_____ been selling a Canadian variety known as the Serpentine turtle. In adult form, it can weigh (15)_____ much as 34 kilos. Now that really is a monster!

C Error correction

Most of the lines in this text contain an unnecessary word. A few of the lines are correct. Read the text carefully, find the extra words and mark them. Tick any lines that are correct. Two examples are given.

0	It sounds like the plot of a film, but it is the true story of how	✓
00	a boy <u>who</u> aged 12 went on a 10-day spending spree at Disneyland	
1	Paris, spending his parent's money on other children he met up,	
2	hiring with a chauffeur-driven car and sleeping in a luxury hotel.	
3	The Parisian, who has been identified himself only by his first	
4	name, Lamine, spent over 40,000 francs enjoying himself until he	
5	amazed security guards at the theme park finally asked to the	
6	police to investigate. Lamine turned it out to be an experienced	
7	runaway with a serious spending habit. This was the third time he	
8	had been run away from his home to visit Disneyland Paris.	
9	Knowing how the cost of the attractions at Disneyland, Lamine had	
10	pocketed 70,000 francs which his parents had in cash at their Paris	
11	home. By the time he was being caught, he had less than half left.	
12	Lamine was obviously knew his way around. He selected a luxury	
13	hotel as his base, and hired a six-door, chauffeur-driven limousine	
14	one day to drive him to another theme park the north of Paris.	
15	People think that, if he gets on the chance, Lamine will do something similar again in the future.	

D Key word transformations

Complete the second sentence so that it has a similar meaning to the first sentence. Use up to five words including the word you are given. Do not change this word.

1 They moved here six years ago today. **living**

They _____ exactly six years.

2 You should take two tablets every four hours. **be**

Two tablets _____ every four hours.

3 Most students can work very hard when they feel like it. **capable**

Most students _____ very hard when they feel like it.

4 I'm really sorry I didn't invite her to the party. **wish**

I really _____ her to the party.

5 'Do you know where Tony is by any chance?' I asked my brother. **was**

I asked my brother if _____ by any chance.

6 People say the driver was using his mobile phone at the time of the crash. **said**

The driver _____ using his mobile phone at the time of the crash.

7 He's always forgetting to turn off the lights and close the doors. **remember**

I wish _____ to turn off the lights and close the doors.

8 My flute is being repaired at the moment. **am**

I _____ at the moment.

E Writing

Choose one of these titles and write an answer in 120–180 words.

1 You see the following announcement in an English-language magazine for young people and you decide to write an article.

> YOU WRITE – WE PRINT
> Imagine that you could spend as much money and time as necessary on a holiday.
> Write us an article describing this ideal holiday.

Write your **article.**

2 A local radio station in your area is planning a new music programme. They have asked you to carry out a survey, to find out what kind of programme other people of your age would like. Write a report on the results of your survey for the radio station.

Write your **report.**

Unit tests key

Unit 1

1 gave /have given
2 took
3 have
4 get
5 set
6 c
7 e
8 a
9 b
10 d
11 grocer's
12 chemist's
13 travel agent's
14 butcher's
15 greengrocer's
16 ironmonger's
17 stationer's
18 sweetshop
19 baker's
20 fishmonger's
21 would work / used to work
22 used to leave / would leave
23 ate
24 washed
25 went
26 do
27 tend to start / start
28 have
29 are always complaining / tend to complain
30 think
31 never got used to
32 I used to smoke
33 they are used to looking after themselves
34 get
35 did you use to live
36 on
37 by
38 on
39 in
40 at

Unit 2

1 was pouring / poured
2 froze
3 shines
4 had been snowing
5 blew
6 heavy
7 thick
8 bright
9 strong
10 light
11 make
12 went
13 run
14 take
15 Have
16 at
17 on
18 on
19 in
20 in
21 will be
22 I'm going to faint
23 I'm going
24 leaves
25 you will have been working
26 I'll turn
27 I'm going to learn
28 We'll be thinking / we'll think
29 I'm going to burst
30 I'll carry
31 X
32 the
33 a
34 the
35 the
36 X
37 an
38 X
39 a
40 the

Unit 3

1 encores
2 magician
3 lines
4 subtitles
5 audience
6 row
7 perform
8 conductor
9 plot
10 set
21 losing
22 working
23 laying
24 to meet
25 to see
26 stealing
27 to be
28 getting
29 having
30 paying

11 security
12 darkness
13 loneliness
14 admiration
15 fitness
16 popularity
17 shyness
18 sincerity
19 changing
20 to take
31 to open
32 going out
33 going
34 sleeping
35 to tell
36 joining
37 being
38 to ask
39 to announce
40 to demonstrate

Unit 4

1 uncle
2 twin
3 widower
4 niece
5 grandfather
6 mother-in-law
7 cousin
8 widow
9 nephew
10 relations or relatives
11 caretaker
12 telephonist
13 electrician
14 shop assistant
15 accountant
16 author
17 solicitor
18 plumber
19 receptionist
20 optician
21 the most difficult
22 further
23 more common / commoner
24 the most popular
25 better
26 the most depressing
27 busier
28 more comfortable
29 wettest
30 the most frightening
31 d
32 a
33 f
34 c
35 b
36 with
37 in
38 for
39 on
40 in

Unit 5

1 dived
2 beat
3 drew
4 served
5 won
6 was ridden
7 hadn't missed
8 trains
9 took
10 saw
11 had spent
12 go
13 costs
14 to come
15 shrank (shrunk); shrunk
16 rose; risen
17 brought; brought
18 froze; frozen
19 chose; chosen
20 held; held
21 laid; laid
22 bled; bled
23 stung; stung
24 caught; caught
25 Whenever
26 Before
27 as soon as
28 after
29 As
30 Then
31 ✓
32 hung
33 have / had never seen
34 ✓
35 Having had / eaten
36 I've been working
37 ✓
38 had been looking
39 ✓
40 been

Unit 6

1 play
2 take
3 making
4 do
5 run
21 stops
22 would not have told / wouldn't have told
23 I'd give
24 I would be able

6   said
7   tell
8   to speak
9   told
10 speak
11 a nostril
12 lips
13 calf
14 blood
15 teeth
16 fist
17 blink
18 shin
19 swallow
20 waist

25 wears
26 were
27 meet
28 had been
29 gets
30 had checked
31 unless
32 as long as
33 If
34 provided that
35 Unless
36 to
37 for (in)
38 on
39 from
40 In

Unit 7

1   middle
2   mid
3   medium
4   average
5   plump
6   slim
7   thin
8   skinny
9   unenthusiastic
10 illogical
11 impatient
12 irresponsible
13 disorganized
14 inconvenient
15 unreliable
16 insecure
17 turn up
18 turn down
19 turn into
20 turn down

21 turn up
22 turn over
23 in
24 over
25 by
26 in
27 ✓
28 that
29 which
30 which
31 that
32 which
33 that
34 that
35 who
36 Ø
37 ✓
38 that
39 ✓
40 which

Unit 8

1   punishment
2   forgiveness
3   arguments
4   security
5   population
6   occurrence
7   witness
8   blackmail
9   verdict
10 smuggler
11 judge
12 was / has been
    banned
13 was arrested
14 are investigating
15 Stealing
16 to take
17 set
18 set
19 keep
20 went through

21 to go over
22 had gone out
23 don't go with
24 didn't go off
25 me to go
26 not to be late
27 me if I could work late
28 not to start smoking
29 that we left early
30 to give it to her
31 would see me the
    following day
32 where the post office was
33 In fact
34 besides
35 On the whole
36 On the other hand
37 besides
38 On the other hand
39 on the whole
40 In fact

Unit 9

1   lose
2   make
3   did / has done
4   have
5   reaching
6   addictive
7   lucky
8   envious
9   amusing
10 observation
11 traffic
12 voyage
13 lane
14 hitch-hike
15 check-in
16 cruise
17 tube
18 land
19 motel
20 luggage

21 You'd better
22 Whatever you do
23 How about
24 I suggest we
25 We could
26 Could
27 should / ought to
28 should / ought to
29 could
30 should / ought to
31 b – Although
32 c – However
33 e – Despite
34 d – In spite
35 a – but
36 to
37 with
38 On
39 at
40 in

Unit 10

1   take
2   find
3   make
4   have
5   change
6   gloves
7   shorts
8   trousers
9   glasses
10 trunks
11 jeans
12 pyjamas
13 boots
14 socks
15 Sandals
16 leather
17 silk
18 rubber
19 wool
20 cotton

21 needn't
22 have to
23 must
24 mustn't
25 needs to be
26 should
27 I needn't have brought
28 don't have to
29 didn't need to cook
30 must
31 flat
32 too
33 freely
34 very
35 rough
36 for
37 in
38 to
39 with
40 out

Unit 11

1   reasonable
2   uncomfortable
3   Unreliable
4   available
5   inadvisable
6   changeable
7   battery-
8   remote control
9   portable
10 research
11 speedometer
12 fax
13 Experiments
14 discover
15 satellite
16 microscope
17 gone
18 can't

19 may
20 can't
21 could
22 were / was
23 had
24 could swim
25 hadn't argued
26 had gone
27 hadn't promised
28 would stop
29 could
30 hope
31 were
32 so that
33 Unless
34 in case
35 despite
36 my father

37 (The fact that) school dinners are much better than they used to be.
38 to buy the tickets in advance
39 nuclear power
40 (The fact that) the climbers have been missing since Wednesday evening.

Unit 12

1 fry
2 boil
3 bake
4 poach
5 stew
6 tender; tough
7 ripe; unripe / green
8 fresh; stale
9 cooked; raw
10 on
11 at
12 on
13 for
14 on
15 down
16 on
17 over
18 away
19 by
20 out
21 raises
22 lay / (is) was lying
23 rose / was rising
24 is lying
25 lay/have laid
26 raised
27 be handed in
28 was directed
29 will be announced
30/31 has been booked / is booked; have been sent out
32 not be brought
33 is fed
34 was following
35/36 is delivered; are emptied
37 be seen
38 has been painted
39 is made
40 has been sold

Unit 13

1 stare
2 brainy
3 sight
4 deaf
5 talented
6 genius
7 emotions
8 articulate
9 colour-blind
10 short-sighted
11 remind
12 didn't remember
13 remember
14 reminds
15 don't remind
16 out
17 up
18 back
19 down
20 out
21 Does Nicola know **how** to play poker?
22 ✓
23 I **have** never been able to run very fast.
24 The whole class succeeded **in passing** the exam.
25 I **would be able** to see better if I wore glasses.
26 ✓
27 Jeremy's never been good **at** languages.
28 Ryan is certainly capable **of** running 100 metres in under 11 seconds.
29 Fortunately the doctor **was able to** remove the object the woman had accidently swallowed.
30 Did the pilot manage **to land** the plane safely?

31 haven't you?
32 doesn't he?
33 will you?
34 shall we?
35 do they?
36 aren't I?
37 won't you?
38 aren't they?
39 didn't we?
40 did you?

Unit 14

1 went
2 pass
3 make
4 did
5 lose
6 infant
7 secondary
8 graduate
9 day
10 degrees
11 intelligent
12 scientific
13 revision
14 qualification
15 examine
16 recovery
17 prescription
18 injuries
19 treatment
20 injection
21 run out of
22 go along with
23 catch up with
24 gone down with
25 come up with
26 d - cause
27 c -makes
28 e - makes
29 a - causes
30 b - makes
31 is having it delivered
32 are having their bedroom redecorated
33 to have it repaired
34 I'm going to have it cleaned
35 had it cut down
36 for
37 on
38 at
39 in
40 of

Progress tests key

Note: Award one mark for each correctly answered question, apart from answers to the Key word transformations. These should receive two marks if fully correct or one mark if partially correct. Answers to the Writing tasks should be marked out of a possible total of 20, according to the criteria given in the Introduction on page 16.

Progress test 1

A Reading

1 D   2 A   3 E   4 B   5 G   6 C
Sentence F is extra.

B Grammar cloze

1 like	6 more	11 few
2 does	7 have	12 are
3 on	8 every	13 the
4 which	9 to	14 rather
5 however	10 as	15 at

C Key word transformations

1 sometimes be difficult to predict
2 about to go home
3 is looking forward to going
4 (for) such a long time
5 not as expensive as / less expensive than
6 can't / cannot afford to buy
7 didn't mean to embarrass
8 we put off

D Vocabulary cloze

1 D   2 A   3 B   4 D   5 C   6 B

Progress test 2

A Reading

1 C   2 G   3 B   4 F   5 A   6 E
Paragraph D is extra.

B Grammar cloze

1 be	6 of	11 to
2 when	7 had	12 however
3 that	8 an	13 before
4 which	9 was	14 more
5 have	10 enough	15 than

C Error correction

1 at	6 ✓	11 ✓
2 was	7 they	12 the
3 it	8 has	13 ✓
4 being	9 of	14 up
5 as	10 which	15 had

D Key word transformations

1 if I had known
2 is being opened by
3 very good at cooking
4 not used to driving
5 run faster than he can / does
6 last time I saw
7 unless it is repaired
8 more you worry, the more

Progress test 3

A Reading

1 C	5 D or E	9 E or D
2 E	6 E or D	10 B or D
3 A	7 F	11 D or B
4 B	8 D or E	12 F

B Grammar cloze

1 there	6 who / that	11 It
2 has	7 after	12 they
3 to	8 is	13 like
4 if	9 for	14 not
5 were	10 a	15 even

C Key word transformations

1 not dry enough to sit
2 did not succeed in convincing
3 wish you had told
4 believed to have got into
5 is not allowed to go
6 would be able to play
7 don't / do not regret choosing / having chosen
8 get better if you do

D Word formation

1 (e)specially	3 successful	5 preference
2 variety	4 financial	6 satisfactory

Progress test 4

A Reading

1 D   2 F   3 A   4 I   5 G   6 E   7 B
Heading C is extra.

B Grammar cloze

1 are	6 be	11 they
2 in	7 to	12 between
3 the	8 why	13 a
4 been	9 and	14 have
5 so	10 could / can	15 as

C Error correction

1 up	6 it	11 being
2 with	7 ✓	12 was
3 himself	8 been	13 ✓
4 he	9 how	14 the
5 to	10 ✓	15 on

D Key word transformations

1 have been living here (for)
2 should be taken
3 are capable of working
4 wish I had invited
5 he knew where Tony was
6 is said to have been
7 he would remember
8 am having my flute repaired

Phrasal verbs

Introduction

A phrasal verb is a verb used with a particle (an adverb or a preposition). The meaning of the verb and the particle together is idiomatic – it means something different from the separate literal meanings of the verb and the particle. Phrasal verbs are very common, especially in informal English.

In addition to learning the meanings of phrasal verbs, you also need to know how to use them correctly. Most importantly, you need to know whether the verb and the particle have to stay together or whether they can be separated.

The grammar of phrasal verbs

From a grammatical point of view, there are four main types of phrasal verbs.

A Intransitive[1] verb and adverb

Examples   *touch down*
            set off

Verbs like these are always inseparable – the verb and the adverb always stay together and can never be separated by other words.
*The plane **touched down** at 6.25 precisely.*
*We **set off** very early in the morning.*

[1] An intransitive verb is a verb which cannot have an object.

B Transitive verb[2] + adverb + object *or*
transitive verb + object + adverb

Examples   *make out*
            pick up

Verbs like these are separable – the object of the verb can come between the verb and the adverb.

If the object is a noun, it may come before or after the particle. If the object is a pronoun, it must come between the verb and the particle.
*I couldn't **make** the car number **out**.*
*I couldn't **make out** the car number.*
*I tried to see the car number, but I couldn't **make it out**.*

[2] A transitive verb is a verb which can have an object.

C Verb + preposition + object

Examples   *get at*
            take after
            cope with

Verbs like these are inseparable – the object of the verb cannot come between the verb and preposition.
*She really **takes after** her mother.*
*I don't know how I'm going to **cope with** my new job.*

This rule is till true when the object is a pronoun.
*Leave me alone! Just stop **getting at** me.*

D Verb + adverb + preposition + object

Examples   *run out of*
            look forward to
            put up with

Verbs like these are inseparable – the three parts of the verb always stay together, whether the object is a noun or a pronoun.
*When I was driving home last night, I **ran out of** petrol.*
*I don't think I could **put up with** another hot summer.*
*I'm really **looking forward to** it.*

Meanings

Some phrasal verbs can have two meanings. This is sometimes the case when the particle can be used as an adverb or as a preposition. Here is an example with *get over*.
*I knew what I wanted to say, but I couldn't **get** it **over** to anybody else.*

Here, *over* is an adverb, so *get over* meaning *communicate* or *convey* is a Type B phrasal verb.
*It took me about a week to **get over** the accident.*

Here, *over* is a preposition, so *get over* meaning *recover from* is a Type C phrasal verb.

This table shows some more examples of verbs with two meanings.

	Verb Type B meaning	**Verb Type C meaning**
turn on (e.g. a light / the TV)	start something	attack suddenly and unexpectedly
make up	invent (e.g. a story)	constitute / form